CYBERIMPERIALISM?

CYBERIMPERIALISM?

Global Relations in the New Electronic Frontier

Edited by Bosah Ebo

Westport, Connecticut
London

Library of Congress Cataloging-in-Publication Data

Cyberimperialism? : global relations in the new electronic frontier / edited by Bosah Ebo.
   p.   cm.
   Includes bibliographical references and index.
   ISBN 0–275–96562–7 (alk. paper)
   1. Internet (Computer network).   2. World Wide Web.   3. Information technology.   4.
Competition, International.   I. Ebo, Bosah L. (Bosah Louis).
   HD30.37.E36   2001
   303.48′33—dc21   00–022831

British Library Cataloguing in Publication Data is available.

Library of Congress Catalog Card Number: 00–022831
ISBN: 0–275–96562–7

First published in 2001

Praeger Publishers, 88 Post Road West, Westport, CT 06881
An imprint of Greenwood Publishing Group, Inc.
www.praeger.com

Printed in the United States of America

The paper used in this book complies with the
Permanent Paper Standard issued by the National
Information Standards Organization (Z39.48–1984).

10   9   8   7   6   5   4   3   2   1

To my parents, Louis and Catherine

Contents

Preface

Is the Internet a messiah or a demon? What contributions will the technology make to the human condition? The Internet remains a mystery even as it continues to dramatically redefine the nature of social relationships between nations and within nations. The technology has already introduced complex dynamics between political institutions, commercial enterprises, nongovernmental agencies, and national interests. The ability of the Internet to bypass the gaze of official structures is redefining global politics. Geographical enclaves once separated by distance and time are developing new virtual relationships that are uninhibited by conventional notions of political territory and national sovereignty. The implications of these new types of cross-national contacts for the traditional notion of the nation-state as a mutually recognized sovereign entity preserved by identifiable geographic boundaries are still not clear.

While the Internet is still immature and many vicissitudes surround the technology, some of its tendencies are becoming obvious. The technology is less accessible and much more expensive in the developing nations than in the industrialized world. Because of the initial cost of hardware and continual on-line charges, Internet services are beyond the reach of many people in the developing nations. Necessary infrastructure for the use of the technology, such as telephone lines and electricity, are either nonexistent or obsolete in those parts of the world. In fact, 80 percent of the world's population still lacks the most basic telecommunications provision, such as telephone lines.

Only 1.5 out of 100 people in the Third World have access to telephone lines, and those lines are located in affluent urban areas. Thirty-five of the forty-nine nations that have less than one telephone per 100 people are in Africa. More than half of the connected computers in the world are in the United States, whereas less than ten countries in Africa are directly connected to the Internet. The six most-wired countries based on networks per million of population are in the West. The implications are obvious when we realize that there is a direct correlation between telephone line density and economic growth.

What appears to be emerging as the technology continues to evolve are innate characteristics that fit into the classic notion of cultural imperialism. We may be witnessing another technology driven by Western transnational media conglomerates and poised to control or suppress indigenous social and economic activities in weaker nations. In this case, the process could aptly be conceived of as cyberimperialism.

Yet the Internet has tantalizing possibilities for inclusive globalization. The technology potentially offers the developing nations the best avenue to join the global economy because it is cheaper than other forms of telecommunications. Entrepreneurs in the Third World could use the Internet to inexpensively pool their resources to develop lucrative global commercial ventures. Small investors in the Third World could tap into economic resources and markets in developed nations. Advocacy groups could be linked electronically to vast transnational cooperatives and coalitions to share ideas for tackling social problems. Educators in the developing nations could have quick and easy access to professional databases and archives in the developed nations.

This book attempts to address some of the nagging questions about the Internet. What new notions of national identities will emerge because of the Internet? Will the technology produce true globality by giving people all over the world an opportunity to participate in a wide range of regional and global activities? Will all nations actively participate in building the information superhighway or will the Internet simply replay perennial global technological inequalities? Will global cybercooperatives provide better ways to manage and share resources within nations and between nations? Will the Internet narrow the knowledge gap between the technology rich and the technology poor within nations and among nations?

I must express my gratitude to some people for making this project possible. I thank the authors for contributing their work. Their professionalism and dedication made the project a pleasant experience. I thank Greenwood Publishing Group for giving voice to this project. I thank Assistant Acquisition Editor Pamela St. Clair for being the consummate professional. I thank my four wonderful daughters, Chineze, Noni, Dumebi, and Chikodi for the inspiration.

CYBERIMPERIALISM?

1

Cyberglobalization:
Superhighway or Superhypeway?

More than 50 million people worldwide have access to the Internet, a collection of computers around the world that disseminate digitized information through telephone and cable lines. Over the last ten years the number of interconnected servers has grown by 100 percent, and there are predictions that it will grow by 700 percent by 2001. Over 100 countries have direct Internet access, with at least one host computer in the country. If you include e-mail networks, about 168 countries are linked to the Internet. All countries in the North and most of Eastern Europe, Latin America, and Southeast Asia have direct access to the Internet. Parts of Africa and Central and South Asia have only e-mail capability. The Internet has become the fastest-growing communications medium in history, doubling in size every year from 1988 to 1994. Messages can be sent around the world to one person or a thousand people in a matter of minutes.

The Internet is dramatically redefining the nature of social relationships within nations and between nations. Virtual environments and cybercommunities are sprouting up all over the world, deemphasizing the significance of time and space. As the Internet becomes an everyday appliance and accessible from every point on the globe, more and more disparate geographical enclaves separated by distance and time will be linked into all sorts of cyberrelationships (Castells 1996). The ability of the technology to link diverse cultures, economies, and political systems into new cyberrelationships that are uninhibited by conventional definitions of geographic territory and national sovereignty could create a true global village.

But the Internet relies on technology, which is less accessible and much more expensive in the developing nations than the industrialized world. Users need a computer and modem, affordable telephone lines, and reliable electricity, which are not readily available in the developing nations. In fact, 80 percent of the world's population still lacks the most basic telecommunications provision, such as telephone lines. India, for instance, has 8 million telephone lines for 900 million people. The need for a high-tech communications infrastructure has seen the rich countries race ahead while much of the developing parts of the world lag behind (Haywood 1995).

There are more telephone lines in Manhattan, New York, than in the whole of sub-Saharan Africa. And the telephone system that works in much of Africa still relies on the colonial infrastructure. Calls from Dakar in Senegal to Lusaka in Zambia are still routed from Dakar to Banjul, to London, and then to Lusaka. More than half of the connected computers in the world are in the United States, whereas less than ten countries in Africa are directly connected to the Internet. In 1995, 70 percent of the 5 million "host" computers connected to the Internet were in the United States (Panos 1996).

Even if the Internet becomes available in the Third World, it is unlikely to be readily accessible to the people who may need it the most. Internet service is a commercial activity and is more likely to be located in areas of Third World nations where telephone lines and other telecommunications infrastructures are available and in good working condition. This eliminates rural areas, because lucrative businesses and middle-class markets in the developing nations are generally located in urban centers. This is important, because 63 percent of the people in the Third World live in rural areas.

Education and cost may also be prohibitive. More than half of the population of the developing nations do not have secondary education. While it costs $20 a month for Internet services in North America, people in Africa, for instance, pay about $100 for similar services. So the Internet may remain an unaffordable luxury for most people in the Third World unless telecommunications infrastructures and education improve and computers become affordable.

Many governments in the Third World see the Internet as nothing more than another hegemonic tool for the export of Western cultural and political ideology. Some of these countries have introduced policies ranging from restrictive pricing to registration and licensing requirements to control the Internet. In 1996 the Chinese government cut access to hundreds of Web sites to eliminate what it called "cultural rubbish," and began requiring all Internet service providers (ISPs) and users to register with the police. The Chinese government actually issued a detailed list of computer crimes, which included using the Internet to defame government agencies or to encourage support for the Dalai Lama or the independence of Taiwan.

The Burmese government outlawed the unauthorized possession of a computer with networking capability. Anyone found guilty of using a computer to send or receive information on the economy and national culture could go to prison for seven to fifteen years. The Iranian government centralized access to the Internet through the Ministry of Posts and Telecommunications, which effectively bans sites of the Mujahedeen, the B'ahai religion, and other opposition groups. Some non-English-speaking developed nations have also expressed concern about the Internet. France sees the dominance of English and American cultural idiosyncrasies on the Internet as a form of cultural imperialism, and has been pushing for the development of on-line French searching software and French vocabulary programs.

The developing nations may have legitimate concerns about the Internet. The seven most-wired countries based on networks per million of population, in descending order, are Canada (192), United States (114), Australia (110), France (37), Britain (24), Germany (22), and Japan (15) (*Toronto Globe & Mail*, 23 May 1997). Conversely, thirty-five of the forty-nine nations that had less than one telephone per 100 people in 1992 were in Africa. Also, the Western transnational corporations produce, market, and distribute much of the global information products. The United States, Japan, and the European community account for 75 percent of the global telecommunications market.

There also is the issue of language and the cultural environment of communications technology. Since academics and businesspeople in the United States dominate interactions on the Internet, much of the information on the medium originates in the United States. Most Web designers are North American, and are naturally inclined to favor their cultural prerogatives, oblivious to the connotations and nuances of other cultures and languages. English has become the preferred language of the Internet, and the cultural environment of the Internet reflects the free-market libertarian philosophy of the United States.

But many optimistic observers of communications technology believe that the Internet may yet offer the Third World the best opportunity to leapfrog into the global technological revolution. The Internet is cheaper than other forms of telecommunication and could give access to huge numbers of people. This could dismantle much of the global information elitism by narrowing the huge communications gap between the developed and the developing nations. Traditional hierarchical global relationships could be replaced by horizontal alignments, spearheaded by coalitions of multinational citizenry and nongovernmental organizations (NGOs) working together to redistribute global resources. The Internet could also make it easy for development of cross-national strategies to combat global problems.

Traditional notions of international relationships could be redefined as global networked communities and cyberdriven interest groups build new nongovernmental coalitions that are oblivious to classical notions of national sovereignty and geographic territories. Because of its decentralized format and ability to bypass the gaze of power structures, the Internet has strong grassroots appeal. Activists and advocacy groups all over the world could develop interorganizational networks of resources and tactics across national boundaries on common issues, such as human rights, nuclear nonproliferation, and the environment (Wriston 1992). As powerful cross-national coalitions, these groups would be in a better position to mobilize publicity and put legitimate global pressure on governments.

Increased communication across geopolitical boundaries and time zones because of the Internet could also increase other kinds of professional cooperative activities between nations. Physicians and health-care professionals in the developed nations could use the Internet to diagnose and deliver cybermedicine to patients in remote parts of the world. Physicians in the developing nations could use the technology to seek advice from specialists in the developed nations or tap into medical databases. Education professionals could use the Internet to deliver virtual learning materials to audiences all over the world. Education professionals in the developing nations could gain quick and easy access to archives of advanced knowledge and professional information from experts in the developed nations. The Internet could potentially slow down the perennial massive brain drain the developing nations have been experiencing if professionals in those nations could have access to training and professional-development programs in the developed world through the Internet. On the economic side, the convenience of cybershopping and lower transaction costs could revolutionize global retailing and direct marketing (Tapscott 1996). Sellers and consumers could trade and buy products from all over the world from their homes.

More than ever, access to communications technology by the citizens of a nation will be crucial in determining the stature of that nation in the world community and its placement in the global political and economic hierarchies. The presence of the Internet means that telecommunications will become even more important for national development (Ohmae 1991). An important issue with regard to the Internet, then, is whether we are dealing with an information superhighway that we will all travel on or an information superhypeway that will only sustain global communications elitism.

The Internet has the potential to enhance the notion of a global village if telecommunications infrastructures in the Third World are developed (Richard 1996). Physical communal neighborhoods may become less important as new global cybercommunities demand more loyalty from citizens of all nations. People could become more interested in joint global-development efforts than limited nationally driven issues. The wide gap in the global distribution of telecommunications resources could be redressed. A few Western companies have initiated efforts to improve telecommunications infrastructures in the developing nations. U.S. corporation AT&T has been soliciting investors for Africa One, a $1.9-billion high-capacity fiber-optic cable around the continent. Microsoft has started operations in Zimbabwe as part of its multimillion-dollar program to build an African market for its products.

Other good news is that proportionally the developing part of the world is witnessing a faster acceleration in the use of the Internet than other parts of the world. By the year 2001 the number of Web users in Africa, Latin America, the Caribbean, and East and Central Europe will quadruple from 7.6 million to 25.6 million. Relatively, Africa does not appear to be doing as well as other parts of the Third World. Only 700,000 people, about 0.1 percent of the population, is now using basic Internet services. South Africa alone accounts for 90 percent of the Internet growth on the continent (Panos 1998).

There is a long way to go before a broad global acceptance of the Internet develops. New global institutional arrangements for access to cyberspace that recognize the technological deficiencies of the developing nations must be in place. Developed nations must not use the Internet to undermine the political integrity and economic stability of developing nations. Developing nations and repressive societies must not impose unnecessary restrictions on the Internet. National governments must articulate nonrestrictive economic policies and predictable legal environments that promote free-market cybercommerce. Inevitably, the key issue is whether all citizens and all nations will actively participate in building the information superhighway. And what types of global cooperatives, coalitions, tendencies, divisions, tensions, stresses, and conflicts will emerge as the Internet matures?

Part I of the book examines emerging theoretical issues in cyberglobalization. Rusciano argues that while the Net and the World Wide Web may not sustain characteristics of traditional notions of imperialism (since the messages are market driven), a new cyberimperialism, driven by corporations instead of nations, may be emerging. Kraidy offers "glocalization" as a new radical theory of global communications in the information age, focusing on the role of media technologies in cultural hybridization, economic decentralization, and political fragmentation. Mendilow uses the theories of Tocqueville and Carlyle to assess the challenge the Internet poses for government legitimacy and national sovereignty. Tong examines the myths about "wiring" the developing world, and argues that the creation of the (Third) World Wide Web is little more than a high-tech manifestation of traditional forms of imperialism.

Part II looks at global politics in cyberspace. Gunkel argues that the view that the Internet will bring multicultural empowerment is a myth because the technology, in both form and content, is hardwired into the traditions of cultural imperialism. Emery and Bates see Central and Eastern Europe as probably the best sociopolitical context to explore the potential of the Internet to restructure global relationships. Segell uses the May 1997 general elections and May 1998 local elections in the United Kingdom to show how the Internet is changing the established system of government in Britain, and acting as an agent of regionalization and globalization.

Part III examines how the Internet is reshaping global economics. Vehovar argues that the Internet will bring new dimensions to the globalization process by introducing virtual monopolies that will create disadvantages for small countries. Blevins argues that the inordinate influence communications empires have over ideology is not a grand conspiracy, but rather reflects the tendencies of free-market capitalist society. Payne argues that new information technologies can help activists for sustainable development in the global South mobilize material resources and connect with sympathetic individuals and organizations in the wealthy North. Yang uses current Internet regulations in the Asian region to identify some critical issues that are arising from a global communications network, and proposes future directions.

Part IV examines emerging notions of national identities and grassroots movements in global cyberspace. Lengel and Murphy explore the Internet's transformative role in international communications and issues of cultural identity, considering disparities between the technologically rich and poor nations and the emergence of the global village. Kole argues that unless certain sociopolitical and organizational conditions are met, nongovernmental organizations connected to the Internet become skilled netizens, but alienated from their grassroots and unable to represent them adequately. White concludes that the U.S. Agency for International Development's Leland Initiative on Internet connectivity and the World Bank–funded African Virtual University will have a substantial impact on African development and may predict some trends. Cooks examines the implications of the movement from the physical space of the nation to the virtual space of the computer for nationalism, and wonders if this could indicate the end of nation as "territory" and the reorganization of economic space.

REFERENCES

Castells, M. 1996. *The Rise of the Network Society*. Cambridge, Mass.: Blackwell.

Haywood, T. 1995. *Info Rich Info Poor: Access and Exchange in the Global Information Society*. London: Bowker Saur.

Ohmae, K. 1991. *The Borderless World: Power and Strategy in the Interlinked Economy*. New York: Harper.

Panos. 1998. <www.oneworld.org/panos>.

Richard, J. 1996. Connecting Developing Countries to the Information Technology Revolution. *SAIS Review* 16 (Winter-Spring): 93–108.

Tapscott, D. 1996. *The Digital Economy*. New York: McGraw-Hill.

Wriston, W. B. 1992. *The Twilight of Sovereignty: How the Information Revolution Is Transforming Our World*. New York: Scribner.

PART I

THEORETICAL ISSUES
ON CYBERGLOBALIZATION

2

The Three Faces of Cyberimperialism

Frank Louis Rusciano

> For the United States, a central objective of an Information Age foreign policy must be to win the battle of the world's information flows, dominating the airwaves as Great Britain once ruled the seas.
>
> Rothkopf (1997, 39)

Nations garner power that they may project internationally, both as a means of national defense and as an instrument to dominate and impose their will on others. Indeed, for certain analysts the two purposes gradually become indistinguishable, so naturally does one lead to the other. In steps, "the primary reason for a state firstly to develop and then use a war capacity is fear for its own security"; this fear leads to "subjugation of other states by war or diplomacy," which, in turn, "provides the impetus for *imperialism*" (Reynolds 1981, 25, emphasis added). The British may have justified ruling the seas out of an altruistic sense of the "white man's burden," but their intentions were clearly imperialistic, stemming from a desire to establish a "relationship of effective domination or control, political or economic, direct or indirect, of one nation over another" (Cohen 1973, 16).

It is a truism that in an information society knowledge is power; further, in an Information Age, such instruments as the Internet and the World Wide

Web provide the potential means by which this power can be projected globally. The implications are clear: If one nation could rule the airwaves as another dominated the seas in a different era, the potential for a new form of imperialism, dubbed here "cyberimperialism," must exist. By this definition, knowledge is selectively distributed or withheld as a means of controlling the international environment. Whether "imperialism" is the correct term for the relations that result, however, depends upon whether the terminology and structures previously associated with this term retain their legitimacy in the Information Age.

To this end it is necessary to distinguish three different types, or theories, of imperialism: metrocentric, pericentric, and systemic (Doyle 1986, 22). These forms of imperialism rest upon a distinction between "core" and "peripheral" nations that dates back at least as far as Lenin's classic analysis:

Lenin [argued] that the most important feature of world-scale imperialism—"the *essence* of imperialism"—is the division of the world into "oppressor" and "oppressed" countries, with the former being the imperialist powers, the latter including all the colonial and semi-colonial periphery, as well as many small countries in Europe. . . . This seems to be the origin of the core-periphery model that underlies modern theories of underdevelopment, dependency, and imperialism, both Marxist and non-Marxist. (Blaut 1997, 386)

In systemic imperialism it is the interaction of both core and peripheral nations that determines their relations; according to this theory, core nations dominate peripheral nations because all nations must expand their influence to avoid decline, and the peripheral nations simply begin, and remain, at an increasing disadvantage in terms of power. In metrocentric imperialism forces emanate from a metropole, or core nation, to encourage an expansionist foreign policy by which smaller nations or regions are dominated for profit; according to this theory, core nations initiate relations with peripheral nations in order to exploit them economically. Finally, in pericentric imperialism the conditions of peripheral nations, and not those of the dominant nations, determine power relations among the systems; according to this theory, peripheral nations are dominated due to classes within their borders who find profit in collaborating with the core powers of other nations (Doyle 1986, 22–30).

Each of these theories of imperialism finds its equivalent in potential versions of cyberimperialism. First, systemic imperialism is manifested in a form of cultural imperialism imposed by core nations upon less-advantaged ones. Here, each state attempts to export its culture, doing so by whatever means it has at its disposal. However, the core states are simply more favorably positioned to disseminate their cultural norms due to their dominance of the language, outlets, and means of access to the Internet. As a result, the peripheral nations find themselves at an increasing disadvantage in the struggle to give their cultural mores and norms voice in the international arena, and to counter the cultural influences of the dominant nations.

A form of metrocentric imperialism, which I refer to as "hegemonic discourse imperialism," is related to the cultural form, but differs from it in fundamental ways. Here, the core nations consciously or unconsciously define and disseminate language and linguistic constructs for understanding the world through the media of cyberspace. By describing the world, however, the core nations come to control it by affecting how other nations view political events, ideologies, or even other civilizations (see Huntington 1996). Control over Internet technology and resources thereby becomes control over the discourse on global issues and events, with the advantage remaining with the core nations.

Finally, pericentric imperialism is manifested in a form of economic imperialism practiced by core nations in relation to peripheral nations. In the classical version of this theory, certain elements seeking profit in the peripheral nations form alliances with the core nations, providing the latter with access to markets and raw materials for manufacturing. The core nations then sell the finished products back to the peripheral nations in a manufactured, processed, and more-expensive form. In a knowledge society this exchange may refer to the collection of information and knowledge from disadvantaged nations through the Internet and the World Wide Web, and the return sale of these "raw data" in a processed, more expensive form. Consider, for instance, that Microsoft and other software companies basically license the means to organize information, and these means are also used by international consultants who collect information about a nation's businesses or operations and sell it back as "advice." The "processed goods" in this scenario may have changed from shirts or automobiles to data organized in a more useful form, but the process remains strikingly similar.

Sufficient parallels exist between past theories of imperialism and their potential equivalents in a cybersociety to warrant further discussion; in this chapter, the discussion will be divided into four parts. In the first part I will evaluate the potential for a cultural imperialism that might arise due to the advantages core nations have in the competition to "make themselves heard" in a cybersociety. In the second part I will evaluate whether cultural imperialism can, in fact, become a form of hegemonic discourse imperialism, particularly as it might be practiced by nations attempting to spread their ideologies using the Internet and the Web as means. In the third part I will evaluate whether we have moved into a period of economic imperialism in which data become the raw materials sold, reprocessed and in more expensive form, to the peripheral nations where they originated. The final section discusses whether nations themselves remain the primary actors in any of these forms of cyberimperialism that might exist. Recalling that imperialism has traditionally been a means to define relations between nation-states, this section asks whether, in a global "Internet society," there might be entities other than nations that are dominant or subordinate in this process. If the relations instead are between core and peripheral groups of elites and nonelites, respectively, whose membership crosses national borders, for instance, can these relationships still be referred to as imperialist?

CULTURAL IMPERIALISM ON THE NET

The theories of cultural imperialism had their origins in the late 1960s, primarily among Latin American analysts; in the 1970s their numbers had increased and spread globally to the point that their efforts and critiques were joined by many critics from nations in the nonaligned movement (Roach 1997, 47). Generally speaking, the theorists sought to link the expansion of capitalism by the United States into the Southern hemisphere with the parallel exportation of American mass culture, mass-media products, and communications technology. In Roach's description, the arguments

focused primarily on the following points: first, these communications/cultural enterprises supported the expansion of TNCs [transnational corporations] in general; second, these enterprises were in their own right increasingly important TNCs; and third, these enterprises were part of a military–industrial–communications complex that had expanded prodigiously since the 1960s. It was assumed that the economic structures of capitalism were complemented by communications structures and cultural industries. (p. 48)

Can these initial claims about communications technologies be extended to Internet penetration into underdeveloped nations? Certainly, the expansion of the Net and the World Wide Web is generally perceived as growing in tandem with the expansion of transnational corporations—indeed, the former is generally considered a necessary condition for the latter in an Information Age. For this reason, nations such as China, which have usually been loath to allow uncensored contact between its citizens and the outside world, now find it nearly impossible to encourage global business ties without allowing Internet access to some portion of its population (Wu 1997, 471).

Similarly, the Internet and the Web have become part of the multinational business establishment themselves, whether one discusses companies like Microsoft, which organizes data for transmission on the Web (and which is presently fighting to include its own Web browser in its software); or companies like America On-Line, which sells access through the phone lines; or Web browsers, which serve as a means to access markets around the world while supporting themselves through advertising or charges for more esoteric information (Brady 1997, 417–418). While some multinational corporations are still experimenting with different means to extract value from the new cybertechnologies, it is undeniable that theirs is an industry that promises continued, rapid growth.

Issues arise concerning the third contention, that the union between communications technologies and transnational corporations is a mere extension of the military–industrial complex in the core nations. This claim assumes, first, that the audience for these messages accepts them passively, as if it were a *tabula rasa* upon which the lessons of the core nations would be written; and, second, that the cultural images that are exported contain messages that are generally supportive of particular regimes or ideologies. Many analysts take issue with both these claims, however.

Research by Fred Fejes (1981), for instance, refutes the claim that audiences accept cultural images in a passive fashion. He argues that other factors intervene in the interpretation of these images, including national elites. Katz and Liebes (1984, 1986) expanded on this notion in studies in the mid-1980s by demonstrating how individuals rely upon social networks to interpret imported images, often with different results depending upon their reference group: "The work . . . on [the television show] *Dallas*, for example, challenged the notion of dominant ideology by presenting research that showed how audiences of different ethnic origins in Israel have different readings of the program, and rely upon a web of social relations to decode its meanings" (Roach 1997, 49). Roach notes how in recent years, the notion of the "passive audience" that absorbs certain messages has been replaced by an "active audience" or "resistance" theory in which audiences consciously attach meanings to messages that the messengers did not intend. As a result, cultural images become more difficult to deconstruct, and "there is no longer any one grand, totalizing interpretation ('metanarrative') of media messages" (p. 51).

It follows, in a somewhat complementary fashion, that there might have been little uniformity in cultural images to deconstruct in the first place. It is debatable whether media messages from core nations ever contained a consistent ideological content. This critique applies especially to the Internet. As one analyst states,

I think there is an aspect of the Net that implies a clash of civilizations, but I don't think it's an issue of imperialism. . . . In my view, there is no question that America dominates the meta-world of images, information, and icons. These days, everywhere you look is a Cindy Crawford or a Pocohontas staring out at you like statues of Lenin in the old Soviet Union. Or Madonna and Michael Jackson of the Muzak of world disorder. That's cultural imperialism, perhaps . . . but . . . the world will not go Anglo-Saxon. . . . Every culture will develop its own analogies in cyberspace. (Gardels 1997, 467)

Furthermore, it is unclear that there is sufficient market interest in core nations to sustain any messages directed toward the periphery. According to Claude Moisy (1997), the attention of First World nations has been refocused away from the very global audiences it can now reach: "In the United States, as in many other countries, the news horizon is tending to draw closer—from the international to the national, and from the national to the local. . . . There would be a certain irony in seeing our world turn local just as it was about to become global" (p. 84). It is unlikely that local messages, even if they are broadcast globally, would have a great deal of cultural impact.

There is, however, an aspect of cultural imperialism that might threaten other nations ideologically. But this aspect has less to do with the messages relayed by the *content* of cultural images on the Net, and more to do with the *structure* and *grammar* of communications in these new technologies. These inquiries take us back to Marshall McLuhan's writings about the "grammar" inherent in different means of communication.

REVISITING McLUHAN: DOES A GRAMMAR OF CULTURAL IMPERIALISM EXIST ON THE NET?

In this interpretation we are interested in only one aspect of McLuhan's lengthy analysis of media forms—the contrast between messages sent by the content and those sent by the structure of the medium. Nimmo clarifies this distinction by noting, "For McLuhan, any medium of communication possesses a grammar, i.e. a set of rules derived from the mixture of human senses associated with a person's use of that grammar. . . . Although people may consciously focus upon the *content* of messages conveyed by the medium, the medium's grammar is the key influence shaping a person's perceptions of the *meaning* of these messages. . . . Hence, '*the medium is the message*'" (1997, 20).

One need not accept the full breadth of McLuhan's sensory analysis to argue that the Net, as a medium, offers opportunities for information retrieval, communication, and discourse that might prove unsettling to those in other nations. There has been considerable debate, for instance, about whether the Net is itself a means of creating art. In response to one analyst who argued that the Net is merely a medium in which creation takes place, Anne-Marie Slaughter (1997) replied that "the mode of technology, the decentralization, the multiple perspectives that are possible through the Internet—*changes the way we create because it changes the way we visualize things*" (p. 480; emphasis added). She then goes on to say that this transformation actually creates culture in the process.

Here, the medium is truly the message, for the medium's structure necessarily reinforces the values of openness, decentralization of opinion, and a plurality of views about the world. As Slaughter (1997) notes, "If the provision of information over the Internet creates a *de facto* norm of freedom of information that will change political systems, that's a culture of pluralism and tolerance and of freedom of expression. That's one culture, the traditional Western culture. And it will be imposed on non-Western peoples" (p. 473). One Asian leader even goes so far as to state that Internet access could be tolerated if it were limited to the "top three to five percent of society which can handle this free-for-all, this clash of ideas on the Net"; however, to expose the mass of people in China, for instance, to this interplay would result in a "mess" that would "ruin the whole community" (Gardels 1997, 474).

These arguments assume, of course, that openness and a clash of opposing opinions constitutes an ideology in and of itself. The problem with this assumption is twofold. First, it is tautological; if one assumes that a plurality of ideas or opinions is an unacceptable ideology, one must displace it with a more absolutist worldview. However, there are also a variety of absolutist worldviews from which to choose, leading one back to the clash of a plurality of ideas that one wished to avoid in the first place. Second, the openness to ideas and perspectives does not imply, as many have fallaciously assumed, that all ideas contain equal truth value as descriptions of the world or as useful principles for organizing the allocation of resources.

Indeed, a counterargument to the cultural imperialism thesis would be that cyberspace provides decentralized opportunities for many of the less-developed countries to have greater control over their images, unencumbered by the vast media apparatus usually needed to transmit messages. As Thomas Friedman (1998) noted in an editorial entitled "Booting Up Africa," "The great thing about the Information Age is that you can move from 0 to 60 much more quickly than in the Industrial Age. . . . We're just two years away from large numbers of people in Africa being able to tell their own story, and that has got to impact politics there" (p. A31). Herein lies a great potential for empowerment, when the ability to "tell one's story" enables one to affect one's political conditions—and these effects occur, not from outside, but from within the less-developed nations themselves. In this sense the Net becomes a positive alternative to the New World Information Order (NWIO) proposed in the mid-1980s. Instead of attempting to control their image by controlling access by the major media outlets, as the NWIO proposed, less-developed nations would make use of an increasingly larger, potentially more powerful and decentralized means to spread their own messages.

This alternative assumes, of course, that those nations that have greater access to the Net's resources will not attempt to control its discourse, as a means of imposing their will or ideologies upon other nations. Indeed, Friedman (1998) notes that "globalization . . . increases the gap, further and faster than ever before, between those partaking of the information revolution and the global economy and those who are not" (p. A31). If one or more major nations attempted to use their information advantage in a conscious fashion to impose their political or economic will upon peripheral nations, the second form of cyberimperialism, hegemonic discourse imperialism, might result.

HEGEMONIC DISCOURSE IMPERIALISM ON THE NET

Before discussing the possibilities for hegemonic discourse imperialism, one must first distinguish it from the cultural imperialism it so closely resembles. Rothkopf (1997), in his article "In Praise of Cultural Imperialism?" blurs the differences between the two forms, or at least implies that one inevitably leads to the other. However, this need not be the case, for several reasons. First, cultural imperialism is an unplanned by-product of the market; if the United States, for instance, dominates the world markets in movies, music, and computer software, it is not due to a desire to export American culture, but rather to search for new markets. If the culture is exported as a by-product, so be it; if the culture interferes with exportation, American companies are more than willing to make allowances for local variations. This is not to say that exported culture is immaterial; the global marketplace is a forum where global consumer tastes are promoted and disseminated, and these tastes are an important aspect of general world opinion (see Rusciano and Hernandez 1998). However, the dominance of one nation or group of nations in this area is due more to an international imbalance in the means to create and spread culture-bearing products. By contrast, hegemonic discourse imperialism self-consciously seeks to use the information advantage to promulgate a message. The epigraph at the head of this chapter clearly portrays control of the airwaves as a means of controlling the international environment.

Second, there is no consistent message in the export of cultural images, despite what some authors claim. One recalls here the statement of the movie mogul who condemned using films to make a political point, stating that if one wanted to send a message they should call Western Union. The only determinant of the products, and hence the culture, exported by nations like the United States is what the market will bear, not whether the messages successfully transmit American values. If one examines the films exported to foreign countries, from *Rocky IV*, which portrayed a tired retread of Cold War conflict, to *Titanic*, which portrays a love affair crossing class lines, one is hard pressed to find a consistent or coherent message in these products. Indeed, one observer seeing the American films exported to Brazil commented that these films present an image of America as a crime-ridden, xenophobic society in which females depend upon males for safety and security (Rusciano 1997).

Rothkopf (1997) attempts to avoid these pitfalls by advocating a form of imperialism directed at "quasi-cultural conflict":

This conflict is primarily ideological and is not deeply rooted enough in tradition to fit within standard definitions of culture, yet it still exhibits most if not all of the characteristics of other cultural clashes. The best example here is the Cold War itself, a conflict between political cultures that was portrayed by its combatants in broader cultural terms: "godless communists" versus "corrupt capitalists." During this conflict, differences regarding the role of the individual within the state and the distribution of income produced a "clash of civilizations" that had a relatively recent origin. (p. 41)

But if we are to include ideological constructs within the paradigm of cultural imperialism, we are working on a different level entirely from the market-based messages. For ideologies attempt to control the world by describing it, and by gaining sufficient support to affect the allocation of enough of the world's resources to make that construct a reality (or at least a realistic approximation of the world as it is to be understood). Promoting ideologies thus clearly falls under the broader rubric of hegemonic discourse imperialism; it suggests that one can use an advantage in communications technologies and access to dominate descriptions of the world, and thereby to construct and control it to one's advantage. Rothkopf (1997) describes this goal as a specific strategy for American foreign policy:

It is in the economic and political interests of the United States to ensure that if the world is moving toward a common language, it be English; that if the world is moving toward common telecommunications, safety, and quality standards, they be American; that if the world is linked by television, radio, and music, the programming be American; *and that if common values are being developed, they be values with which Americans are comfortable.* (p. 45, emphasis added)

The question that remains is whether these aspirations can truly be described as "imperialistic." Here, two caveats—one theoretical and one empirical—are in order. First, Rothkopf (1997) would no doubt object to the characterization of these intentions as imperialistic, due to qualitative differences he cites between these goals and the goals of past imperialist powers. Unlike the exclusive ideologies that promote their own cultures at the expense of others, American values represent a different agenda for Rothkopf:

Many observers contend that it is distasteful to use the opportunities created by the global information revolution to promote American culture over others [after all, no one, least of all Americans, wishes to think of themselves as imperialists], but that kind of relativism is as dangerous as it is wrong. American culture is fundamentally different from indigenous cultures in so many locales. American culture is an amalgam of influences and approaches from around the world. It is melded—consciously in many cases—into a social medium that allows individual freedoms and cultures to thrive. . . . Americans should not deny the fact that of all the nations in the history of the world, theirs is the most just, the most tolerant, the most willing to constantly reassess and improve itself, and the best model for the future. (pp. 48–49)

We return, then, to the question regarding pluralism in the previous section: If openness to other cultures is one's primary value, can promoting openness be interpreted as imperialism? Many would argue that proclaiming an ideology to be nonideological does not necessarily remove its sting. Also, just because Americans embrace pluralistic values for themselves does not necessarily mean that they will extend these values equally to other nations; as Brian Barry (1965, 14) once noted in reference to the British, when they spoke of "justice," they spoke of it for their own citizens, and not for those of another country like India. The final judgment on whether Rothkopf's (1997) disclaimers allow him to avoid the accusation of hegemonic discourse imperialism will likely rest with the citizens around the world whose lives would be affected by it.

A second problem with this analysis is whether it adequately describes the American mission, or the mission of any of the advanced industrialized nations in the Information Age. In an essay entitled "Myths of the Global Information Village," Moisy (1997) claims that a lack of interest, rather than a lack of power, will prevent the major powers from globally exporting their vision of the world:

The Internet is a fantastic tool that makes life easier for a lot of professionals. It is certainly great for global stocks and global smut. But it represents in no way the miraculous advent of the much heralded "global village." For decades now, hazy-eyed apostles of the communications revolution have prophesized about the coming of a world without boundaries where everyone will know everything about everyone else. Since knowing is understanding, we were all going to share our worries and unite in alleviating them. . . .

A careful analysis of the current exchange of foreign news around the world reveals an inescapable paradox. The amazing increase in the capacity to produce and distribute news from distant lands has been met by an obvious decrease in its consumption. This is certainly true for the United States, but it appears the same phenomenon exists, to some degree, in most developed societies. (pp. 78–79)

If citizens are directing their attention away from global issues, it is likely that their governments will do likewise, at least in the democratic countries that define the core nations of the world. One recalls that Moisy argues how Americans' focus has been becoming more localized, even in an era of media globalization. It is practically a truism in American politics that citizens have a greater distrust of the national government than in the past half century or so. These considerations beg the question of how our nation's efforts and ideology may be directed to the purposes described by Rothkopf (1997) when our citizens' attentions are directed elsewhere. One answer, of course, would be that the promotion of a particular ideology or construction of the world would become the province of national elites. The public at large would then only intervene when prompted by the media on some emotional issue:

The day-to-day conduct of a country's international relations will remain the province of a small, informed establishment with the tacit consent of a relatively indifferent public. On the other hand, circumstances may arise in which the public stirs and makes itself heard on foreign policy matters out of a perception, right or wrong, that the very raison d'etre of the nation is at stake. In these cases, the public will not necessarily react on the basis of knowledge and pertinent information, but more likely on the basis of collective emotions aroused by the mass media. (Rothkopf 1997)

It is of course possible for a small elite to lead the domination of other nations in an imperialist fashion. But the project Rothkopf (1997) describes involves a greater level of citizen involvement beyond "tacit consent" and a more sophisticated response than "collective emotion." Further, the public must support the allocation of resources necessary to fulfill the grand purposes Rothkopf advocates. Unless Moisy's (1997) analyses and predictions are false, the publics in core nations are unlikely to be engaged in a regular fashion in global affairs. Hegemonic discourse imperialism could remain an unfulfilled threat, leveled by an elite incapable of rallying a public to support it.

The same critique does not necessarily apply to economic elites, however. Because individuals are by necessity involved in the economic system, citizens at all levels do not have the option of withdrawing from the process and undermining economic imperialism. The question remains whether such a form of imperialism could indeed exist through the media of the Net and the World Wide Web.

ECONOMIC IMPERIALISM AND THE NET

Most classical theories of imperialism were, at base, economic theories. When Lenin first analyzed imperialism as a system, he envisioned it as a short-term solution to the falling rate of profit within capitalist nations. Simply stated, capitalist nations could maintain a somewhat reasonable level of prosperity for their workers (or at least a high-enough level to prevent them from revolting) by exploiting the labor and raw materials of other, less-developed nations. According to this theory, nations are divided into the "core" and "peripheral" nations described. The core nations dominate the manufacturing industries, and therefore have a need for raw materials and expanding markets for their goods. The peripheral nations are generally kept at a low level of development, in which their main products are raw materials. Core nations come to dominate the periphery by buying their raw materials (often at prices cheaper than they would bring in the core nation), and selling these materials back to the peripheral nations as processed, manufactured goods in a more expensive form. The peripheral nations thereby not only remain in an underdeveloped state; they are constantly losing ground, as they buy more expensive forms of the raw materials they originally exported.

This theory has not been abandoned in the wake of the Soviet collapse; instead, certain analysts argue that the instruments by which peripheral nations are exploited have merely changed: "The IMF and the World Bank continue to function as protectors of the imperialist system, acting as the enforcers for core capitalisms: *to make the periphery behave as suppliers of raw materials, provide opportunities for investments and trade, and last, but not least, to make sure the debts to the bankers in the money centers are properly serviced*" (Magdoff 1993, 4, emphasis added). One observes the same processes occurring as were described in classical definitions of imperialism. The peripheral nations supply raw materials to the core nations, give them ample markets for the manufactured goods traded in return, and accumulate debts in the process that are serviced by international institutions to keep the periphery in a constant state of underdevelopment and virtual servitude.

It is beyond our purposes here to evaluate the usefulness of Magdoff's (1993) thesis for the whole of the international system. However, the question arises whether a form of economic cyberimperialism is possible in the Information Age. One might argue that the trend in recent years has been away from economic imperialism, as nations formerly on the periphery provide goods previously manufactured in the core nations. The battle over the North Atlantic Free Trade Agreement (NAFTA), for instance, centered around the accusation that it encouraged companies to move their factories south to Mexico, where labor was cheaper and costs were therefore lower. A similar argument was raised against the Global Agreement on Trade and Tariffs (GATT). It would seem that these agreements actually reverse the traditional direction of economic imperialism, opening markets in the core nations for goods manufactured in the (now rapidly growing) peripheral nations.

However, this argument neglects the point that one of the main products of a postindustrial society is information (see Bell 1973). Consider that the classic theories of imperialism depended upon the peripheral nations remaining in a state of underdevelopment relative to the core nations. In Lenin's time this meant that the periphery would remain mainly agricultural and the core would be in an advanced industrial state. The core nations have since moved into a postindustrial society, where the basis of wealth is no longer land (as in agricultural societies) or capital and control over the means of production (as in industrial societies), but knowledge and expertise. Under these circumstances it may be possible for core nations to still retain an imperialistic relationship with the periphery, keeping the latter in an underdeveloped industrial state while the core countries move into the postindustrial Information Age.

What might imperialism in this age look like, though? If one considers information processed in a form useful to the customer as the "product" in a cybersociety, then there are several options corporations (or nations) could take for creating value and profit on the Net. The first option would be to control the "means of production" through licensing the software used to translate raw data into usable form; as Branscomb (1997) notes, controlling these programs would be equivalent to controlling the Internet: "Now the most obvious candidates for ownership [of the Net] in the future are some of the major software companies, led by the most obvious and most pervasive, Microsoft" (p. 451). If one company or nation could "own the Net" in this manner, it would be the virtual equivalent of Britain ruling the seas for their own profit in an earlier era of imperialism.

Another means of creating value on the Net would be to control access to cyberspace, without necessarily "owning" it. As one analyst notes,

I think it's more like asking who owns the earth's navigable waters. Because in a way, I think the Internet and cyberspace is a lot like what our seafaring ancestors faced when they went out sailing—they saw water as a means to get places, to conduct commerce, to discover far-off lands, to bring back spices and slaves. And in the process they created maritime and admiralty laws, rules of the sea, and regularly battled pirates. *It sounds like what a lot of people on the Internet, and certainly those in government and industry, are trying to do today, which is create the rules of the highway or the rules of the Internet and cyberspace.* (Fowler 1997, 453, emphasis added)

It would be naïve, however, to assume that if governments and industries were making the rules of access for the Net they would create conventions that did not preserve some advantage for their respective nations or corporations. The efforts of such groups as the World Intellectual Property Organization (WIPO), for instance, are directed toward making sure that copyrighted material available on the Net does not get distributed without the requisite charges. While such protections are no doubt necessary to guarantee that commerce can occur on the Net, they clearly serve the interests of those who have a monopoly on the information or images that are so protected.

A response to these criticisms might be that access to the Net and the World Wide Web, once established, tends to be free for most of the services provided. Although the on-line services do charge for access, one could argue that this is no more imperialistic than charging for phone calls or other forms of communication. In fact, most companies provide their search services free of charge, and support their efforts through advertising placed upon the headings of the various search engines.

However, there are indications that this situation may be changing, particularly regarding the specialized information needed by consultants and experts in various fields. First, while the Net and the World Wide Web provide a huge quantity of information, the quality of that information, especially when it must be used in making authoritative decisions about resource allocations, is questionable. As a result, "Users looking for extremely specialized information will have to pay for it" (Brady 1997, 418). Second, there is more of a demand for the corporations that provide access to the information themselves to exercise some degree of quality control over the contents. As one analyst stated about the Magellan service on the Net,

The art of looking for and finding information is truly an art and not a science. At Magellan, our focus is on adding value to content, not just by going into Internet resources, but by actually evaluating them, rating them, and helping people to decide which resource would be most helpful to them. . . . We have a unique ability to recognize very strong intellectual capital, to bring it onto the Net, and to publish that content in a new way. . . . We do believe that people will be prepared to pay for value-added information as it becomes more accessible on the Net. (Maxwell 1997, 420–421)

How might this contribute to a form of economic cyberimperialism, though? One answer lies in the individuals who would have access to the quality information. If it is a truism that knowledge is power in an Information Age, it is equally certain that *accurate* knowledge is the only true source of such power. This insight shifts the image of the Net from a resource all can access equally (assuming that all citizens ever would have equal access) to one that requires experts to "filter" the wheat of useful data from the chaff of misinformation.

It is in this manner that a new form of economic cyberimperialism might arise, led by a class of elites who specialize in selling access, information, and advice using the Net. This class is described by Robert Reich (1991) in his essay, "Why the Rich are Getting Richer, and the Poor Poorer." Here, the author describes those "symbolic analysts" whose products dominate the global economy:

Symbolic analysts at the top are in such demand worldwide that they have difficulty keeping track of their earnings. Never before in history has opulence on such a scale been gained by people who earned it, and done so legally.

Among symbolic analysts in the middle range are American scientists and researchers who are busily selling their discoveries to global enterprise webs. They are not limited to American customers. . . . America's ubiquitous management consultants . . . are being sold for large sums to eager entrepreneurs in Europe and Latin America. . . . American design engineers are providing insights to Olivetti, Mazda, Siemens, and other global webs; American marketers, techniques for learning what worldwide customers will buy; American advertisers, ploys for ensuring that they actually do. (pp. 219–220)

These "symbolic analysts," whom Reich (1991) defines as those with the ability to "manipulate oral and visual symbols" in a manner customers desire, have the most to benefit from cyberspace. Indeed, they constitute a class whose activities are similar to those described in classic definitions of imperialism. By licensing the software to organize raw data into a usable form, companies like Microsoft basically "sell back" other individuals' original information in a processed, more-expensive composition. The only difference with the original core–peripheral relationship between nations is that here the rights to the means of production are guaranteed through licensing rather than outright ownership in the producer's own country.

Similarly, the experts who offer advice in a variety of different areas are also taking the "raw material" of data from the original customers and selling it back as processed information at a higher cost. Those symbolic analysts in the entertainment industry often function in the same way, using materials or locations accessible to others to produce goods they will sell at higher prices. The reason why these individuals may be poised to practice a form of economic cyberimperialism, though, does not relate to their activities alone, but to the resources on the Web which allow them to pursue their trade on a global level. As Reich (1991) notes,

The most important reason for this expanding world market and increasing global demand for the symbolic and analytic insights of Americans [as well as other nations' symbolic analysts] has been the dramatic improvement in worldwide communication and transportation technologies. . . . A new invention emanating from engineers in Battelle's laboratory in Columbus, Ohio can be sent almost anywhere via modem, in a form that will allow others to examine it in three dimensions through enhanced computer graphics. (pp. 221–222)

Still, these activities do not qualify as imperialistic unless they involve some form of political or economic domination as a result, either intended or unintended. Here, Reich (1991) argues that the global market for symbolic analysts made possible by such instruments as the Net has created three distinct classes within nations: the symbolic analysts, the routine producers who work in the old manufacturing industries, and the in-person servers, who are service workers in businesses from banking to dry cleaning. Of these, only the symbolic analysts are thriving; the global market for their services and products ensures that they are well compensated (p. 261). However, the other two classes are rapidly losing ground, just as the citizens in peripheral nations lost ground under other forms of imperialism.

During the industrial era those on top of the economic ladder in a given nation could not afford to limit the compensation for workers on the lower rungs, for fear of losing their markets. As a result, in individual nations, relationships between labor and top management tended to be somewhat equitable, and whatever exploitation did occur would follow the traditional theories of imperialism by exporting it to other countries. With a global market for goods and services, however, those at the top of the economic ladder no longer consider their economic fate to be tied to the fate of workers in their own nations. Under these conditions, manufacturing jobs can be exported overseas without undue harm to the symbolic analysts who sit atop the economic hierarchy (Reich 1991, 265–266). Such moves reduce job opportunities in core nations while improving the living standards in peripheral nations only marginally, due to low wages. As such, differential development once again serves the class that masters the means of production, but in this case the product being sold in a cybersociety is information and images, flowing from a core of elites to a periphery of nonelites working in the traditional industries.

The question that remains, then, is whether this arrangement is correctly described as imperialism. After all, the classical definition of imperialism involved the political or economic dominance of one nation over another. Can imperialism exist when practiced by a class that knows no national boundaries in its markets or activities?

AN IMPERIALISM WITHOUT NATIONS?

Imperialism is both a description of exploitative relationships between entities and a specific paradigm for the character of associations between or among nation-states. All the classic definitions of imperialism described the nation-state as a primary actor in the relationship. However, the global reach of the Net and the World Wide Web has led some analysts to predict the appearance of an imperialist class that reaches beyond national borders: "An elite will be needed, but this elite will be the structure of a new imperialism. *It will not be an imperialism of a nation but an imperialism of a new group would be internationally minded by structure.* And the Net will certainly be a tool. Actually, I said they would be nomads. They will form a virtual tribe of a new elite" (Attali 1997, 475).

There are problems with predicting the rise of this new form of imperialism, however. First, the class divisions Reich (1991) describes may not be inevitable. If the Net is an instrument that can release creativity in new forms, those who profit from it might turn their attention to relieving the fate of displaced industrial and service workers. This suggestion is not entirely idealistic when one considers that the alternative would be for those on the top of the economic hierarchy to exist in relative isolation from the vast sectors of society they have abandoned. Second, the decentralized nature of the Net does allow for access by those who in the past might have been disenfranchised from other means of economic advancement. While market solutions have generally not proven useful for redistributing economic rewards in the past, the Net's unique nature in this regard might reverse this trend, assuming most citizens could access its resources.

Even if Reich's (1991) direst scenarios were realized, however, it would seem that imperialism is best left as a term to describe the relations between states. Recall that Lenin and other theorists who originally advanced this theory did so in order to explain how capitalist nations could avoid the upheavals associated with the falling rate of profit by exploiting the resources of other countries. Once this paradigm moves beyond the nation-state it loses most of the reasoning behind the original theory.

Such a shift might indicate more about the condition of the nation-state in the Information Age than about imperialism, however. One reason why imperialism is perhaps an inappropriate term to describe the relationships between the new elites and nonelites relates to the inability of national governments to control the global markets and global forces unleashed, in part, by the Net and the World Wide Web. As such, we may be witnessing the end of the age of "imperialisms." But replacing these with a form of cyberexploitation that operates without regard for national borders would hardly mark an improvement in the human condition.

REFERENCES

Attali, Jacques. 1997. Cultural Imperialism on the Net. In *The Internet and Society*, edited by Jim O'Reilly and Associates. Cambridge: Harvard University Press.

Barry, Brian. 1965. *Political Argument*. London: Routledge and Kegan Paul.

Bell, Daniel. 1973. *The Coming of Post-Industrial Society*. New York: Basic Books.

Blaut, J. M. 1997. Evaluating Imperialism. *Science and Society* 61: 382–393.

Brady, Tim. 1997. The New Economics: How Will Value be Created and Extracted? In *The Internet and Society*, edited by Jim O'Reilly and Associates. Cambridge: Harvard University Press.

Branscomb, Anne. 1997. Who Owns the Internet? In *The Internet and Society*, edited by Jim O'Reilly and Associates. Cambridge: Harvard University Press.

Cohen, Benjamin J. 1973. *The Question of Imperialism: The Political Economy of Dominance and Dependence*. New York: Basic Books.

Doyle, Michael W. 1986. *Empires*. Ithaca: Cornell University Press.

Fejes, Fred. 1981. Media Imperialism: An Assessment. *Media, Culture, and Society* 3: 281–289.

Fowler, Peter. 1997. Who Owns the Internet? In *The Internet and Society*, edited by Jim O'Reilly and Associates. Cambridge: Harvard University Press.

Friedman, Thomas. 1998. Booting Up Africa. *New York Times*. 5 May 1998, A31.

Gardels, Nathan. 1997. Cultural Imperialism on the Net. In *The Internet and Society*, edited by Jim O'Reilly and Associates. Cambridge: Harvard University Press.

Huntington, Samuel. 1996. *The Clash of Civilizations and the Remaking of the World Order*. New York: Simon and Schuster.

Katz, E., and T. Liebes. 1984. Once Upon a Time, in Dallas. *Intermedia* 3 (12): 28–32.

———. 1986. Mutual Aid in the Reading of Dallas: Preliminary Notes from a Cross-Cultural Study. In *Television in Transition*, edited by P. Drummond and R. Patterson. London: British Film Institute.

Magdoff, Harry. 1993. What Is the Meaning of Imperialism? *Monthly Review* 45 (4): 1–7.

Maxwell, Christine. 1997. The New Economics: How Will Value Be Created and Extracted? In *The Internet and Society*, edited by Jim O'Reilly and Associates. Cambridge: Harvard University Press.

Moisy, Claude. 1997. Myths of the Global Information Village. *Foreign Policy* 107: 78–87.

Nimmo, Dan. 1997. Mediated Democracy in the Global Political Village. *Current World Leaders: International Issues* 40 (2): 12–32.

Reich, Robert. 1991. *The Work of Nations: Preparing Ourselves for Twentieth Century Capitalism*. New York: Alfred A. Knopf.

Reynolds, Charles. 1981. *Modes of Imperialism*. New York: St. Martin's Press.

Roach, Colleen. 1997. Cultural Imperialism and Resistance in Media Theory. *Media, Culture, and Society* 19: 47–66.

Rothkopf, David. 1997. In Praise of Cultural Imperialism? *Foreign Policy* 107: 38–53.

Rusciano, Francesco Fiske. 1997. Popular Culture and America's False Image. Paper for Fulbright Foundation Essay Contest.

Rusciano, Frank Louis, and Sigfredo Hernandez. 1999. World Opinion and the Global Market. In *World Opinion and the Emerging International Order*, edited by Frank Louis Rusciano. Westport, Conn.: Praeger.

Slaughter, Anne-Marie. 1997. Cultural Imperialism on the Net. In *The Internet and Society*, edited by Jim O'Reilly and Associates. Cambridge: Harvard University Press.

Wu, Xiaoyong. 1997. Cultural Imperialism on the Net. In *The Internet and Society*, edited by Jim O'Reilly and Associates. Cambridge: Harvard University Press.

3

From Imperialism to Glocalization: A Theoretical Framework for the Information Age

Marwan M. Kraidy

The "information society," wrote Machlup in 1962, refers to those sectors specialized in the "production and distribution of knowledge" (cited in Beniger 1986, 21). In contemporary discourse, references to the "Information Age" and the "information revolution" have become commonplace. They are based on the recognition that the world has become increasingly dependent on the production, distribution, and consumption of information. Whereas enthusiasts proclaim a better world awash with information for everyone, skeptics raise issues of availability, access, and cost of information. The discussion has to a large extent been polarized between "techno-utopians" and "neo-Luddites" (Doheny-Farina 1997).

The concern about an information gap between industrialized and developing countries is no novel preoccupation. In the field of international communication several paradigms have looked at information inequities and ensuing social and cultural disparities. "Communication and development" (Lerner 1958; Rogers 1976; Schramm 1964), "cultural imperialism" (Mattelart 1979, 1983; Schiller 1976, 1985, 1992), and an emergent and ill-defined "cultural pluralism" (Sreberny-Mohammadi 1987) have examined the structure, direction, ideology, and volume of international information flows. Focusing on traditional pre-Internet media such as radio, television, film, and satellite broadcasting, these three currents of thought were motivated by a variety of perspectives, followed disparate methods, reached divergent conclusions, and proposed different solutions.

Since the mid-1980s, the multidisciplinary concept of globalization (Giddens 1990; Robertson 1992, 1994) gradually took center stage as an arena for the debate on international flows of information, technology, and capital. At the same time, the advent of the Internet radically compounded the complexity of international communication processes, harboring new technological possibilities, cultural realities and ideological tensions. This complexity mandates a theoretical model more sophisticated than traditional international communication and globalization frameworks. Such a model needs to take into account global economic and technological inequities, cultural and ideological differences, and the needs and realities of industrialized and developing nations alike. Besides, this theoretical framework will need to accommodate and explicate the multidirectional and multifaceted realities of contemporary global communications. This chapter will propose "glocalization" as a new conceptual framework for understanding international communications in the Information Age.

As a theoretical model, glocalization is broad enough to accommodate the myriad elements of international communications and focused enough to understand the complex duality of the Internet with its forces of fragmentation and cohesiveness, restriction and emancipation. The concept of glocalization originated in economics as a "guiding principle of original economic thought which interacts simultaneously on modes of production and on lifestyles" (Moinet 1996, 2), but gained a broader definition as a "global outlook adapted to local conditions" (Robertson 1994, 36). After reviewing the conceptual underpinnings of cultural imperialism and globalization, glocalization will be proposed as a more adequate framework.

CULTURAL IMPERIALISM

In the 1960s several bodies of literature coalesced around the umbrella concept of cultural imperialism. Tomlinson (1991) distinguishes four types of cultural imperialism. These are cultural imperialism as media imperialism, cultural imperialism as a discourse of nationality, cultural imperialism as a critique of global capitalism, and cultural imperialism as a critique of modernity. These four categories overlap, since modernity itself is constructed by intersecting discourses of technology, nationalism, and capitalism. For instance, Kerr's (1964) theory of cultural convergence argues that social and economic convergence results when a technologically advanced society introduces its values to a weaker culture. Theorists of cultural dependence examined patterns of economic, technological, and cultural dependence of peripheral (developing) countries on central (industrialized) ones (Evans 1979; Hamelink 1983).

Cultural imperialism is an ambiguous umbrella concept. Mattelart (1979) conveyed the "apprehension" with which "the problem of imperialism is approached," because the concept "has too often been used with ill-defined meaning" (p. 57). Several definitions have attempted to capture the essence of the concept. Whereas Beltran (1978) defines cultural imperialism as "a veritable process of social influence by which a nation imposes on other countries its set of beliefs, values, knowledge, and behavioral norms as well as its overall style of life" (p. 184), Tunstall (1977) states that "the cultural imperialism thesis claims that authentic, traditional and local culture in many parts of the world is being battered out of existence by the indiscriminate dumping of large quantities of slick commercial and media products, mainly from the United States" (p. 57). These definitions, ranging from cultural influence to annihilation, illustrate the confusion surrounding the concept.

With the rise of global communication technologies, media imperialism became the dominant current of thought in the 1970s (Beltran 1978; Mattelart 1979, 1983; Schiller 1973, 1976). From a political economic perspective on international communication, Schiller (1973) focuses on the global reach of American mass media. He argues that American media are neither free nor independent; rather, they are controlled by what he calls the "mind managers." These managers "create, refine and preside over the circulation of images and information which determine our beliefs and attitudes and ultimately our behavior" (p. 1). Schiller (1992) contends that five constituents form Western information policies and are oriented to preserving a firm grip over markets in Asia, Africa, and Latin America through the mass-mediated dissemination of "packaged consciousness" (p. 1).

Armand Mattelart (1979, 99) offers a "Third World" formulation of cultural imperialism. Mattelart's focuses on multinational corporations, mainly in the media and cultural industries. Mattelart describes the threefold activity of multinationals in terms of the (1) production of electronic warfare, (2) provision and enforcement of the "New Education," and (3) internationalization of cultural products. Mattelart's metaphor of "electronic warfare" comes from what he describes as a close alliance between media industries and the military. He argues that advanced communication technology developed by the military is transferred to media industries once its military cycle is over. Mattelart offers the example of satellite technology as a civil application of a technology that was restricted to military use at its beginning. The brief history of the Internet, which started as a nuclear-war emergency communication system for the U.S. military, supports Mattelart's point. Mattelart also describes the dependent relations created by Western providers of advanced technology and non-Western recipients as "subimperialism" (p. 102). Electronic warfare and global universities, Mattelart (1983) contends, produce the internationalization of cultural commodities, characterized by an unequal exchange favoring industrialized over nonindustrialized nations (p. 15). Schiller's (1996) more recent work echoes similar perspectives.

Rooted in a radical humanist conceptual framework, cultural imperialism's merit lies in its identification of issues of inequalities in global media and cultural dynamics. A wide variety of empirical studies was generated by this paradigm, and described inequalities in media and cultural exchanges. A central concern in those studies was about the fear of the "cultural homogenization" and "cultural synchronization" (Sreberny-Mohammadi 1987, 120) that global media messages could cause in local cultures, described in terms such as "indigenous" and "authentic."

In the 1990s the concept of imperialism lost intellectual and ideological ground. Its ideological absolutism failed to take notice and accommodate rapid and complex developments in international communication (Salwen 1991; Straubhaar 1991; Sreberny-Mohammadi 1997). Sreberny-Mohammadi echoed earlier reservations when she wrote that "the concept was broad and ill-defined, operating as evocative metaphor rather than precise construct, and has gradually lost much of its critical bite and historic validity" (p. 47). In the meantime, another concept has to a large extent replaced imperialism as the central framework for international flows: globalization (Tomlinson 1991).

GLOBALIZATION

The concept of globalization was born in the 1980s and has now entered popular and professional vocabularies. Waters (1996) reveals that although the word "global" is more than four centuries old, terms such as "globalize" and "globalization" only appeared in the late 1950s. In 1961 one of the Webster's dictionaries became the first major dictionary to define globalization (Waters 1996), but the concept did not gain academic currency until the early 1980s (Robertson 1992). Like imperialism in the 1970s and postmodernism in the 1980s, globalization has been defined from a variety of standpoints. Whereas Giddens (1990) defines globalization as the "intensification of worldwide social relations which link distant localities in such a way that local happenings are shaped by events occurring many miles away and vice versa" (p. 64), Waters describes it as a social process decreasing geographical constraints on social and cultural modalities. The transcendence of physical distance is achieved mainly through transnational information and media technologies. Robertson, one of the pioneering academic voices in the globalization debate, defines it as "the compression of the world and the intensification of consciousness of the world as a whole" (p. 8).

Robertson (1994) advocates the use of the term "globalization" rather than "internationalization" because the latter refers to channeled and thus traceable exchanges between nation-states. Globalization, Robertson contends, better describes the complex and manifold cultural interconnectedness that characterizes the world today (p. 19). Robertson lists the ever-increasing number of multinational organizations, international institutions, and agencies, the adoption of a unified global time, and especially the accelerated growth of communication technologies as both causes and symptoms of globalization. These, in Hannerz's (1994) words, have constituted the world as a global "ecumene," defined as a "region of persistent culture interaction and exchange" (p. 137). Similarly, Appadurai (1994) sees globalization occurring through flows and disjunctures between what he refers to as ethnoscapes, finance-scapes, technoscapes, mediascapes, and ideoscapes, referring to the continuous movement across the globe of people, capital, technology, images, and ideologies.

Globalization has thus superseded cultural imperialism as a paradigmatic framework for information and other international flows (Tomlinson 1991). This paradigmatic shift does not mark the end of inequities, but their reconfiguration. Hence, there is a discourse with a focus on the information gap, the cleavage between "haves" and "have-nots" in the information age (Schiller 1996; Wresch 1996). We are often reminded that while members of a largely Western, male, and affluent cyberelite "amuse themselves in cyberspace, half the human race has never made a telephone call" (Tele-Haves and Have-Nots 1996). Quantitative differences are crushing: A 1992 study reports that whereas North America boasted 5,396 databases, Africa only had 8, Western Europe had 1,797 and South America had 54 (Wresch 1996). Hence the argument that entire regions of the globe are at risk of becoming irrelevant to a global economy whose principal and arguably most important currency is information.

Lacking basic telecommunications and computing infrastructures necessary for the exchange of information, a majority of developing countries may recede into cultural isolation and economic irrelevance. At special risk of being left behind by globalization is Africa. Africa produces 0.3 percent of the world's scientific knowledge (Renaud and Torres 1996) and one source credits Manhattan, New York, with more phone lines than all of sub-Saharan Africa (Panos 1996).

In *Disconnected: Haves and Have-Nots in the Information Age*, Wresch (1996) paints a revealing vignette of two residents of Windhoek, the capital of Namibia, Theo Schoeman and Negumbo Johannes:

Theo Schoeman washes his BMW at 5:00 A.M. He is out early in part to beat the heat. . . . Mostly Schoeman is up early because he faces a very full day. President of the family business, Schoeman Computers, he has an endless stream of business information he must absorb. Besides his e-mail connections to the business centers of Europe, he also receives CD-ROMs with thousand of business and technical articles from periodicals around the world. . . . But not all his connections are electronic. Fluent in English, German and Afrikaans, he travels at least once each year to trade shows in Germany and the United States. . . . When people in the technology field started talking about forming a group, he helped found the Namibian Information Technology Association. . . . In many ways Theo Schoeman could be the ideal "Information Man." . . .

Across town is Negumbo Johannes—everyone's nightmare about the information age. Johannes wakes every morning at six. He sleeps on the floor of a friend's house in Wanaheda. The house is a concrete block rectangle about the size of a one-car garage

in the United States. Wanaheda is on the Northern outskirts of Windhoek, north because that is where blacks were allowed to live under South African rule. His street is
gravel. Water and electricity are planned but none has arrived yet. . . . Most days
Johannes just stands on his corner waiting for work. . . . Negumbo Johannes leads a
life of brutal poverty. He has no money, he has no skills, he has very little hope. . . .
The Information Age has arrived in Africa and new systems are being established.
Those systems totally exclude him. (pp. 1–3)

Wresch's (1996) depiction of two diametrically opposed portraits in the
information age is both revealing and cautionary. It repudiates pervasive images of rich, educated, connected, information-saturated Westerners with poor,
ignorant, isolated, information-hungry others. The two contrasting portraits
are more revealing in what they do not explicitly reveal: that the vignette
could be in New York City, Bombay, London, or Saõ Paolo; that it could be
telling the story of a Wall Street broker and a homeless person in New York,
where the wealthiest fifth of the population earn an average of $110,199 per
year while average earnings for the poorest fifth is $5,237 (Schiller 1996).
Looking at these two men, we think that "they may as well be living on separate planets" (Wresch 1996, 4). Yet they live in the same city. The information gap is as deep between countries as it is within societies.

Whereas imperialism is seen as a planned, systematic, monolithic endeavor,
globalization is seen as a more complex phenomenon, "a dialectical process
because . . . local happenings may move in obverse direction" (Giddens 1990,
64). Instead of a structured, one-way dependency, we now speak of a complex interdependency. There are those who see globalization as a Western
victory in that "the First World and its paradigms no longer need to be argued;
they are simply displayed through the logic of consumption and fashion"
(Lomnitz 1994, 263). Nevertheless, global consumerism has superseded the
one-way flow of raw materials from developing nations to the industrialized
ones and the reverse one-way flow of commodities from the West to the rest.

GLOCALIZATION

Globalization is a dialectical "stretching" of local events, according to
Giddens (1990), because "local transformation is as much a part of globalization as the lateral extension of social connections across time and space" (p.
64). As a dialectical process then, globalization is not, as is widely believed,
a homogenizing, Western force that coerces local cultures into adopting its
norms and values or erases local cultural arrangements altogether. Rather than
a coercive monologue by the industrialized world, contemporary international
cultural relations appear more like a dialogue, albeit unbalanced in favor of
industrialized countries, but a dialogue still.

With its connotations of standardization, homogenization, and universalism, the term "globalization" falls short of rendering the complexity of inter-

national flows and exchanges of culture, information, capital, and people. Specifically, it fails to take account of, and give due attention to, local factors in international relations. "Glocalization," by accounting for both global and local factors, is a more appropriate conceptual framework to capture and accommodate international communication processes. Formed by "telescoping global and local to make a blend" (Robertson 1994, 36), the concept originated in Japanese agricultural and business practices of "global localization, a global outlook adapted to local conditions" (p. 36) and made its way to the social and human sciences (Galland 1996; García-Canclini 1995; Mattelart 1998; Robertson 1994). Glocalization is proposed as a theoretical framework for international relations in the Information Age.

Economic Decentralization

Transnational financial transactions reveal that in 1996 more than 60 percent of foreign direct investment (FDI) is being poured into the industrialized world. South Korea's *chaebols* are transnational corporations: Samsung alone has eleven factories in four European countries (Fine for Some 1996). Current financial upheavals in Asia notwithstanding, this reveals an emergent trend of previously peripheral countries becoming international economic players, upsetting centuries of center-to-periphery economic relations. Besides, local companies have developed competitive tactics to undermine the dominance of transnationals. By spicing burgers in Malay and Indian flavors and offering rice dishes, Jollibee, a Philippino fast-food company, out-performed McDonald's and has twice as many locations in the Philippines as the golden-arch multinational. Jollibee's local knowledge and exploitation of consumer taste gave it a competitive edge over a fast-food juggernaut whose standardized policies were too rigid and ignorant of local norms beyond its national base. Jollibee has become popular from Hong Kong to Middle Eastern countries with large Asian migrant populations (The Lesson the Local Learnt a Little Too Quickly 1996).

This decentralizing trend of the world economy, in which the outcome of intersecting local and global forces is unpredictable, is also manifested in the role of information technologies in international relations. Operating on both global and local levels, simultaneously enabling and restricting, uniting and fragmentary, new information technologies are the engine of glocalization.

The Dual Impact of Information Technology

Historically, the emergence of new information technologies has unleashed forces of cohesion and dispersal. The French Revolution hailed the optical telegraph in 1794 as a great instrument of universal unification and social justice under the values of the Enlightenment, only to see it monopolized by rulers who used it to preserve and expand their control, increasing social, economic, and cultural disparities (Mattelart 1996, 1998). Later the telephone was the harbinger of real-time, interactive communication and brought about one of the most centralizing and cohesive forces of modern social organization: the skyscraper. By making possible communication between hundreds of people concentrated in a reduced space, the telephone made skyscrapers sociologically possible several decades after advances in engineering made them physically possible (Galland 1996). Similarly, radio and television were hailed at their debut as public providers of solutions to social problems by bridging differences and creating shared experiences among people, only to fall into private hands and harbor unabashed consumerim appealing to consumers' most individualistic tendencies (Schiller 1996). The result is a blurring of the boundary between citizenship and consumption (García-Canclini 1995). History unequivocally demonstrates the dual centrifugal and centripetal impact of emerging technologies on society.

The information superhighway is no exception to this historical trend. From its military origins as a nuclear-proof communication system for the U.S. military in the 1960s and 1970s through its development as a tool for scientific research in the 1980s, the Internet came of age as a full-blown communication, entertainment, and commercial medium in the 1990s. The Internet gave new garb to old discourses of utopia and doomsday, reviving fears about increasing technological dependence, a deepening information gap, and global cultural homogenization. Both forces of technological inequality and cultural synchronization cannot be completely discarded. However, technological and cultural counterforces lead to a more complex picture of international relations in the age of the Internet.

Technological innovations have a tendency to spread and take root faster in nonindustrialized countries (Tele-Haves and Have-Nots 1996). The phenomenon of "leapfrogging," which consists of skipping generations of intermediate technologies to adopt more recent technological products, may signal a more hopeful future for developing nations. These countries typically have low investments in national telecommunications infrastructure, so they adopt new and cheaper technologies faster because they have no substantial investments in older and more traditional technologies.

The spread of cellular phones in developing countries is a case in point. In much of South America remote villages have for some years been connected via fixed wireless phone networks, in contrast to Britain, whose first such network began providing services in 1996 (Tele-Haves and Have-Nots 1996). Lebanon, one of the world's smallest nation-states, leads the Arab world in cellular-phone use and has the world's lowest airtime tariffs, while richer states such as Saudi Arabia, Kuwait, or the United Arab Emirates lag behind (Haddadin 1996). Paris has fewer mobile phones than Saõ Paolo, and two out of three phones in Cambodia are mobile phones. It is true that the proliferation of cellular phones in Nigeria, Lebanon, and Brazil is to a large extent due to unreliable state-operated traditional telephone networks. The fact remains that these countries tend to adopt technologies faster than more industrialized nations.

This tendency toward leapfrogging made the expansion of the Internet into developing countries a possibility. It is true that highly industrialized countries such as Sweden and the United States boast sixty-eight and fifty-one telephones per 100 people, respectively, while Africa's teledensity (number of telephones per 100 people) hovers around one (Wresch 1995), and that a high teledensity is essential for an electronic infrastructure. Yet it is important to note that the Internet grows at a faster rate in developing countries than in industrialized countries: In the first half of 1995, for instance, the progression of the number of Internet domains in Africa was 53 percent (35 percent in South Africa, the most industrialized country in the continent), 51 percent in Asia (44 percent in India and China), while it was 40 percent in Western Europe and 35 percent in the United States, the most interconnected country (Renaud and Torres 1996, 25). Although these figures do not reflect a full recession of inequities, since less than 5 percent of the world's population is connected to the Internet, they point to potential for future growth.

Even as connections to the Internet remain relatively rare in developing countries, they are fully exploited, quantitatively and qualitatively. In Tunis, Tunisia, and Lima, Peru, unlike in Western cities, all Internet connections are used (Renaud and Torres 1996). Besides, there are reports from Latin America and Eastern Asia of more than 100 electronic mail accounts accessed via one computer terminal (Renaud and Torres 1996). In other developing countries, universities have found creative ways to connect to the Internet at an affordable cost. Consider the University of Namibia's store-and-forward strategy: Every evening its server collects outgoing electronic mail, connects to a Pretoria, South Africa, link, sends outgoing messages, and receives incoming mail. In spite of the short delays, this approach reduces the university's electronic mail bill to an affordable US$30 a month (Wresch 1995). Burkina-Faso is another example of a successful Internet operation in Africa. A combined effort of nongovernmental agencies, a university, a hospital, and a committed team of engineers has placed Burkina-Faso on a lane of the information superhighway (Renaud 1996). After an initial six users in its early days, Internet traffic in Burkina-Faso now grows by around 100 percent a year, a higher rate than many Western countries.

Visionaries in other developing countries have developed other means to connect to the Internet. The organization *Red Cientifica Peruana* was created in 1991 to establish an Internet infrastructure in Peru. Nongovernmental organizations, a university, and research centers were mobilized under the leadership of José Soriano, an academic. A massive campaign was conducted to convince decision makers and financiers to associate themselves with the project. By 1993 a first (64kbs) permanent connection was established via satellite, and by 1995 data debit grew eightfold and more than 263 institutions were using the networks. All this was achieved with no government subsidies and no international aid. Keeping in mind that Peru is one of most lacking countries in terms of information technology, with only three telephones per 100 people (Renaud and Torres 1996, 25), this is truly a laudable achievement.

Such technological breakthroughs in the developing world gain more importance when they are fully used to advance social and cultural causes. In many cases their use has a direct positive impact on people's quality of life: Due to new communication networks and wireless telephony, rural medical doctors in Zambia can solicit information from hospitals in the capital, and the *Mujer a Mujer* association in Mexico gathered substantial data on a U.S. textile company and succeeded in negotiating a contract with better working conditions for Mexican women (Gresh 1996, 17). The Burkina-Faso network is now used by the Food and Agriculture Organization of the United Nations (FAO) to distribute early crop-alert bulletins, and also by the World Bank, which sends a "Population and Health" newsletter (Renaud 1996, 25). Other countries in Africa are following the example of Burkina-Faso in cooperation with NGOs and other scientific organizations, or with commercial ventures such as British Telecom in Ghana and Compuserve in Gambia, and virtually all of Africa, with a couple of exceptions, is nearly certain to be connected in the near future (Renaud and Torres 1996, 25).

The implications of this glocalization process of local players acting on global avenues are indeed far-reaching. If the trend of eroding centers and emerging peripheries is real, this will make it possible for developing nations to emerge on the international scene. Relatively affordable and available technologies provide a starting point for the development of specialized and information-based industries. Efficient interconnections to the information superhighway and the availability of working opportunities for highly qualified individuals will also reduce the brain drain devastating many developing countries. In turn, this will bring a degree of scientific autonomy that could bring about local industries, possibly curtailing technological dependency.

Linguistic Fragmentation

Besides technological inequalities, concerns about cultural homogenization have been raised as the Internet expands its reach. These concerns revolve around two main issues: the predominance of the English language on the Internet and the fear that local cultures lose their cultural identities under the weight of Western popular culture. Since the Internet is primarily a U.S. phenomenon, and since most producers and consumers of Internet material are based in the United States, English became the de facto language of the network. In 1996, 80 percent of all information on the Internet was in English (The Coming Global Tongue 1996). This justifies fears of cultural homogenization through language. Some trends, however, point to a more fragmented linguistic landscape on the Internet. These trends are primarily the changes that English is subjected to on the Internet, the revival of old or minority languages, the rise of machine translation, and the possible resurgence of languages that could compete with English as the lingua franca of the electronic age.

Whereas the contemporary United States and Britain alone account for 70 percent of the 320 million people whose first language is English, there are more than 57 million speakers of creolized English is countries such as Jamaica and Liberia (The Coming Global Tongue 1996). Other English-speaking countries such as Belize, Australia, and New Zealand further diversify the world map of the English language. Besides, English-speaking countries such as India and Jamaica have exploited their knowledge of English and their cheap labor to sell a variety of data-processing services to more industrialized countries. The mixture of language and technology also produces interesting results.

Technological innovations are a fertile ground for new terminology. Like any specialized language, elements of cyberjargon are bound to make it into the mainstream. The magazine *Wired* has already produced a "Principles of English Usage in the Digital Age," and a "Hacker's Dictionary" with more than 2,000 entries is available on several World Wide Web sites. The availability of a variety of software for electronic "chatting" has also created the written conversation. This new genre features broken sentences, abbreviations, and a "get to the point" attitude (The Coming Global Tongue 1996). To compensate for facial and other nonverbal cues, a variety of "emoticons" were introduced, such as the "smiley" and other graphical renderings of human emotions. The rapid drop of the number of native-English speakers on the Internet has led to the advent of more creolized forms of the language. All these factors have led to fractured, hybridized strains of English.

The myriad cybercultures and other virtual communities have developed new vocabularies and linguistic modes. Electronic subcultures have developed their own jargon, while diasporic communities have created a variety of linguistic reconversions to celebrate their native cultures. For one thing, the Internet has witnessed a relatively strong presence of ethnic or minority languages. Without the Internet, individuals speaking these minority languages have to forfeit them because of the absence of exile communities large enough to sustain the native language. In the United States, for instance, the Armenian and Arabic communities are large enough to sustain their respective languages. Languages of smaller exile communities, such as Catalan, Breton, Gaelic, Macedonian, or Yoruba, however, profited when the Internet connected relatively isolated expatriates. Furthermore, while "larger" languages such as Chinese and Arabic have developed software, smaller linguistic groups have creatively developed transliterations to transcend the Latin alphabet and converse in their native languages.

Finally, two factors can in the future undermine the dominance of English on the Internet. One of them is direct machine translation. Translating machines adequately translate denotative language, but fail to render connotations and other culturally bound meanings. Still-more-sophisticated translating machines adopted on a wide scale in the future may decrease the usage of English on the Internet. As early as 1994, AT&T released a corporate video outlining the company's "vision of the future," featuring direct-translation multimedia telephones. The second factor is the possible rise of a world language that could compete with English. The French government has instituted a wide variety of measures and earmarked a massive amount of funds to create, advance, and preserve a strong Francophone presence on the Internet. However, observers see Spanish, the fastest-growing language, or Chinese, the language of the largest national population, as more probable competitors to English (The Coming Global Tongue 1996).

Consequently, the reign of English on the Internet is not absolute. In the Middle Ages, Latin was the lingua franca of letters, science, and religion in Europe. Although its usage may have dominated other languages during that era, few of them died as a result. The same can be said of the Arab–Muslim empire that stretched from Spain to China for several hundred years. Arabic's dominance was in no way total. The Soviet empire is a more recent example of the failure of a dominant language, even when supported by systematic integrationist policies, substantial resources, and even physical violence, to eradicate smaller, local languages. If historical evidence is to be believed, the current dominance of English as the world language may be only temporary.

Cultural Hybridization

The fragmentation of English and the questioning of its dominance are part of a larger phenomenon of cultural hybridization. A variety of studies have documented how local communities adapt to global media and popular culture (Featherstone 1994; García-Canclini 1988; Hannerz 1994; Kraidy 1996). Instead of the destruction of local traditions, we see these traditions rearticulated within the globalizing force of modernity. Rather than a monolithic imposition of Western values and ways of life, mainly from the United States, we see the emergence of hybrid cultural forms and social arrangements. Most of these studies have focused on traditional media forms, such as popular music, film, and television. Although this kind of reception research is virtually nonexistent within the context of the Internet, the factors already discussed lead us to think that similar hybridizing patterns will be found. In many cases, language can function as a barrier to Western popular culture carried by the English language. Smaller English-speaking countries such as New Zealand are more prone to cultural invasions than non-English-speaking nations. Besides, ironically, how can we speak of West-to-East or North-to-South cultural imperialism via the Internet when less than 5 percent of the world's population is connected, and when large population segments throughout the world remain illiterate?

Political Fragmentation

Besides cultural hybridization, the end of the Cold War triggered an unprecedented fragmentation of the international political landscape. Instead of a world of nation-states polarized under the influence of two superpowers, we now see a decline in the sovereignty of nation-states and numerous subnational and supranational actors yielding greater influence than ever before. Within countries, we see regions and provinces, such as Cataloña in Spain and Québec in Canada, gaining in autonomy and visibility, while developing countries witness the burgeoning activity of social, environmental, and health-related nongovernmental organizations, and international organizations such as the Red Cross and the International Monetary Fund. Above all, transnational corporations are gaining the power that state governments are losing.

This decentralization and loss of power by states is also manifested at the level of the means of information and communication. Numerous local events have achieved global visibility because of the exploitation of the Internet. When members of the Tupac Amaru rebel Peruvian group stormed the Japanese Embassy in Lima, Peru, in 1997, dozens of sympathetic sites on the World Wide Web promoted the cause of Tupac Amaru in English, French, and Spanish. Islamic groups are highly active on the Internet, propagating their faith to millions of Muslims scattered across the globe. Throughout the world, local dissidents have put the Internet at the service of political action (Alfonso 1996), while activists participate in electronic debates and make their voices heard. This leads some observers to refer to the Internet as a "new weapon" for democracy (Bissio 1996).

DISCUSSION AND CONCLUSION

Concerns about an information gap are warranted, but the view that the gap between information-rich and information-poor is irreversibly widening is questionable. A plethora of social and economic factors provide the basis for a hopeful perspective on the possibilities of the gap being bridged between the industrialized and developing worlds. Glocalization, understood as a blending of global forces with local elements, adequately accounts for the complexity of global relations in the Information Age. The argument developed in this chapter demonstrates that glocalization is a conceptually viable and empirically defensible theoretical framework. Unlike cultural imperialism, with its assumptions of one-way information flow and intentional cultural domination, and unlike globalization, with its notions of cultural synchronization and world homogenization, glocalization recognizes and conceptualizes the technological developments, linguistic creolization, cultural hybridization, social decentralization, and political fragmentation that characterize contemporary international relations.

Phenomena such as leapfrogging and low-cost technologies have the potential to bring a level of scientific autonomy and curtail technological dependency, therefore halting the brain drain from developing countries. This can be achieved by research and development made accessible by information networks, by which some regions of the developing world have already started using technology as a producer good rather than a consumer good. This might signal the dawn of an era of emergence in the developing world of new healthy, independent, but interconnected sustainable economies.

Although the English language currently dominates the Internet, current and future trends point to increased creolization of English vocabulary, potential competition, and technological developments that may undermine English as the language of choice in the information age. Research on mass media and popular-culture reception around the world points to cultural hybridization rather than synchronization, whereas information technologies contribute to the decentralization of societies and local political groups disseminate their messages to a global audience via the Internet. These developments point to receding center–periphery international arrangements and to emerging decentralized, fragmented, and multifaceted patterns, best captured theoretically by the concept of glocalization.

When conceptualizing glocalization, it is important to keep in mind that inequalities persist among haves and have-nots. Glocalization by no means glosses over these disparities. It rather argues that boundaries between the information-poor and information-rich are constantly redrawn, and centers and peripheries are continuously rearticulated. It defends the possibility that both rich and developing nations can meet the challenges of the future. In the glocalization framework, the road to a just, prosperous, and peaceful world lies in the acknowledgment of the complexity of, and a tolerance for the ambiguities of, international technologically mediated relations. The future lies in the construction of information bridges over the information gap. Rather than a hypocritical technoutopian celebration of the information age, and instead of a self-defeating technophobic condemnation of its impact, we should focus on grasping its complexity, protecting ourselves from its perils, and taking advantage of its promises. In doing so we should remember that "it is unlikely that the information age will be as good as we hope or as bad as we fear. It will certainly be far different than we imagine" (Wresch 1996, 247).

NOTE

The author wishes to thank Ute Sartorius, Department of Industrial Technology, University of North Dakota, for helpful comments on this chapter.

REFERENCES

Alfonso, C. A. 1996. Au service de l'action politique. *Manière de Voir*, October, 44–45.

Appadurai, A. 1994. Disjuncture and Difference in the Global Cultural Economy. In *Global Culture: Nationalism, Globalization and Modernity*, edited by M. Featherstone. London and Newbury Park, Calif.: Sage.

Beltran. J. 1978. TV Etchings in the Minds of Latin Americans: Conservatism, Materialism, and Conformism. *Gazette* 24: 61–85.

Beniger, J. 1986. *The Control Revolution*. Cambridge: Harvard University Press.

Bissio, R. 1996. Nouvelles armes pour les démocrates. *Manière de Voir*, October, 42–43.

The Coming Global Tongue. 1996. *The Economist*, 21 December, 75–78.

Doheny-Farina, S. 1997. *The Wired Neighborhood*. New Haven: Yale University Press.

Evans, P. 1979. *Dependent Development: The Alliance of Multinational, State and Local Capital in Brazil*. Princeton, N.J.: Princeton University Press.

Featherstone, M., ed. 1994. *Global Culture: Nationalism, Globalization and Modernity*. London and Newbury Park, Calif.: Sage.

Fine for Some. 1996. *The Economist*, 8 September, 72–73.

Galland, B. 1996. De l'urbanisation à la glocalisation. *Terminal*, Autumn, 71–72.

García-Canclini, N. 1988. *Culturas híbridas: Estrategias para entrar y salir de la modernidad*. México, D.F.: Grijalbo.

———. 1995. *Consumidores y ciudadanos: Conflictos multiculturales de la globalización*. México, D.F.: Grijalbo.

Giddens, A. 1990. *The Consequences of Modernity*. Cambridge, Mass.: Polity Press.

Gresh, A. 1996. Et les citoyens du Sud? *Le Monde Diplomatique*, May, 17.

Haddadin, H. 1996. Lebanon Leads Arab World in Cellular Phone Subscriptions. Beirut, Reuters, 16 October.

Hamelink, C. 1983. *Cultural Autonomy in Global Communication*. New York: Longman.

Hannerz, U. 1994. Cosmopolitans and Locals in World Culture. In *Global Culture: Nationalism, Globalization and Moderntiy*, edited by M. Featherstone. London and Newbury Park, Calif.: Sage.

Kraidy, M. 1996. Towards a Semiosphere of Hybrid Identities: A Native Ethnography of Glocalization. Ph.D. diss., Ohio University.

Kerr, C. 1964. *Industrialism and Industrial Man*. New York: Oxford University Press.

Lerner, D. 1958. *The Passing of Traditional Society*. New York: Free Press.

The Lesson the Local Learnt a Little Too Quickly. 1996. *The Economist*, 28 September, 71.

Lomnitz, C. 1994. Decadence in Times of Globalization. *Current Anthropology* 9: 257–267.

Mattelart, A. 1979. *Mutinational Corporations and the Control of Culture: The Ideological Apparatuses of Imperialism*. Newark, N.J.: Harvester Press.

———. 1983. *Transnationals and the Third World: The Struggle for Culture*. London: Bergin and Garvey International.

———. 1996. Les "paradis" de la communication. *Manière de Voir*, October, 11–13.

———. 1998. Généalogie de nouveaux scénarios de la communication. In *L'Après-Télévision: Multimédia, virtuel, Internet*. Actes du Colloque "25 images/seconde," edited by J. Berdot, F. Calvez, and I. Ramonet. Valence, France: CRAC.

Moinet, N. 1996. Stratégie de réseaux et intelligence économique. *Stratégie et Contexte/MC*. Poitiers, France: Université de Poitiers, May 30.

Panos. 1996. <http://www.oneworld.org/panos/>.

Renaud, P. 1996, Un exemple Burkinabé. *Le Monde Diplomatique*, February, 25.

Renaud, P., and A. Torres. 1996. Internet, une chance pour le Sud. *Le Monde Diplomatique*, February, 25.

Robertson, R. 1992. *Globalization*. London and Newbury Park, Calif.: Sage.

———. 1994. Mapping the Global Condition: Globalization as the Central Concept. In *Global Culture: Nationalism, Globalization and Modernity*, edited by M. Featherstone. London and Newbury Park, Calif.: Sage.

Rogers, E. M., ed. 1976. *Communication and Developmemt*. Beverly Hills, Calif.: Sage.

Salwen, M. 1991. Cultural Imperialism: A Media Effects Approach. *Critical Studies in Mass Communication* 8: 29–38.

Schiller, H. 1973. *The Mind Managers*. Beacon Press: Boston.

———. 1976. *Communication and Cultural Domination*. White Plains, N.Y.: International Arts and Sciences Press.

———. 1985. Electronic Information Flows: New Basis for Global Domination? In *Television in Transition: Papers From the First International Television Studies Conference*, edited by P. Drummond and R. Paterson. London: British Film Institute.

———, ed. 1992. *The Ideology of International Communication*. New York: Institute for Media Analysis.

———. 1996. *Information Inequality*. London and New York: Routledge.

Schramm, W. L. 1964. *Mass Media and National Development: The Role of Information in the Developing Countries*. Stanford: Stanford University Press.

Sreberny-Mohammadi, A. 1987. The Local and the Global in International Communications. In *Mass Media and Society*, edited by James Curran and Michael Gurevitch. London: Edward Arnold.

———. 1997. The Many Faces of Imperialism. In *Beyond Cultural Imperialism: Globalization, Communication and the New International Order*, edited by P. Golding and P. Harris. London and Thousand Oaks, Calif.: Sage.

Straubhaar, J. 1991. Beyond Media Imperialism: Assymetrical Dependence and Cultural Proximity. *Critical Studies in Mass Communication* 8: 29–38.

Tele-Haves and Have-Nots. 1996. *The Economist*, 18 May, 19–20.

Tomlinson, J. 1991. *Cultural Imperialism*. Baltimore and London: Johns Hopkins University Press.

Tunstall, J. 1977. *The Media Are American*. Beverly Hills, Calif.: Sage.

Varis, T. 1984 The International Flow of Television Programs. *Journal of Communication* 34: 143–152.

Waters, M. 1996. *Globalization*. London and New York: Routledge.

Wresch, W. 1995. New Lifelines. *Internet World*. Available http://www.Internetworld.com/print/monthly/1995/11/lifelines.

Wresch, W. 1996. *Disconnected: Haves and Have-Nots in the Information Age*. New Brunswick, N.J.: Rutgers University Press.

4

The Internet and the Problem of Legitimacy: A Tocquevillian Perspective

Jonathan Mendilow

One of my favorite science-fiction short stories makes literal use of the *deus ex machina*. It turns on an experiment, foretold far into the future. The computers on all the populated planets were linked so as to share knowledge and to consult one another in total joint cooperation. Then the ultimate question was posed: "Is there a God?" Lights flashed and there came the ultimate answer: "Yes, *now* there is." The terrified questioner, leaping too late to switch the computer off, was struck by a bolt of lightning from the sky.

This, of course, is more than a modern version of the Frankenstein plot, where a human creation breaks loose and turns on his creator. Here the roles are reversed, with the machine assuming command. But more interesting still is a further dimension. Now that a God has been created by the very question, it is the machine that determines human values and penalizes the questioner seeking desperately to preserve control.

The appeal of the story lies equally in what it perceived and in what it failed to perceive about the transformations beginning at the time of writing and in the midst of which we are still caught up. First published in 1954 (Brown 1976), it did not actually use the term "computer" at all, but rather "cybernetic machine." Nevertheless, it is alive to the fact that an information revolution is taking place and that it is inextricably related to a revolution in communication. Thus, the question concerning God was posed at a particular place, but it travelled the entire universe, from computer to computer, yielding a cumulative instant answer representing, as it were, the entire computer "species." What the story did not envision was the rapid progress of the information and communication revolution. The "far future" turned out to be much closer to the time of writing, and the huge electronic brain-machine, linked to others of its kind and consulting them at the speed of light, is small, cheap, and simple enough to sit on my desk, as well as on some hundred million other desks in the United States alone.

This, however, did not prevent the author from putting his finger on the uniqueness of what is now going on. The use of the term "machine" and the echoes of Mary Shelley invite a brief comparison. Like the Industrial Revolution of the eighteenth and nineteenth centuries, what is happening today is bringing about interrelated changes in the conditions of day-to-day living as well as in the mind-set and values of the time. And yet the former revolution hinged on the invention and exploitation of devices geared to save labor power, with the dislocations in the mind-set as a by-product.

The current revolution centers on the maximization of brain power: the production and transmission of knowledge and ideas. Changes in the mind-set and values are direct and rapid, and so are the effects on the modes of organization and behavior. This is true of society as a whole, though for individuals such changes may seem relatively slow. Still, the change for those directly exposed to the computer may be virtually instantaneous. In terms of the story, once a question had been posed to the computer, the answer came too rapidly for the questioner to catch up.

But the most interesting perception offered by the story relates to the question of authority. Legitimacy does not inhere naturally in, nor is it a permanent feature of, political arrangements. It is a social construct, directly related as cause and effect to conceptions of the private and collective self and to the socioeconomic practices based on them. As attested by the relationship between the questioner and the computer, rapid shifts in knowledge, values, and ideas may consequently lead to the breakdown of legitimacy and to its corollary, the establishment of new forms of government.

Again, what the author did not, and probably could not, envisage in this context is no less interesting. In the story, humanity is depicted as a unified "public," and so are the computers. This is being changed by the proliferation of Internet use. It is common today to refer to the information superhighway; in the famous words of Al Gore, it is a set of "high-speed networks . . . that tie together millions of computers, providing capabilities that we cannot even imagine." Yet the analogy is taken from an earlier phase of American history and simply does not fit the Internet. If we were to update it, we would have had to consider the fact that the Internet serves to link individuals into communities that are not based on territorial contiguity or personal acquaintance, but are located in cyberspace.

In brief, we would have had to come up with a superhighway with an infinite number of lanes, leading instantaneously from everywhere to everywhere in the world. There is no such thing, since a highway serves societies with a degree of stability, whereas the Internet potentially undermines existing societies while creating an endless number of borderless new ones based on the common interest, knowledge, or values of often anonymous individuals. The possible result of such tendencies is foreshadowed in the phenomenon of Internet addiction: the absorption of individuals, each in his or her own "virtual" Internet "society," at the expense of relations in the "real world" and the norms these engender. And whereas the total disappearance of the traditional forms of society is not in the offing, government becomes less relevant, the relations between it and the infinite number of Internet societies and among themselves becomes increasingly unclear, and the question of legitimacy is greatly exacerbated.

These, of course, are still embryonic tendencies, but it must be remembered that as the changes resulting from the previous Industrial Revolution percolated throughout society they led to the questioning of authority and the gradual rise of today's "brave new world." Nor is the awareness of such dangers completely lacking. In the Third World it explains attempts made by such authoritarian regimes as Iran or China to ban the Internet or at least to censor its use. The common assumption, however, is that in such contexts the Internet will act as a carrier of information and, knowledge being power, as an agent of individual freedom and Western democracy. The Internet is understood, then, as a highway leading to a preexisting destiny and, furthermore, as bringing about processes that are essentially comparable to those brought by industrialism in the First World.

As for the West itself, the superhighway image fosters the tendency to conceive the Internet as no more than a quantitative improvement on what already exists and hence as not causing any dislocation. Even here there are new voices. For example, the president of the company that makes the black boxes that connect the Internet around the world predicted that the Internet "will have every bit as much impact on society as the Industrial Revolution . . . but instead of happening over a hundred years, like the Industrial Revolution, it will happen over seven years" (Friedman 1998). Yet such voices are few and no full-fledged analysis of the relationship between the Internet and government legitimacy in the West has, I believe, appeared so far.

In what follows I suggest that by applying to the twentieth century a neglected theory of crises of authority propounded by Alexis de Tocqueville we may enhance the way the impacts of the Internet are theorized and point to some serious issues for the future. This is not for any a lack of more recent studies of legitimacy crises. The present century has witnessed three major waves of interest in the subject: between the two World Wars, between the early 1970s and mid-1980s, and resulting from the wholesale collapse of communist systems in the late 1980s and early 1990s. However, between the time of Marx and the end of the 1980s focus was chiefly laid on crisis tendencies in advanced capitalist systems or in specific capitalist countries, as though crises of authority were peculiar to them.

Many of the critics actually were strongly influenced by Marx himself. Left-wing scholars have commonly prophesied an imminent crisis bred of the contradictions between the forces and the relations of production, between the functions of accumulation and those of legitimation of the capitalist state, and between democracy and liberalism (e.g., O'Connor 1973; Offe 1972; Wolfe 1977). Non-Marxists, too, assumed that if a *Götterdämmerung* occurred (or, as in Nibset's [1977] version, *The Twilight of Authority*) it would be, to quote another title, *The Breakdown of Democratic Regimes* (Linz and Stepan 1978).

Even neoconservatives warned of the dangers of government bankruptcy and of the ungovernability following excessive commitments to spend, especially on welfare, more than capitalist economies could provide through growth. The loss of favor of such predictions following the fall of the Berlin Wall caused researchers of crises of authority in the USSR and other communist systems to treat their subjects with little reference to the accumulated work in the field. Ironically, they thereby fell into the same weakness of analyzing legitimacy crises as though they were phenomena unique to the type of system they were studying.

The upshot is that today we are left with many specific studies, but only two theories of wider applicability that could be of use to us in assessing the possible consequences of the information revolution: those put forward by Gramsci of the first and Habermas of the second "wave" of interest in the subject in the twentieth century. The former defined "organic crises" as resulting from the withdrawal by the masses of their passive acceptance of an ideology, one that reflected the interests of the ruling class that had bound them to the established order. Such a crisis may result from a failure in some major national undertaking, or from the emergence of new demands on the part of segments of the population who have suddenly become politically conscious. The latter, in an analysis which he later partly disavowed, ascribed "legitimation crisis" to the results of societal inadaptability. It arises when the state can no longer adapt to major changes, whether external or internal, that threaten its established constitutive tradition.

Irrespective of the differences between the two, they give rise to similar reservations. Apart from occasional comments, Gramsci confined his analysis to capitalist systems, while Habermas explicitly limited his arguments to the advanced industrial countries. The former did not clarify what he considered to be a major undertaking or its failure. Nor did he take into account the complexities and contexts that make it difficult to predict effects arising out of similar situations. The latter offered a discussion so abstract that no weight was given to any contextual variation. What emerges is a checklist of conditions common to advanced capitalist countries that may precipitate a crisis of authority, but no explanation why these led to a crisis in the one case or time and not in another case or time.

The appeal of Tocqueville's theory lies in that he brings us back to the pre-Marxist era of thinking about legitimization crises while offering ideas that could be applied to modern society. Social scientists, he believed, ought to aim at influencing social behavior and promoting human values. In his magnum opus, *Democracy in America* (1969, iv, 18–19, 311, 315), he specifically stated that his purpose was to facilitate the understanding of the new democratic trends and to make use of the lessons offered by the new world to the main problem that the old world was wrestling with, namely, how to reap the benefits of democracy while avoiding its dangers.

Similarly, his passionate concern with making sense of the French Revolution and its occurrence in France rather than in any other European country was fueled by his urge to anticipate the future of French politics and to pinpoint dangers inherent in the new democratic dispensation (Tocqueville 1955, x). On the other hand, he had little trust in grand theories "that make all the events of history depend on great first causes linked together by the chain of fate." These, he argued, "banish men from the history of the human race. Their boasted breadth seems to me narrow, and their mathematical exactness false. . . . I believe . . . that man's important historical facts can be explained only by accidental circumstances" (Tocqueville 1970, 62).

The reconciliation between his aim and this realization lay in the belief that accidental circumstances themselves occur and acquire meaning because of something that is not accidental. "Chance can do nothing unless the ground has been prepared in advance." To use his words again, what takes place is "born of general causes fertilized by accidents. And to make the whole thing depend on the former is as superficial as attributing it solely to the latter" (Tocqueville 1970, 62). His effort to comprehend the history and to trace the development of his native country led him, therefore, to come up with a general theory of what lies beyond specific political arrangements, and what allows them to persist or collapse. It is this effort to elucidate underlying causes of legitimacy crises that facilitates the application of his arguments to a context so different from his own.

In what follows I shall first attempt to offer an account of what Tocqueville himself had in mind and how it relates to theories propounded by other thinkers of his time, especially Thomas Carlyle. In the final part of this chapter I shall offer a brief discussion of the way this can enrich our speculations about the possible political effects of the Internet, and of what all this could tell us about "cyberspace imperialism."

• • •

It is perhaps a sign of our own times that the term "crisis" has deteriorated through overuse to indicate any serious situation. It is consequently important to begin a discussion of Tocqueville's notions by pointing out that he was using the term in its original, medical sense: the turning point in a disease when a decisive change takes place leading either to full recovery or to death. This largely explains why he commonly compared societies to persons and tended to replace the term malady or disease for crisis. It is not that all social diseases necessarily lead to a crisis. He distinguished between what can be compared to a passing childhood disease which renders "the health of the body social . . . more vigorous and more durable" (Tocqueville 1985, 215) and complaints of which "the sources of the illness are deeper" (p. 6), thereby leading eventually to a crisis.

At first sight this does not differ greatly from the usage of the term by modern critics like Habermas (1976, 1). But illness in the latter's use of the metaphor could have somatic as well as psychosomatic sources. Tocqueville, by contrast, insisted that "whatever anyone says, it is ideas that stir the world" (Tocqueville 1968, 58), and it is they that "in the end govern society" (Tocqueville 1862, vol. 1, p. 351). Hence, sicknesses that derive from somatic sources "inoculate" society, whereas those fueled by psychological sources may lead to crises even if the physical symptoms do not manifest themselves immediately: "Malad[ies] of men's minds [are] suddenly brought to a crisis by an unforeseen chance accident" (Tocqueville 1970, 35). This, however, should not be taken as indicating an idealist position, nor did Tocqueville consider, as did Burke or the Romantics, that society was a collective organism. Rather, what he had in mind was a dialectical, mutually determining interrelationship between the underlying assumptions of society and what he referred to as its mores, its social conditions, laws, and circumstances. But to get at his full meaning, we must clarify what he understood by "consent."

By the second quarter of the nineteenth century radical thought was less concerned with establishing the proper limits of government rule and more with the way in which it can be made responsive to the wishes of the governed. Consent therefore came to be measured by the specific arrangements and procedures by which governing was carried out. This, in turn, rested on the fundamental premise that human beings are essentially alike in thought and action, and hence that similar political arrangements will yield similar results. For Tocqueville this required the ignoring of an essential human attribute, namely, that thought and activity are causally interrelated and that consequently neither can be taken as existing by itself, each being an artifact of the other. Hence, social interaction is conditioned by the way people think of themselves and of others, whereas such thoughts are largely created by their social interactions.

All societies must organize to get things done, and all must have their methods of rendering interrelations predictable. Such organization however is not directed by natural laws or mere technical considerations, but by the meanings attached to the activities and the norms and standards that have developed to regulate them in the society in question. Consent, in sum, is a psychological phenomenon, a function of the individual's identification with the community and his or her acceptance of what it stands for as a natural way of life. Whether the institutions and practices by which the way of life is regulated are liberal or not is irrelevant, for without such consent government cannot last, irrespective of its nature. "Whatever anyone says, the principle of the sovereignty of the people is at the base of all forms of government, and it hides [even] under the least free of institutions" (Tocqueville 1970). For Tocqueville, the blank assertion common in the West that the immense power of the Russian Czar rested on nothing but naked force, for example, merely reflected lack of sensitivity to the fact that the Russians lived, as it were in a different world, one which "had no contact with West and the new spirit stirring it" (p. 117). In truth, the Czar's power rested on the "firmest foundations" of "the wishes and ardent sympathies of the Russian people. . . . [They] saw the Emperor not only as the legitimate ruler, but also as God's representative and almost as God himself" (p. 239). This explains the refusal to generalize about the consequences of the spread of egalitarianism and democracy in America and the various countries of Europe. Parallel developments could bring about diverse results because of differences in social structure, geography, ways of doing things, and culture. Thus, the English and the French had a common starting point in the Middle Ages. Yet the former developed free institutions that made them so different "that they form almost a distinct species of men" (Tocqueville 1862, vol. 2, p. 336). The French, by contrast, had ways of looking at things and of conducting affairs that rendered the dangers of democratic tyranny more acute.

This argument faces the reader with a problem, for if legitimacy does not result from any specific arrangement, where does it spring from? Tocqueville's answer leads to what he called "the hidden source of energy," or "the life principle" of society, a set of axiomatic premises, conceptions, and perceptions that, though "independent of the organs which perform the various functions needed" serve as the condition of their existence (Tocqueville 1955, 79). This has reverberations in the thought of the period. Hegel had already referred to the *Sittlichkeit*, the often tacit perceptions, conceptions, and values taken as axiomatic by society that underlay its moral codes and customs, its institutions, laws, and policies. In England, Burke asserted that societies have an "innate nature" and "prejudices" that direct it as it unfolds in time.

Even a century later, something similar can still be discerned in Mosca's concept of the "political formula." But the critic closest to Tocqueville's own time, and the one who offered an argument that is the closest to Tocqueville's own, is Thomas Carlyle. In fact, though Tocqueville never mentioned the English thinker, it is inconceivable that he was not familiar with his "best seller," the *French Revolution*, which was published a short time after Tocqueville began his own writing career and which opens with a synoptic overview of his thesis. Yet Carlyle's clearest formulation was in the earlier "Characteristics," which the Frenchman may indeed not have read: "Every polity has a spiritual principle. . . . All its tendencies of endeavor, specialties of custom, its laws, policies and whole procedure, are prescribed by [an] idea and flow naturally from it. . . . This idea . . . is properly the soul of the State, its life" (Carlyle 1907, vol. 28, pp. 13–14).

Be that as it may, neither the French philosopher nor the English man of letters gave meanings a precise form. Their analysis of stable societies and their treatment of authority crises clearly imply, however, that they were dealing with the factors that endow society with its identity and distinguish it from mere aggregations of unrelated individuals and from other societies. This rests on tacit assumptions regarding the permanent features of the collective and its environment serving as a kind of a prism through which members select and interpret information about the group itself and the world in which it finds itself. It also includes resulting conceptions taken for granted concerning what Edward Shils (1972) called "the center," that is, the broad ethical standards that determine the distribution of benefits, the permissible range of disagreements, the unarticulated understandings of what society should strive for, and the benchmarks for the evaluation of the workings of the institutions of authority.

Because what is in question is not a logically structured sequence but a metalogical world picture, Tocqueville often employed the term "passion" for political sentiments deriving directly from it, unmediated by conscious thought or interest. Despite, and perhaps because, he was far from accepting the Rousseauistic call for a civil religion, it is noteworthy that he recognized a "family tie" between political and religious passions: "On both sides general goods, immaterial to a certain degree, are in sight; on both sides an ideal of society is pursued, a certain perfecting of the human species, the picture of which raised souls above contemplation of private interest and carries them away" (Tocqueville 1985, 192).

For both Tocqueville and Carlyle, such a "life principle" or "idea" fosters what today we would refer to as the political culture of society, the habits of thought and attitudes toward political matters and customs that typify it and give a degree of predictability to the behavior of its members. This is wide and flexible enough to permit considerable variation, and the range of possible governments is similarly wide. But whatever the differences, to enjoy a degree of longevity, governments must be firmly rooted in the political culture of their societies. Their policies should aim at goals within the parameters agreeable to it, their procedures ought to be considered acceptable, and the means should accord with what is generally regarded as admissible. Thus, when writing on America, Tocqueville could assert that it was the unique Puritan world picture that explains the society it created, together with its characteristic ways of perception and behavior. The principle aim of his work was, in turn, to show that its political institutions were rooted in and explicable by "the practical experience, the habits, the opinions, in short the customs of the Americans" (Tocqueville 1969, 47).

At bottom, we have here an epistemological argument. The evaluation of government implies some system of reference. In brief, government behavior, like any behavior, is defined and assessed by a reality. But realities are not absolute. They are social constructs, formed with time by societies as they give meaning to their world. What is involved is not "the thing" in itself but what we make of it, and what we make of it is a function of what we bring to it. This is not to say that individuals give an identical meaning to changing realities or that the construction of meanings is a onetime affair. Rather, it is a dynamic process working itself out on several interrelated levels. What Tocqueville called the "life principle," and Carlyle the "Idea," refers to the more-stable and less-detailed comprehension that provides the framework on which everything else depends.

To use an analogy, it serves as the foundation of a building supporting the walls of society's political culture. These are not to be equated with the foundation itself, but are determined by it. In turn they determine the space within which particular divisions may be made and the range of usages to which each room and the entire building may be put to. The comparison of this last level to the comprehension of individuals in society explains why each individual forms his or her own reality and why one can assume a diversity that reflects different times and circumstances; yet there exists an underlying world picture and a unifying collective reality that establishes the contours of every individual mind-set and serves as the foundation of government legitimacy.

A brief comment on Gramsci's (1971) notion of hegemony may clarify the issue further. The concept refers to the legitimacy conferred upon a class when its philosophy is absorbed by society at large to become part and parcel of the people's "common sense." By this Gramsci meant the sense common to all, or in his terms, the uncritical "philosophy of non-philosophers" (p. 419). It is the worldview of the average man, compounded of the accumulated experiences, opinions, beliefs, assumptions, and knowledge of his group. Language, popular religion, customs, and ways of life in which the common sense is embedded thus become instruments of hegemony. This explains the common denominator in the way Tocqueville, Carlyle, and Gramsci conceptualized crises of authority as the outcome of the dispersal of society's "source of energy" (Tocqueville), the "death of the idea" (Carlyle), or the rejection by the masses of the ideology that has infiltrated their common sense (Gramsci).

But the differences are no less illuminating. Writing from within the Marxist tradition, Gramsci devoted his analysis to class conflict. His common sense comes from class ideology and serves to justify government by a particular class. The failure of such a government in some major political undertaking or the rise of a powerful contending class may terminate the hegemony of the ruling ideology and bring about a crisis of legitimacy. By contrast, the two pre-Marxist thinkers drew a distinction between crises of particular governments and crises of legitimacy. As we have already mentioned, Tocqueville actually regarded the former type of malady as a potential source of strength, as one might say, an inoculation of the body politic. The latter form of crisis is of an altogether different species. It is the end result of processes that bring about the growing disparity between institutions of authority and their output, on the one hand, and the political culture and deeper hidden principles on which governments are ultimately based, on the other.

To return to our previous analogy, this is what happens when the walls and the foundations can no longer cope with the excess of interior changes and additions. The building may then collapse and a new one will have to be erected if a stable form of government is to be set up at all. In fact, Tocqueville was tormented by the fear that France would never see the termination of the effects of the French Revolution in his own time.

Tocqueville and Carlyle both further agreed that such processes have their source in the corrosive effects that realities have on the deep structures and basic assumptions held by society. Yet it must not be assumed that they played the same tune exactly in the same key. For Tocqueville, processes culminating in legitimacy crises are driven by government failure to respond to "changes that the mind of man is apt to undergo as a result of changes in his material environment" (Tocqueville 1955, 113). The retaining of government structures, laws, and policies irrespective of shifts in their contexts must of necessity create a widening gap between two factors: the inability to react satisfactorily to needs and demands arising from among the governed, and the basis of legitimacy that rests on the claim that those in authority act on behalf of society and in return earn its approbation. The outcome is a situation where structures of authority and old ways of doing things become "meaningless anachronisms," which, "while keeping their original forms, had been drained of substance" (p. 30). Together with the sense that government has become irrelevant, what then arises are doubts about the basic premises sustaining its rule. In such cases an inverse proportion is established between the antiquity of institutions and their lack of credibility (p. 17).

Changes in the material environment may derive from any number of causes, notably, technological innovations and their socioeconomic repercussions, as Tocqueville claimed, in the France of his day (e.g., Tocqueville 1970, 63, 75). A special instance, however, is when the activities of government or of those in authority are out of line with the infrastructure that confers legitimacy upon them. One reason for the shattering of the ancient regime, for example, was the abandoning of the principles informing it by the landed nobility, which had abnegated its local responsibilities and flocked to the court in Versailles. The persistence of obsolete laws regardless of the ensuing social and economic realities were, Tocqueville argued, at the root of the fury that prompted the Revolution.

Admittedly, outdated feudal arrangements obtained not only in France. However, the old order there was perceived to be less tolerable than in other European countries because the peasant had freed himself from dependence on the aristocracy and became a petty landlord in his own right. As such, he himself felt directly the burden of the feudal laws that had lost any justification they had once had, while the continued demand by the aristocracy for all their benefits were perceived as outrageous. This explains the radicalism of the pre-Revolutionary ideologues who "enounced theories so strongly opposed to those that were still regarded as basic to the social order" that they demanded the total remodeling of the society founded on their own logic alone (Tocqueville 1970, 140).

Carlyle (1907), in contrast, held legitimacy crises to be the potential outcome of inevitable, natural, and cyclical causes. Every Idea has "its period of youth, of maturity, of perfection, of decline, nothing born but to die" (vol. 10, p. 57). Our basic assumption must rest on knowledge, conscious or not, of the world in which we act. Yet knowledge is never exhaustive, nor is it necessarily accurate. Consequently, while activity based on the Idea is purposive, it need not succeed in attaining its preconceived objective. It is rather a process performed more or less consciously with more or less certainty as to its outcome, depending on the nature of any particular act and on the capacity of the actor.

Moreover, social and political activities may create new sets of relationships or alter existing ones, so that basic premises become inapplicable. As a result, the Idea is in constant flux as old truths are discarded and new ones incorporated to become part of the general consciousness. Every age "fashions for itself" its own version of the Idea, Carlyle (1907) wrote, and every generation asks itself incredulously how its parents could have held such strange beliefs as they did (vol. 29, p. 60). To use Carlyle's central metaphor of clothes in *Sartor Resartus*, the impact of social and political activities on the Idea is its constant patching and repatching. This may lead to an Idea so different as to become new. Alternatively, the Idea may become so divorced from reality that it ceases to be meaningful and must be replaced. Man, Carlyle wrote, covers himself with a "clothes-Thatch." Yet, "day after day [he] must thatch himself anew; day after day this despicable thatch must lose some film of its thickness; some film of it, frayed away by wear and tear, must be brushed off . . . till by degrees the whole has been brushed thither, and [he] gets new material to grind down" (vol. 1, p. 147).

The two thinkers, then, regarded crises of legitimacy as issuing from processes that develop in diametrically opposite directions. In the case of Carlyle they can be compared to the wave shocks of an earthquake traveling upward till they reach the roof. For Tocqueville the collapse begins with a faulty roof that damages the stories one after another till the basement is reached. The two processes need not, however, be mutually exclusive; moreover, they lead to the same corollary.

Unlike Gramsci, neither Tocqueville nor Carlyle maintained that legitimacy is something that either exists or does not exist. Instead, they viewed it as a continuum stretching between the poles of what could be called active and passive legitimacy. The former obtains when government is regarded as acting in accordance with the predominate mind-set. Though there may be varying shades of opinion and conflicts over resource allocation, the members of society are attached to the basic principles informing the regime and identify with the activities government undertakes in their name.

The passive form of legitimacy is when more and more people become alienated from a government that nevertheless persists in retaining outdated forms and practices. Conformity in this case springs mainly from blind habit, indifference, or fear of consequences. There is little meaningful contact between the wielders of power and those subjected to it, and the seeds of crisis of legitimacy have now been sown. This is what Tocqueville (1955, 29, 203) defined as "the period of gestation" of legitimacy crisis: an "unstable equilibrium" that every "shake of destiny" could destabilize. Such a situation was true of France on the eve of the revolution, when "the laws [were] the same, the rules seemed to be the same, the same principles [were] professed, on the surface everything [was] the same; but at *bottom*, the *methods*, the *habits*, and the *spirit* all [were] changed" (Tocqueville 1862, vol. 2, p. 284). Elsewhere he employed an almost unbelievably modern metaphor of "a vehicle still moving with the motor shut off" (Tocqueville 1959, 164). Carlyle's metaphor was of a more sombre cast. There are situations in which the "soul politics" has departed and what is required is "that the Body Politic be decently interred" (Carlyle 1907, vol. 1, pp. 76, 71–72).

The question now arises as to the factors that propel the shift from passive legitimacy to a full-blown crisis of authority. Here one can turn to Habermas (1976). He drew a distinction between economic crisis, crisis of rationality or administrative capacity, crisis of legitimacy, and crisis of motivation. These are four propensities that are likely to develop from one another where the general principles or organization no longer allow for the solution of new problems to the degree necessary for the continued existence of the system. Neither Tocqueville nor Carlyle drew such distinctions, yet their analyses do not differ greatly except that they turned the progression on its head. In Habermas's terminology crisis of motivation stands for the situation in which the socioeconomic system undergoes such changes that "its outputs become dysfunctional," that is, where it generates demands the state cannot meet.

For Tocqueville, likewise, the "dispersal of the source of energy" entails the loss of whatever social solidarity existed before. With the dissolving of the glue that holds society together in its common apprehension of reality and in the values and goals deriving from it, society itself splits into "thousands of small groups," each "living only for itself and, quite literally, minding its own business" (Tocqueville 1955, 96). Every one of the minisocieties and of the individuals within them seeks to maximize selfish benefits and is disgruntled by any requirement laid upon him or her. The inevitable outcome is Habermas's crises of administrative capacity, what Tocqueville called "a sort of apoplectic torpor" (Tocqueville 1985, 81).

The inability to fulfill increasing demands leads in turn to the withdrawal of legitimacy, a situation complicated by the widespread perception of government as serving the narrow interests of its supporters. Tocqueville described such a situation when before the February 1848 Revolution government acquired "the features of a trading company whose every operation is directed to the benefit that its members may derive therefrom" (Tocqueville 1970, 5). If other segments of the population regard government policies that demand obligation as an intrusion, this is likely to generate actual animosity. Carlyle, for his part, summed up the situation in his comparison of society in such a condition to an overcrowded lodging house, where the guests "each, isolated . . . turns against his neighbor, clutches what he can get and cries 'Mine.'" Paralysis of this kind, Tocqueville (1955, 203) argued, is a temporary "state of unstable equilibrium," for it can last only as long as no serious problems besets the government or the society.

The critical moment would come when authorities that are already faltering are weighed down by an accumulation of unresolved problems or are confronted by some unforeseen problem of yet greater magnitude. At such a time, precisely when it is most in need of support, government will not be able to count on the loyalty of the people and may even confront active hostility. It is "at the mercy of that final stroke of destiny," which would cause the "scission of the lifeline" (Tocqueville 1955, 203). Whether the "crunch" derives from an economic breakdown is immaterial, for any accident may bring the same result. This is why the otherwise trifling incidents preceding the French Revolution brought about such momentous consequences: "The grandiose edifice built up by our kings was doomed to collapse like a card castle once disturbances arose within the social order on which it was based" (p. vii), whereas in 1848 the ineptitude of King Louis-Philippe "was the accident that made the illness fatal" (Tocqueville 1970, 6).

However, such a progression was not a foregone conclusion. Segments of society lose faith in particular political arrangements, though not at the same time, so that the process as a whole may extend over long periods. The growing heterogeneity of society tends to expand the time taken for a crisis to develop yet further because there will always be those whose interest is in the perpetuation of existing practices. This allows a window of opportunity for such reforms as will restore faith. Tocqueville considered two relevant variables. One is the nature of the political culture. Some cultures, he argued, promote "restraint" and consequent "tranquillity." This was typical of America, where "self-interest rightly understood" fostered "temperance, moderation [and] self-command" (Tocqueville 1969, 48). The absence of centralization contributed considerably to this effect by prolonging the time it took any shock waves to travel throughout society. Such was not the case in France, where, by contrast, the culture fostered bitterness and the "system of centralization made [its] . . . fate depend in a single blow struck in Paris" (Tocqueville 1862, vol. 2, p. 92).

The second variable that determines the possibility of preventing a legitimation crisis is the quality of leadership. Charismatic leaders may enjoy personal legitimacy even if they head a faltering order, and they may exploit their popularity to introduce fundamental reforms; a revolution from above, as it were. Had an individual of the "caliber and temperament" of Frederick the Great been the monarch of France, for example, "He would certainly have initiated many of the sweeping changes made by the Revolution . . . and thus not only have preserved his crown but greatly added to his power" (Tocqueville 1955, 165). Turning to the crisis that was deepening in his own day, Tocqueville therefore wished a hero would come forth to rescue the country.

At this point again the similarity with Carlyle is striking. The Englishman is perhaps most widely known today for his *Heroes and Hero-Worship* (1841), in which he portrayed history as the record of a succession of heroes. Frederick the Great was his model, too, and for most of his creative career he was steadfast in his hope that a person like him would come to save the day. But Tocqueville was cast in a more skeptical mold. For him, even where the need to change is recognized by those in power what is required is a vision that surpasses both self-interest and the immediate present. Leaders endowed with these qualities are always rare, and especially at times of crisis in gestation. "I see no signs of . . . great men, and in fact, have no faith in the sudden apparition of heroes, while I see round me swarms of mischievous pigmies," he wrote. "I am very uneasy and much alarmed" (Tocqueville 1862, vol. 2, p. 94).

• • •

As our first parents were driven out of Paradise, Dean Inge tells us, Adam remarked to Eve "My dear, we live in an age of transition" (1966, 391). Since then every age has been one of transition, but there are some that are patently more so than others. Such periods, often referred to as "revolutions," are marked by concentrated processes of change in society in relation to its environment and its mind-set. As Tocqueville acutely recognized, revolutions of this kind are unique complex events, involving multiple patterns of transformation and their interacting consequences. In addition, individuals and circumstances play so major a role that any generalization must be restricted to the most rudimentary outlines. With this as a given, I shall limit myself to a few comments from a Tocquevillian perspective on only one prominent political trend that has already begun to reveal itself and that I believe will become increasingly clear in the next millennium. As societies enter the more advanced stages of the Internet Age, the relationships between their members and their governments is steadily being altered. The pace of transition varies with the status, personal background, and age of the individuals involved, but the general tendency is to widening disjunction between them, proceeding from both the communication and information components of the revolution we are undergoing today.

A term commonly associated with the Internet is "globalization," indicating interactions across national boundaries beyond government control. This immediately brings to mind Marshal McLuhan's (1967) global village. To some degree it is a valid association. However, his notion hinged on the uni-directional potentialities of radio and television. The Internet differs from these in that it is interactive, providing nodes where like-minded individuals with common interests can come together. To appreciate the difference better, we can recur to another of McLuhan's dicta, "The medium is the message." By this he contended that the medium determines the kind of organization in which it is employed. Thus, the personal word-of-mouth befits the village, tribe, or similar intimate social mode.

By contrast, the modern nation-state would be unthinkable in the absence of mass media that extend the range of communication spatially and shorten the process in time. The Internet, global as it is in reach, re-creates the multi-directional, one-on-one communication that defines a community of people who link up with one another to pursue common interests. It could be termed an unusual kind of village, where no one enjoys superior power accruing from privileged knowledge or access to the media and no hierarchical structure prevails. This oxymoron of a global intimate community is likely to be enhanced in the near future with the introduction of hybrid media combining the effects of the Internet with the personal elements of the telephone and the TV. What is at stake, it seems, is the kind of society Tocqueville encountered and admired in the America of the 1830s. It was there, he argued, that geographical size enabled individuals to freely join communities of like-minded citizens with whom they could collaborate in getting things done. Small local communities thus truly represented the nature and concerns of their members, while the need for the nationwide government was limited to overarching issues such as defense. On the face of it, the appearance of cyberspace as analogous to the geographical extent of the New World not only opens up the possibility of regaining this paradise lost but of exporting it to the rest of the world, including Europe.

On reflection, however, this is clearly not the case. What Tocqueville meant was the structure of society in the phenomenal world. Internet users, by contrast, do not actually converse with the network in the "real world," and even in the chat room they do not meet their partners and possibly do not even know who they really are. It is a community that exists in the mind and cannot replace actual organization. This, however, does not imply that governments remain unaffected.

As noted earlier, Tocqueville regarded the decentralized network of communities in America as an antidote against the disease of legitimation crises. Ironically, cyberspace communities may become a source of government weakness in the real world that has so changed since his day. Not only do they offer more meaningful participation, but they disseminate knowledge in an egalitarian way and link interested parties, thereby empowering their members to act in the ostensible world in matters of concern to them so that they are released from dependence on services hitherto offered by various organizations. Furthermore, they operate in a way opposed to that of governments. They are based on the equality of voluntary participation rather than on the exercise of authority and the fundamental inequalities of power; they do not demand loyalty, nor do they depend on lines drawn on the map, but include anyone and anywhere who wishes to join in and are characterized by immediate accessibility and action free from red tape.

At this point one must consider yet another aspect of globalization that had already begun with the spread of multinational corporations some decades before the introduction of the Internet. The activities of such corporations established spheres where states had little say as to the circulation of information, capital, and even investment decisions. The Internet is bringing about the intensification and egalitarian spread of such interactions, emphasizing the inability of governments to control ever-growing areas of activity. This has already had a major domestic effect on market demands for labor and their results in terms of the composition of the workforce and the changing socioeconomic structures of societies. Governments may react by setting up retraining programs, instituting changes in their welfare systems, and shifting their education policies, but all these are still no more than attempts to adjust to forces over which they have no power. In 1999, the recession in Japan and the troubles in Southeast Asia with their spreading effects on Europe and America are vivid proof of the magnitude of the forces at work and the problems governments must face up to.

So far the discussion has turned on processes that could lead to a growing disjunction between two measures of time: one marking the tempo of change in the realia of individuals, the other the tempo of change in the structures, *modus operandi*, and outputs of government. In the spirit of Tocqueville we shall argue that such a lack of synchronization may well affect the basic premises and values on which government legitimacy rests. But concurrently there is a growing likelihood that another sort of disjunction might take place, this time between the tempo of knowledge expansion and the tempo of changes in what Carlyle called the Idea.

A basic common denominator of all the critics mentioned was the postulation that shifts in our comprehension of the world and consequently in our basic assumptions and sets of socially constitutive general principles, though varying in rate, nevertheless proceed at a more-or-less moderate or at least comprehensible pace. Tocqueville's "source of energy," Carlyle's "Idea," Gramsci's "dominant ideology," Habermas's "Constitutive tradition"—all require time to establish themselves, percolate through society, become translated into action, and eventually change. And yet, the characteristic of the Internet Age is a revolution in the acquisition, transmission, and indeed the very nature of information and knowledge (Lyotard 1984, 4–5), all leading to new and constantly changing social linkages. A situation is developing where along with the different generations of computers, the growing rapidity of the production and assimilation of knowledge, and its light-speed communication, specialized branches of knowledge become assimilable only by limited groups within society, and at different rates according to needs and interests. One can stipulate that the unconscious impact of such knowledge on social values, norms, and attitudes will increasingly vary, resulting in a plethora of ideas replacing any common Idea. At the same time, "the increasing strength of the principles . . . [that] society exists and progresses only if the messages circulating within it are rich in information and easy to decode" gives rise to a situation in which the nation-state is progressively perceived as a mere "factor of opacity and 'noise'" (p. 5).

When nondemocratic regimes are fully exposed to the effects of the Internet they will clearly become increasingly susceptible to legitimacy problems arising from both top–bottom and bottom–top processes. The nature and the operation of the cybernetic communities utterly contradict the mode of operation and the standards of dictatorial governments at the same time that citizens' uncontrolled access to information deprives them of one of their most potent sources of authority. The need to react to global trends and the concomitant powerlessness to engage in large-scale social and economic engineering all tend to conflict with their claims for legitimacy.

To have to cope constantly with a spread of knowledge that is not consonant with the proclaimed ideology subjects them to yet further pressure, and the fact that this spread is not uniform across society only exacerbates the weakness. To retain an unchanged Islam in the face of globalization and Internet proliferation, whether in its Wahabi version of Saudi Arabia or its Shi'ite version in Iran, becomes a highly questionable exercise. Rulers in such quandaries may of course resort to the systematic use of intimidation as a means of ensuring conformity, but where popular compliance depends on sheer self-interest or fear we have exactly what Tocqueville and Carlyle meant when they spoke of crisis in gestation. Alternatively, rulers may make efforts to adapt the regime so as to moderate reform by leading it themselves. This, we have seen, was a solution considered by Tocqueville, save that he had the strongest suspicions of any possibility of a *deus ex machina*. His skepticism can be justified by the Chinese style of reform, while the notorious events at Tiananmen Square may serve as a warning that such an approach may easily get out of hand.

All this, it could be claimed, may be true of Saudi Arabia, Iran, or China, but whether it could apply to liberal democracies is questionable. These governments, after all, derive their authority from the will of the people as tested in periodic elections, and they are ousted from office upon losing that support. Nevertheless, the difference may turn out to be one of degree rather than of kind.

Precisely because of the ongoing revolution in the means of communication, I would suggest that it is today more imperative than ever to recall Tocqueville's widely known argument that a stable democracy hinges on a balance between centrifugal and centripetal forces: the interests of individuals and particular publics defined by the pursuit of their own gain, and the interest of the community as a whole, which justifies the allocation of resources that override immediate individual and group gain. Where the two come into conflict, the preservation of law and social institutions becomes a function of the priority given to the latter. Where this is not the case, society must rely on specific interests to motivate the support for law and those institutions that originate and administer the law. This will demand rule by sectional interest and the imposition or the threat of sanctions on nonbeneficiaries, thereby increasingly reducing liberty. No less important, where compliance rests on sheer self-interest, the Thrasymachean principle holds; namely, that the only sin is that of being caught.

Such a situation is precisely what Tocqueville had in mind when he spoke of the fragmentation of society and the reduction of government into a form of "trading company." Carlyle's comparison, it will be recalled, was of an overcrowded inn where each guest at the common table grabs what he can and the stronger appropriate the food of the weaker. In short, it is the acceptance of government as acting on behalf of, to quote Anderson's (1994) definition, "an imagined community" (p. 6) that enables democracies to serve as arenas where private interests can be best pursued and individual liberties maintained. Taken together, the tendencies discussed as likely to materialize with the spread of the use of the Internet are liable to gradually upset this balance, thus rendering the democratic arrangements progressively hollow.

Both at the individual and the collective levels, identity derives meaning through the exclusion of the self from the other, the us from the them. The process of globalization presents us, therefore, with an ever-deepening problem of collective identity: How does one define the us within the perception of humanity as a single society? To clarify the implications it must be appreciated that identification with the general public hinges on the ability to distinguish it from the local community and that of humanity as a species, and on the perception of it as a good. The consequence of the intensification of Internet use is the diminution of the meaning of geographical propinquity. When the Internet user can join in a cross-border global network, literally in a moment and with the aid of only the keyboard and the mouse, the distinction between all those communities not restricted to face-to-face contact with family, friends, and neighbors is bound to be blurred. This trend may even be accelerated with the appearance of hybrid forms of telecommunication, combining the potentialities of the computer with those of the TV and the telephone. Of course, all such communities, whether the general public of the democratic state, the Internet network, or humanity at large, are mental constructs.

But the more the users form groups united by common interests and knowledge which separate them from other members of their geographically bound community, the more the network becomes concrete and meaningful at the expense of the national community. Indeed, the ability to belong to one or more communities linked by common interests but lacking geographical loci is likely, at the cost of the national community, to give meaning to the concept of humanity at large. Those spatially distant from one another may become close in knowledge and interest and vice versa. Moreover, against the new possibilities of direct action afforded to the individual through the Internet, the imagined communities may appear to be not only less relevant but also less efficient. That all this will lead to a revolution, as Tocqueville feared in 1848, is out of the question. No change in the basic structures of democratic rule is likely to occur overnight. As long as no single state conterminous with the whole of mankind comes into being, the nation-state will persist to concentrate resources and provide services beyond the power of individuals and local communities.

As distinct from dictatorial regimes, it is also difficult to perceive the kind of structural or procedural reforms that would restore the conception of the general public to its pre-Internet status. What is more likely is the spread of general apathy, which, together with the reduction of the need for bureaucracy and the lowering of the costs of decentralization by the Internet, could generate persistent demands to strip the central powers of national governments as much as possible in order to transfer them to local authorities. An alarmist might foresee this apathy as allowing freer reign to powerful individuals and groups to pursue their selfish interests, thereby deepening the apathy yet further. Tocqueville's vision of "thousands of small communities" conducting their self-centered lives would then sound almost prophetic. In short, democracies may find themselves in a perpetual crisis in gestation, but without any final crunch.

One may briefly conclude by referring to the theme of this book, cyberspace imperialism. This metaphorical attribution of a human form of conquest to the revolutionary communication technologies of today usually evokes the cultural and economic consequences of their use. In this chapter it serves a different purpose: to denote the encroachment of the geographically amorphous Internet on the space monopolized in the past centuries by territorially defined governments of nation-states. The term "space" here does not refer to any physical dimensions but to a concept, that of the place that a government as expression of the state holds in the mind of its citizens.

No man is an island. Every individual constitutes in himself a node of interrelationships and communication networks. As the twentieth century draws to a close, the complexity of the networks is dramatically increasing at a pace unknown before, through the agency of the Internet. The argument that was offered here was based on the premise that this involves not only quantitative but qualitative changes. Along with the extension of our contacts with the external world there comes an alteration in our view of that world and of our place within it; that is to say, we are subject today to an uncommonly rapid and fundamental shift in our *Weltanschauung*, or mind-set. Though no one can predict where this will lead, it is already clear that the idea of nation-states as the largest meaningful human communities is no longer at the core of our political consciousness. Gone likewise is the traditional deference given to national governments as corporate entities compounding the partial knowledge of many individuals, managing it, and applying it to the benefit of all.

With the free trade and availability of knowledge to anyone who can press computer keys comes also the awareness of the new egalitarian possibilities of joint action without the various state mechanisms. Another basic assumption is being eroded as bureaucracies and hierarchical organizations, the trademarks of governments, are, in more and more spheres of life, being rendered obsolete. Finally, what is increasingly coming under pressure is perhaps the most critical legitimation-producing assumption, that there is a general public that transcends all specific groups within society, and that governments represent that public rather than any sectional interests. The Internet, while linking humanity, disintegrates national groups into congeries, each of which is linked to others beyond the map borders. Whether the wearing away of all these assumptions results from the inability of governments to adjust to the new realities, as Tocqueville would have insisted, or whether the change in our basic assumptions causes governments to lag behind, as Carlyle would have maintained, the upshot is the same. Democracies and nondemocratic regimes are exposed to different legitimation problems, and the consequences may vary with circumstances. But, ironically, in a world drawing closer together, a common denominator is likely to be that all national governments will fall victim to cyberspace imperialism.

REFERENCES

Anderson, B. 1994. *Imagined Communities: Reflections on the Origin and Spread of Nationalism*. Rev. ed. London: Verso.

Brown, F. 1976. Answer. In *The Best of Fredrick Brown*, edited by R. Bloch. New York: Nelson Doubleday.

Carlyle, T. 1907. *The Works of Thomas Carlyle in 30 Volumes*, edited by H. D. Traill. London: Chapman and Hall.

Friedman, T. L. 1998. The Internet Wars. *New York Times*, 11 April, A25.

Gramsci, A. 1971. *Selections from the Prison Notebooks*, edited by Q. Hoare and G. Nowell. New York: International Publishers.

Habermas, J. 1976. *Legitimation Crisis*, translated by T. McCarthy. London: Heineman.

Inge, Dean. 1966. *The Book of Unusual Quotations*, edited by Rudolf Flesch. New York: Harper and Row.

Linz, J., and A. Stepan, eds. 1978. *The Breakdown of Democratic Regimes*. Baltimore: Johns Hopkins University Press.

Lyotard, J. F. 1984. *The Post Modern Condition: A Report on Knowledge*, translated by G. Bennington and B. Nasswin. Minneapolis: University of Minnesota Press.

McLuhan, Marshall. 1967. *The Medium Is the Message*. New York: Random House.

Nibset, Robert. 1977. *Twilight of Authority*. New York: Oxford University Press.

O'Connors, J. 1973. *The Fiscal Crisis of the State*. New York: St. Martin's Press.

Offe, C. 1972. *Strukturprobleme of Kapitalistichen Staates*. Frankfurt: Suhrkamp.

Shils, Edward. 1972. *Center and Periphery*. New York: Random House.

Tocqueville, A. de. 1862. *Memoir, Letters, and Remains of Alexis de Tocqueville: Translated by the translator of "Napoleon's Correspondence with King Joseph."* 2 vols. Boston: Ticknor and Fields.

———. 1955. *The Old Regime and the French Revolution.* Garden City, N.Y.: Doubleday.

———. 1959. *The European Revolution and Correspondence with Gobineau,* translated by J. Lukas. Garden City, N.Y.: Doubleday.

———. 1968. *Journeys to England and Ireland,* translated by G. Lawrence and K. P. Mayer. Garden City, N.Y.: Doubleday.

———. 1969. *Democracy in America,* translated by J. P. Mayer and M.G.L. Lawrence. Garden City, N.Y.: Doubleday.

———. 1970. *Recollections,* translated by G. Lawrence. Garden City, N.Y.: Doubleday.

———. 1985. *Selected Letters on Politics and Society,* edited by R. Boesch, translated by J. Toupin and R. Boesch. Berkeley and Los Angeles: University of California Press.

Wolfe, A. 1977. *The Limits of Legitimacy.* New York: Free Press.

5

Cybercolonialism: Speeding Along the Superhighway or Stalling on a Beaten Track?

Deborah Tong

"What makes power hold good, what makes it accepted, is simply the fact that it doesn't only weigh on us as a force that says no, but that it traverses and produces things, it induces pleasure, forms knowledge, produces discourse. It needs to be considered as a productive network which runs through the whole social body, much more than a negative instance whose function is repression."

Michel Foucault

"At the basis of the entire construction, one finally finds a common motive; the colonizer's economic and basic needs, which he substitutes for logic."

Albert Memmi

The notion of the Internet as a tool of oppression contradicts virtually everything that is published today on the World Wide Web. The contemporary discourse surrounding the communications revolution is dominated by those spearheading the industry. Articles in leading cyberculture magazines are rife with assertions that the Internet is a politically potent, democratic, and uniting force. The rhetoric is all pervasive, and indulges us to believe that a ubiquitous networked computer system will yield all the benefits that come with job creation, democracy, and freedom: in effect, the American Dream. But all too easily we forget that we have been down this road before. This "dream" has a track record of crashes. Somewhere along the line it always skids into a nightmare.

There is a skewed reasoning that propels the seemingly inevitable Information Revolution. As the group Interrogate the Internet (1996) suggests, it is often proposed that information is the proverbial first step on the road to freedom; the logic, summed up in the following linear equation, demonstrates the professedly benevolent consequence of Western science:

data = information = knowledge = wisdom = truth = freedom (p. 125)

However, as this chapter seeks to point out, the idea that a free flow of data means an equally free society requires a huge leap of faith rather than logic; but then, as I shall argue, this is the neohegemony of cybercolonialism.

There certainly are positive aspects to possessing information; as the old adage reminds us, "Knowledge is power." However, there is comparatively little analysis on the imposition of Western knowledge and technology onto the newly industrializing countries (NICs) (Howard and Howard 1996). Instead, the key to today's development rhetoric is that access to information will serve only to empower and free the peoples of the South. What is conspicuously absent in the wealth of the pro-Internet discourse is the question of how this system is actually generated and sustained: That is, who in effect does the Internet serve? Does it cater to the people *en masse* as we are told? Or are there other vested interests involved? And what does this imply for all the plans and (nonvirtual) realities for those who are next in line to get wired up? Inasmuch, this author forwards another equation to keep in mind when examining the *telos* of the "decentralized" Information Age, one that is often applied but not often implied:

knowledge = technology = speed = efficiency = control = power

It should be remembered that the Internet is not a neutral technology. Like any technology, contained within it are the inherent biases of those who designed it (i.e., the American military). Western ideas, knowledges, and communications practices largely dominate the structure, system, and culture of the Internet. The notion that the Web is an equal and open forum for all the world's voices is a far cry from today's reality. But again and again the rhetoric encourages us to not think of today, but think of tomorrow, think of the future. In fact, this same utopic vision was called upon during colonial times, the primary difference being that religion was the soothsayer instead of science. The civilizing missionaries' advice to the "savages" was to forget the toils of the moment, as "short term pain begets long term gain." But it was exactly these promises of future salvation that sustained the exploitation. The promise of a glowing future is something that no one can really be held accountable for, and thus, unsurprisingly, is often not delivered.

SHIFTING METAPHORICAL GEARS

Cyberspace is explicitly referred to as the "New Frontier," a place that challenges the brave mavericks and outlaws of cybersociety to chart new territory. As the Progress and Freedom Foundation (1994) document *Cyberspace and the American Dream: A Magna Carta for the Knowledge Age* declares:

The bioelectronic frontier is an appropriate metaphor for what is happening in cyberspace, calling to mind as it does the spirit of invention and discovery that led ancient mariners to explore the world, generations of pioneers to tame the American continent and, more recently, to man's first exploration of outer space. . . . Cyberspace is the land of knowledge, and the exploration of that land can be a civilization's truest, highest calling. The opportunity is now before us to empower every person to pursue that calling in his or her own way.

What this romanticisation cleverly omits though, is what *really* occurred during the conquest of the new territories. The metaphor valorizes the pioneers while veiling the actual consequences of the voyages of discovery. Could we have already forgotten the motive of greed that was masked under the "spirit of adventure"? And the genocide of millions of indigenous people as the march of conquest expanded over the new territories (Sardar 1996)? Ziauddin Sardar argues that the frontier metaphor generates the myths of freedom by placing the act of domination into the hands of the populace. He writes, "The frontier is the agency through which power elites get everyone to do their work while thinking they are acting on their own volition" (p. 18). The "hero" is thus a mere puppet of hegemony.

U.S. Vice President Al Gore's oft-quoted analogy of the Internet as a superhighway is another prevailing Netaphor. Within the American mythology the car and the highway denote all the positive aspects of progress. The parable suggests that like the cars that speed along the highways, ultimately the users of the Net will find a new sense of freedom and autonomy. Not surprisingly, it was Gore's father who oversaw the building of the extensive U.S. interstate highway system in the 1960s. Brushing aside the sleek ad-campaign metaphor however, the shadow of the analogy exposes a much more telling reality, one that elucidates the intimate links between the giant corporations and the strategic manner in which they created, and still profit from, a situation of mass dependency. A brief history may illustrate the point more clearly:

In the 1920s trolleys were the primary mode of transportation in most U.S. cities. However, in the 1930s and 1940s the National City Lines Company (backed by General Motors, Firestone, Standard Oil, Phillips Petroleum, Mack Truck, and others with obvious vested interests), purchased and shut down more than 100 electric trolley systems in forty-five U.S. cities (Mechanic 1996). The car soon became the primary "choice" of transportation within the urban centers. With the increasing availability of the new auto(nomous)-mobiles, people began migrating out of the cities and into the suburbs. Urban planning began to shift around the vehicle rather than vice versa. This spurred the advancement of urban sprawl and rendered a tremendous dependence on the car: The roads designed to serve as routes for communication paradoxically increased the numbers of isolated individuals. Inasmuch, the 1960s saw a boom in the creation of extensive highway systems that served to reconnect the communities. This "boon" has instead resulted in a network of traffic jams (similarly reflected in the slowed transmissions due to Net congestion) filled to the brim with agitated-single-occupant vehicles.

The American dream accompanied by its success symbol has also been exported to less-developed countries (LDCs). The effects in the South, however, have been questionable in terms of success. As Albert Memmi (1965) notes, "The purpose of the highway system is without regard to the needs of the colonized—but absolutely in line with those of the colonizer" (p. 113). Instead of freedom, the creation of roads in Brazil, Korea, Bangladesh, and many countries in Africa has created a plethora of complications for the people of those communities (e.g., flooding, congestion, pollution, relocation, etc.; for a more detailed examination, see Wresch 1996; Reiss 1992).

The superhighway acts to reconnect people without physically moving them at all. If we compare the car to the computer and the Internet to the highway system, it soon becomes apparent that those who profit from its export are the corporations and not the people, for how can this "freedom" that is espoused paradoxically be dependent upon technology? The creation of the highway system simply perpetuates the problems and sustains the industries that surround the remote individual; this is because the corporate ethic is to never directly address "the problem," as it is "the problem" that generates business. The beauty of cybercolonialism and the new electronic highway however is that it is invisible, as are the powers behind it. It is an escape from all the problems and ugliness in the real world. Which is why perhaps, one never meets poverty on the Internet.

ROADBLOCKS ON THE INFOBAHN

> There once was a monk in Tibet
> Who ached to join the Internet.
> He'd bought a fast modem
> When somebody told him,
> "ISPs aren't near Lhasa yet."
> PC Magazine Limerick Contest Winner, Richard Tjoa

The first barrier to Cyberspace is the most obvious: affordability. Getting on-line requires a computer, and the average cost of a new system far exceeds the annual income of most individuals in the Third World. The poverty clock keeps ticking with nearly forty countries having an annual per capita income of less than $150 (Gonzalez-Manet 1988, 13). It must be evident that in nations where people can barely afford to eat, the cost one must incur to surf the Net seems utterly ludicrous.

First there is the price of the computer and all the necessary peripherals which amount to between $3,000 and $5,000. This needs to be upgraded or replaced every few years as both the hardware and software become ineffectual due to the constant upgrading of the Internet's capabilities. Second, there is the cost to an Internet Service Provider (ISP) which ranges anywhere from $240 to $300 annually. Third, there are the phone bills, which vary depending on the level of regulation within the state or nation. Generally, calls placed from LDCs to wealthy nations are much more expensive than the reverse. In addition, the cost of equipment varies from country to country. The tariff rates on imported communications technologies are over 40 percent in many African countries (Panos 1995). The Net's superficial "equal access" slogan does not apply to the South. For example, the cost of a modem in India is approximately four times the price of the same model in North America, and the cost of Internet access time in Jakarta, Indonesia, is approximately twelve times higher than it is in Rome, Italy. As such, average Internet users in poor countries have to be even wealthier than average users in affluent nations.

The lack of infrastructure, or what is now being called the "infostructure," is another major barrier for peoples in NICs who want to connect to the network. What is largely taken for granted in the West is that access to the Internet requires a modem that connects to functioning phone lines. Again, there is a huge disparity between the North and South. The International Telecommunications Union's (ITU) 1995 publication *Telecommunications Indicators for the Least Developed Countries* states that the "average level of teledensity among the LDCs is 0.29 or just one phone for every 350 people. The total number of telephone main lines in the 48 LDCs stands at just over 1.5 million . . . [which] . . . is one percent of the total number of lines in the United States" (UNDP 1996, 6). Between China and India, half of the world's population, there is only one phone per 100 people (Wresch 1996). In black African countries the density of phone connections is two per 1,000 (Boafo 1991). Even in countries where people do have the money for a phone line, the waiting lists are long and service is not always available. For example, in Brazil 10 million people want phones but cannot get them, and even after paying $2,000 per line, only 57 percent of the calls actually go through (Wresch 1996, 125). In Zimbabwe, over 400,000 people are on waiting lists to have a phone installed (UNDP 1996). How, in all honesty, can one believe the new tech dreams of democracy when half of humanity has never even made a phone call?

Geography is another factor that limits access to phone lines and thus the Internet. In Africa, telecommunications devices are concentrated in urban areas where only 20 to 25 percent of the population resides (Boafo 1991). In the Third World, vast tracts of land do not even have a phone in sight. In fact, more than half of the world's population lives over two hours away from a phone: 58,000 villages in Indonesia, 535,000 villages in India and 151,000 villages in Africa do not have telephones within the communities at all (UNDP 1996). The majority (i.e., 80 percent) of the world's inhabitants neither have a phone nor regular access to one (Panos 1995). Moreover, phone installation in rural areas is extremely expensive. Telecom Nambia estimates that it costs approximately US$5,000 to install one phone in a rural area (Wresch 1996). Further, it has been estimated that an expenditure of US$28 billion would be required to install enough phones for a ratio of even a single line per 100 people in sub-Saharan Africa (UNDP 1996).

Poor insulation and wiring laid overland create yet another predicament. During the rainy season power surges result, and lightning is said to be "the number one killer of computers and modems in Africa" (Majtenyi and Fleet 1996, 22). Surge suppressers and uninterruptable power supplies are used, but again serve to increase the cost of the systems. And in countries near the equator, the temperature is sufficient to cause computers to simply overheat and shut down (Wresch 1996). Even when these problems are set aside, an additional issue arises: The quality and speed of phone lines around the world is not standardized. Thus, even with a high-capacity modem, transmission may be faulty simply due to poor phone connections. Africa's phone lines are particularly unstable and can rarely handle high speeds. William Wresch (1996) writes in *Disconnected: Haves and Have-Nots in the Information Age* that, although there have been a number of attempts, the United Nations is unable to send e-mail to Madagascar, even at 300 baud, the slowest rate. Other lines lose messages that are sent at a rate faster than 1,200 baud (120 characters per second). As a result, African phones not only cost more per minute but take more minutes to process messages than phones in the United States. Thus, the poorest people in the world pay the highest charges for electronic mail, and the very people who might benefit most from e-mail are the most limited in its use.

The paucity of technical expertise required to build, operate, and maintain telecommunications infrastructures also needs to be considered. There is a shortage of technicians with the requisite skills in the South, and the labor costs are high for those who are adroit in the new technologies. Instead, much of the know-how is often imported through foreign aid programs, and even then problems arise. For example, Zimbabwe has top-of-the-line digital exchanges that were implemented by several European countries. The aid, however, was offered only in conjunction with purchases from the corporations of the donor countries. As a result, Zimbabwe now has five separate digital exchange systems, but also five times the maintenance problems that it would have had otherwise (Wresch 1996).

As will soon become clear, the technical skill required for the information revolution may purposely be kept from the hands of those in the new cybercolonies. In *The Colonizer and the Colonized*, Albert Memmi (1965) argues that a function of colonialism is to obscure technical skills in order to subdue and exploit the colonized: "The colonizer pushed the colonized out of the historical and social, cultural and technical current. What is real and verifiable is that the colonized's culture, society and technology are seriously damaged. He has not acquired new ability and a new culture. One patent result of colonization is that there are no more colonized artists and not yet any colonized technicians" (p. 114).

THE LANGUAGE BARRIER

"Last month, when I was in Central Asia, the President of Kyrgyzstan told me his eight-year-old son came to him and said, 'Father, I have to learn English.' 'But why?' President Akayev asked. 'Because, father, the computer speaks English.'"

U.S. Vice President Al Gore

What is taken for granted is always apparent to those who are not in its possession. Upon finally connecting to the network, the first thing a member of a developing nation would undoubtedly detect is Cyberia's lingua franca: English. English is the mother tongue of data. It encodes 80 percent of all computer messages and data content even though only slightly more than a tenth of the world's population speaks the language (including both primary and secondary language speakers) (Naisbitt 1994; Lockard 1996).

Language is encoded through the digital networks as a binary system. That is, a series of ones and zeros sends shifting high and low frequencies down the wire to represent a particular numeral or letter. The most common of these modes of transmission is ASCII or the *American* Standard Code for Information Interchange (emphasis added). It was written by Americans and has since been widely tele-exported. Although its extended versions do make exceptions for special characters in French, Spanish, or German, neither ASCII nor the rest of the major international codes are designed to encode foreign languages (i.e., Kanji, Sanskrit, etc.) (Wresch 1996). Computer software is also written almost exclusively in English. Though many software houses in developing countries employ indigenous programmers (for a fraction of the salary), they, too, must code according to the language protocol.

Translating the programs for foreign users is one possibility. Unfortunately, due to the slow processes of translation, major applications tend to come into the marketplace years after the original. Further, the rapid changes in software development and the "internationalization lag" lead many of the Anglo-originating programs and applications to become obsolete even as they reach nonanglophone users for the first time (Lockard 1996). Translation programs for text are also being developed on the Web; however, at the present time they are only about 80-percent accurate, with abysmal syntax and style. Aside from this, the unidirectional flow of information is still left unaddressed: All things translate back to English.

The Asian market currently has the highest level of nonanglophone software products and translations. Although this seems to indicate that English speakers may soon not be the only ones exercising power on the Net, it also makes it quite evident that it is competing economic forces rather than communication needs that really dictate the direction of software developments (Lockard 1996).

For now, members of LDCs who wish to participate or work on the Net must be "fortunate" enough to be bilingual. The same colonial ethic holds true: "If he wants to obtain a job, make a place for himself, exist in the community and the world, he must first bow to the language of his masters. In the linguistic conflict within the colonized, his mother tongue is that which is crushed" (Memmi 1965, 107). Similarly, the difficulty for Webmasters in the Third World is that they must not only have the language and the technical skills to have a presence on the Internet, but also the necessary free time to upload and maintain a regular site. If one compares the history of indigenous writers during colonialism, it would be rash to expect a proliferation of Webmasters from the developing world:

The material conditions of the existence of the colonized would suffice to explain the rarity of writers. The excessive poverty of the majority drastically reduces the probability of finding a budding and developing writer. . . . History shows us that only one privileged class is enough to provide an entire people with artists. The fact is that the role of a colonized writer is too difficult to sustain. He incarnates a magnified vision of all the ambiguities and impossibilities of the colonized. (p. 107)

RIGGING THE SPACE RACE

"Not only do we have to spread information technology around, but we have to completely change the whole approach to education and more generally knowledge. We have to turn countries into what I call learning nations."

Jean Francois Rischard, Vice President,
Finance and Private-Sector Development, the World Bank

The same pervasive myths that were used to justify colonization can be seen again with the development and aid projects instituted in the South. The dominant impression is that benevolence and good will motivate these projects. It may be argued however, that today's "aid" is in many ways similar to the "white man's burden" of the last colonial era. The patronizing idea is that people in the LDCs need to undergo a "learning process" to catch up to their "civilized" partners in the West. What is usually obscured, however, is that the benefactors of these loans and assistance projects are not the ones receiving the aid, but rather those who are instituting it.

At the first level, the coercion of the NICs on the Internet is guised by promises of an equal voice for the developing nations, as its decentralized framework supports a multidirectional flow of information. Nevertheless, left out of the discourse is the direct and recurrent imposition of knowledge and knowledge systems from the West, knowledge that is de facto considered far superior to that which is generated in the South. To illustrate, one needs only be reminded of the fact that the bulk of African and black studies are conducted outside of African institutions.

As the keepers of the knowledge then, the West assumes that it holds the responsibility to transfer its scientific knowledge and technical wisdom over to the South, as it is this supposed lack of modern technology that keeps developing nations in an economic quagmire. This notion hides under a linear ideology of technological development that may, in fact, be the real catalyst of the difficulties.

MacBride (1980) has indicated that historically exports of Western technology have actually hindered developing countries in the sense that such transfers

(i) Have consisted primarily in simple exportation of western technology, which reflects the economic and social conditions and practices of one part of the world only; (ii) have generally tended to be capital rather than labour-intensive; (iii) have created dependence upon foreign capital, foreign supply sources and foreign tastes and expectations; (iv) have been effected mostly by transnational corporations, which have maintained control over the technology; (v) have benefited elite sectors . . . more than the masses; (vi) have contributed little to economic self-reliance and co-operation among developing countries; (vii) have fostered the rural exodus and increased migration. (p. 217)

In the past, communications sectors in developing countries have focused more on developing large-scale infrastructures rather than producing endogenous software (Boafo 1991). The consequence within the computing industry is that the infrastructures are set up to fertilize the markets for the imports of foreign computer software and hardware. The tautological failure of "leapfrog economics" is that the NICs must have the newest (and most expensive) equipment in order to stay on the edge and compete in the global marketplace, yet they must also already be on the economic upperground in order to do so. The creation of endogenous communications equipment and technologies is capital intensive. Considering only the current financial restraints in developing nations, it is not surprising that production and manufacturing in this area is limited to, and controlled by, industrialized countries (MacBride 1980).

The platform of "freedom of information" would seem to suggest that information is in itself free, but the actual know-how, skills, and knowledge regarding the manufacture of computer software and hardware is carefully guarded by the transnational corporations and industrialized countries who produce it. As Hamelink (1996) notes, "This is not accidental. . . . [Western technology] is jealously protected from transfer as it is considered private property of the 'technology-producers'" (p. 128). Furthermore, national industrialization programs tend not to give serious consideration to the creation and production of indigenous communication equipment, and very few research-and-development activities take place in this arena. Consequently, those who import the new technologies are often left with equipment that they do not fully comprehend, and must therefore relinquish control over to the experts and technocrats who have mastery over the systems (Boafo 1991).

DIGITAL TOLLS

> "Let us remember that the main purpose of aid is not to help other nations but to help ourselves."
>
> Former U.S. President Richard Nixon

Development agencies are now advocating the creation of a strong information industry in the South as a solid route for improving the fate of the poorer countries. The rhetoric suggests that the countries with strong information structures and networks prosper the most. Facts and statistics are cited as persuaders that the rest of the world needs to join the Information Age in the global race toward progress. Only dismal forecasts are predicted for those who may wish to stay disconnected. As *The Economist* advises, "The losers will be those who stood still and watched" (UNDP 1996, 6). This attitude is particularly directed toward the African continent, which currently has the fewest Internet connections (Panos 1995). Rischard, the World Bank's vice president of Finance and Private Sector Development, has commented that, "Africa needs to seize this [development] opportunity, quickly. If African countries cannot take advantage of the information revolution and surf this great wave of technological change, they may be crushed by it" (Rischard 1996). But won't they be crushed by it anyway?

The World Bank, along with at least twenty other large development agencies, has now redirected its resources toward aid in the communications sector. The World Bank's project InfoDev (or what this author would more critically call InfoDebt) is yet another large-scale financing project that seeks to generate income through trickle-down economics. The idea is that the employment and growth generated in the new sectors will promote a higher standard of living for those in poor countries. The fact that the TNCs are moving to the Third World precisely for the purpose of exploiting the unionless cheap labor is apparently not as important. These altruistic loans are also only approved to projects that hold at least a 10-percent rate of return on the investment (Alberti 1996). As many of the LDCs are in arrears, "tied aid" is usually one of the conditions to lending out the capital. The U.S. Treasury has estimated that for every $1 that is contributed to the World Bank, $2 is returned in procurement contracts that U.S. exporters receive in return (Alberti 1996). Likewise, in the 1994 fiscal year the bank paid out $16 billion in support of 1,900 development projects but took in $20 billion in loan payments and charges. That year the World Bank held a surplus of $4 billion, while many of the poverty-stricken nations were left in an even worse economic condition than they were prior to receiving the loans (Zagorin 1994). As James Halloran

(1994) indicates in *The Global Political Economy of Communication*, forty countries are now in a worse position than they were a decade ago. The amount of interest on debt repayment is only 4 percent for rich countries in contrast to the 17-percent rate that is paid out by the poorer nations. As a result, the flow from South to North in debt repayments amounts to US$50 billion annually.

The same colonial structures and ideologies are resurfacing, but this time they are hidden behind the decentralized and invisible webs that are spinning around the globe. In the *New Internationalist's* "State of the World Report," Chris Brazier (1997) suggests that the resident representatives of the IMF and the World Bank are essentially the new masked colonial governors. Brazier argues that during colonial times the governors were dispatched from the mother country to effectively serve as monarchs in the colonized states. It is well recognized today that these governments were managed in the ultimate interest of the colonizing powers themselves rather than the protectorate states as was claimed. The situation did not change significantly after Third World nations gained independence either; the one exception was that the governors were no longer required as figureheads, since the same process was legitimized within a market system. Instead, the earnings generated by the poor countries from the sale of their resources now had to be directed toward the purchase of the machines and processed goods (which had previously been supplied without charge) from their former masters. There may not be a visible geographic imperial center as there was during the colonial era. The TNCs may be physically decentralized, but their control and power is now cleverly cloaked and consolidated in cyberspace.

SIPHONING CYBERFUEL

"Why not develop an 'INTERNET FRANCHISE' approach, based on the successful McDonald Hamburgers Corporation as a model?"
Tony Villasenor, Manager, NASA Science Internet

It is vital for the TNCs to convince Third World leaders that possessing and importing the latest new technologies is both beneficial and necessary to their future survival in the global economy. This is because the Third World represents a ripe and extremely lucrative potential market, both in the telecommunications and computer industries. Liberalization, or the breakdown of the LDCs national telecommunication monopolies within the phone industry alone, is projected to account for 30 percent of the estimated US$900 billion that will be generated in the telecommunications market by 2005 (UNDP 1996).

Proponents of communications development projects often cite India as a prospering case example; their software manufacturing market has increased at a rate of 30 to 40 percent per year (Graham and Marvin 1996) and, in fiscal year 1994–1995, the country's software exports amounted to US$500 million (UNDP 1996). The numbers look promising; however, a closer examination reveals that the profits are actually the result of the giant computer corporations (Dell, Microsoft, IBM, and Hewlett-Packard), who have been drawn in by the country's cheap domestic labor force (D'Souza 1996; Graham and Marvin 1996).

The South is of vital importance to the North as they are the fuel in the race toward progress. As Howard and Howard (1996) suggest, globalization is intimately tied to the information revolution. The creation of communications technology for development does not occur in a vacuum and is in fact systematically designed. Such globalization projects are "conceived, planned, funded, organized, facilitated, operated and exported within a deregulated free market system. It is this system which 'gives globalisation its dynamic' . . . which reflects and reinforces the total system" (Halloran 1994, 181).

The trend toward deregulation, or what critics are calling reregulation, is accompanied by the myth of the free-market system. The dominant ideology in the politics of communications transfer suggests that by opening up the market to competition, prices will fall in the marketplace, enabling a greater share of the general population to afford the new technological services. However, as Hamelink (1996) has observed, under capitalist conditions a free market inevitably leads to a consolidation of capital, the growth of TNCs, and forms of "industrial oligopolization" that in reality only benefit a select few. The smaller players who cannot keep up the pace get eliminated.

The control may be centered, but the distribution of work is spreading across the globe. As noted in earlier examples, countries with on-line connections are now being exploited heavily by the TNCs, who logically prefer to tap into the South's cheaper labor sources. The advantages for the corporations are substantial: Wages can be less than 20 percent of that in the North, staff turnover rates are only 1 to 2 percent per annum (compared to 35 percent in North America), and the workers are drilled for accuracy to almost military levels (Graham and Marvin 1996). What's more, "back offices" are now proliferating at a rapid rate all across the Third World (Graham and Marvin 1996). That is, routine teletransacted and teledefined services are the so-called new opportunities that are being offered to many citizens in developing nations. Pelton has argued that this creates the growth of "electronic immigration" or "the on-line 'importing' of (often female) labor and skills from cheap 'telecolony' locations around the globe" (cited in Graham and Marvin 1996, 153). We are all familiar with the image of the exploited female labor forces in Southeast Asia who produce the assembly-line microchips, but few are aware that there is now a burgeoning market for the new telemonitoring industries. Just how will some of these aid projects enable LDCs to utilize the latest technologies and enter the world economy? One of the suggestions forwarded by the World Bank is to train African personnel to monitor the closed-circuit TV camera systems in U.S. shopping malls (Graham and Marvin 1996).

It should now be blatantly obvious why the TNCs are so eager to act as "donors" in order to furnish and hardwire the developed world. They are the invisible monarchs. With the assistance of their cybercolonial governors (i.e., the IMF and the World Bank) they have the power to dictate and boss around national governments. The only real difference now is that it doesn't even matter if these governments are elected or not (Brazier 1997).

DISCONNECTED FROM THE (FINISH) LINE

Let us assume for a moment that the infostructures that are currently underway are all successfully implemented. The Internet has become truly ubiquitous. All individuals have access to computers, phone lines, and Internet connections through their local ISPs. What then?

Computer technologies are biased for the simple reason that they are designed with particular notions in mind with regard to efficiency. As such, how useful will the Internet really be to the homeless and poor around the world? The Internet may be a great idea for socially and geographically isolated members of the North to reconnect with each other, but to members of poorer nations who often live close to their kin, would it make sense to use the Internet to reconnect? The fact is that face-to-face contact is the direct communication link and will probably continue to be so for over 1.5 billion peasants and 900 million illiterates in Africa, Asia, and Latin America (Gonzalez-Manet 1988). Moreover, even with the implementation of computers in poor areas (Jamaica being a case in point), Internet access may end up being inconsequential. As the authors of "Contradictions in Cyberspace: Collective Response" write, "If the supercomputer is next to a shanty town bereft of running water, no amount of access to e-mail will remedy the problem: no knowledge will be emancipatory (poor and homeless people in First World countries face a similar situation), as access to unlimited information is unlikely to improve their lot in life" (Interrogate the Internet 1996, 125–126).

Another point to consider is that many countries are still plagued by warfare and internal strife. Many people are too busy fighting their injustices in the real world, let alone a virtual one. Countries under dictatorship or authoritarian rule can also dismiss the freedoms associated with the Internet. That is, aside from the information haves and have-nots, one still needs to take account of the "wills" and the "will-nots." For example, in 1993 China banned the manufacture and sale of all satellite dishes (also used for Net connections). The following year, Saudi Arabia followed suit. In Algeria, Islamic fundamentalists observed that satellites were pointed toward Europe and not Mecca and attacked the satellite dish owners (Wresch 1996). Even if signals are received, they can still be clamped. In China all Internet traffic must run through the Quinghua University, a "choke point" that enables all information to be potentially monitored and/or deleted. And in Singapore the government has created a unique system that enables the direct filtering of Internet content.

The superhighway is not a "superfreeway" either. With the Web's intensifying commercial interests, more and more of the information that is valuable is often not free. Many of the academic on-line journals and e-libraries require hefty subscription fees and require that their customers subscribe through credit card payment. As Hamelink (1996) writes, "Increasingly citizens are required to pay for information services rendered by public bodies. In many countries governmental departments charge for information that is generated through public finance, they levy fees for the use of data collections or sell these through private on-line service operators" (p. 101).

Finally, considering the rapid technological changes in the developed world, the most likely prospect is that the LDCs will become a dumping ground for obsolete technologies (Boafo 1991). That is, even if NICs invest heavily now in the newest technologies, they may not be able to afford to keep pace with the high rates of software and hardware turnover that are exhibited by the industrialized nations. The entire computer industry is based on the rapid advancement of these developments, as the software and hardware manufacturers propel each other by creating the necessity for constant upgrading. Many countries may soon have the infrastructure to support the new technologies, but not a base of consumers with enough capital to afford the ceaseless shifts that go with it.

CONCLUSION

The new (virtual) world promises all of its members unlimited access to information and communication. At the same time, the discourse surrounding the communications revolution veils the nonvirtual realities and contrary consequences of wiring up the Third World. Amidst the hype, the barriers of access capital, infrastructure, language, and technological expertise remain hidden, and the majority of the world's people are silently disqualified from the race on the infobahn. Although slews of development projects have been devised to circumvent these difficulties, more often than not the agendas that are presented are anathematic to the people they claim to assist. The World Bank works to create monetary and technological dependencies for people in the South, and the transnational corporations are the new world imperialists whose vested interests are really dictating the developments in the information era. Until now, the discourse on the World Wide Web has largely been held in the hands of a minority. Isn't it about time we open cyberspace up to the absent critiques of the majority?

REFERENCES

Alberti, Lisa. 1996. *The Development Lending Dilemma: Macroeconomics vs. MicroEnterprise.* <http://psirius.sfsu.edu/IntRel/IRJournal/su96/Alberti.html>.

Boafo, S. T. Kwame. 1991. Communication Technology and Dependent Development in Sub-Saharan Africa. In *Transnational Communications: Wiring the Third World,* edited by G. Sussman and J. A. Lent. Newbury Park, Calif.: Sage.

Brazier, Chris. 1997. State of the World Report. *The New Internationalist* 287: 4–9.

D'Souza, Dilip. 1996. Silicon Valley East. *The New Internationalist* 286: 25.

Dyson, E., G. Gilder, G. Keyworth, and A. Toffler. 1996. Cyberspace and the American Dream: A Magna Carta for the Knowledge Age. *The Information Society* 12: 295–308. Also available at <http://www.pff.org>.

Gonzalez-Manet, Enrique. 1988. *The Hidden War of Information*, translated by L. Alexandre. Norwood, N.J.: Ablex.

Graham, Stephen, and Simon Marvin. 1996. *Telecommunications and the City*. New York: Routledge.

Halloran, James. 1994. Developments in Communication and Democracy: The Contribution of Research. In *The Global Political Economy of Communication*, edited by Edward A. Comor. New York: St. Martin's Press.

Hamelink, Cees. 1996. *World Communication: Disempowerment and Self-Empowerment*. London: Zed Books.

Howard, Pat, and Roger Howard. 1996. Monopolies of Knowledge in Development. In *Monopolies of Knowledge: Essays in Honor of Harold Innis*, edited by A. Beale and Gail Faurshcou. Proceedings of the Monopolies of Knowledge Conference, Simon Fraser University, Vancouver, B.C., November.

Interrogate the Internet. 1996. Contradictions in Cyberspace: Collective Response. In *Cultures of Internet*, edited by Rob Shields. London: Sage.

Lockard, Joe. 1996. Resisting CyberEnglish. *Bad Subjects* 24. <http://english-server.hss.cmu.edu/bs/>.

MacBride, Sean. 1980. *Many Voices One World*. Part 5: Communications Tomorrow. Paris.

Majtenyi, Cathy, and Michael Fleet. 1996. Wiring Africa. *The New Internationalist* 286: 22.

Mechanic, Michael. 1996. *Metroactive*. <http://metroactive.com/features/cars.html>.

Memmi, Albert. 1965. Portrait of the Colonized. In *The Colonizer and the Colonized*.

Naisbitt, John. 1994. *Global Paradox*. New York: William Morrow.

Panos. 1995. *Panos Briefing Document* No. 16. London: Panos.

Reiss, Bob. 1992. *The Road to Extrema*. New York: Summit Books.

Rischard, Jean Francois. 1996. Cited in *Increasing Internet Connectivity in Sub-Saharan Africa: Issues, Options, and World Bank Group Role*. <http://www.worldbank.org/html/emc/documents/africa0395.html#inf_rev>.

Sardar, Ziauddin. 1996. alt.civilization.faq: Cyberspace as the Darker Side of the West. In *Cyberfutures: Culture and Politics on the Information Superhighway*, edited by Z. Sardar and J. R. Ravetz. New York: New York University Press.

UNDP. 1996. *UNDP and the Communications Revolution*. <http://www.undp.org/undp/comm/>.

Wresch, William. 1996. *Disconnected: Haves and Have-Nots in the Information Age*. New Brunswick, N.J.: Rutgers University Press.

Zagorin, A. 1994. The Sins of a Sainted Bank. *Time Domestic* 144 (8): 54.

PART **II**

POLITICS IN THE ELECTRONIC GLOBAL VILLAGE

6

The Empire Strikes Back Again: The Cultural Politics of the Internet

David J. Gunkel

In the March 1996 issue of *Wired*, Nicholas Negroponte (1996) provides one of the more recent expressions of a concept that has been at the heart of on-line interaction for quite some time. In this editorial, titled "Pluralistic, Not Imperialistic," the founding director of MIT's Media Lab argues that the telematic network is not the next stage of American imperialism but rather a free domain that fosters and encourages global pluralism.[1] "The idea that the Net is another form of Americanization and a threat to local culture is absurd. Such conviction completely misses and misunderstands the extraordinary cultural opportunities of the digital world" (p. 216). Contrary to the imperialist aspirations that had accompanied the Mechanical Age, the Information Age has been determined to offer global liberation and multicultural empowerment.[2] According to Negroponte's (1996) assessment, "The Net is humankind's best chance to respect and nurture the most obscure languages and cultures of the world" (p. 216).

I would like to reconsider this rather popular line of argumentation that has had profound effects on the perceived social and political implications of the telematic network. Although the Internet appears to be international, it has distinct national origins and was developed for purposes other than global communication. The Net originates in the Advanced Research Projects Agency of the U.S. Department of Defense (DOD).[3] In the early 1960s, the DOD was experimenting with a new data communications technology called "packet-switching." This technology fostered the development of a new kind of computer network, one that supported multiple users and resisted systemwide crashes by automatically rerouting data around downed circuits. The goal of this experimental network, originally named ARPANET, was not the decentralized global information system that is heralded in current technical and popular discourses. Rather, its original purpose was directed by the exigencies of the Cold War. The DOD researchers who developed ARPANET sought to design the prototype of a national-defense, data-communications systems that would be immune to and survive the devastation of nuclear aggression. The Internet, therefore, traces its genealogy directly to one of the primary agents of American hegemony, and the effects of this paternity can still be read in the very structure and content of the "global network."

AT THE VIRTUAL CENTER OF DECENTRALIZATION

"The decentralized characteristics for which so many praise the net did not arise out of anarchist intention, but out of nomadic military strategy."
Critical Art Ensemble (1998, 142)

One of the more distinctive characteristics of ARPANET and its direct descendent, the Internet, is its decentralized systems architecture. Prior to the development of ARPANET, information networks were commonly designed around a central server that coordinated and controlled all aspects of data communication. The disadvantage of this systems architecture is obvious. To disable the entire network, one only need hinder the central hub. ARPANET, on the contrary, disseminated all operations throughout the network. It was, therefore, comprised of a loose amalgamation of independent computers, or what Negroponte (1995) has called "a lattice of heterogeneous processors" (p. 180). In this way, as Bruce Sterling (1993) describes it, "The network would have no central authority." It is this decentralized systems architecture that rendered ARPANET virtually immune to failure or destruction. And it is this same structure that has been determined to constitute the Internet's resistance to cultural imperialism and control. As Negroponte (1996) asserts, "Colonialism is the fruit of centralist thinking. It does not exist in a decentralized world" (p. 216).

Negroponte's (1996) assurance that colonialism is necessarily allied with centralist thinking is overly simplistic and uninformed by the history of Western imperialism and the struggles of decolonization. Decentralization is not in and of itself opposed to cultural domination, but has been and continues to be one of the strategies of colonial administration. "Decentralized domination," writes Ziauddin Sardar (1996), "solves two problems simultaneously: it makes the new territory manageable and submissive to the structures of control while keeping the citizens happy by giving them a sense of their importance as they are being used" (pp. 38–39). Cultural domination, therefore, not only can but does exist in a decentralized world, and the Internet is not an exception but a prime example.

Operation of the decentralized network that is called the Internet is dependent upon the allocation and designation of separate but equal domains. Currently there are two kinds of top-level domains available to the public. Generic domains (.com, .net, and .org), which are administered by Network Solutions through Internic and are assigned irrespective of geophysical location, and country domains, which are specified in ISO 3166 and administered locally.[4] Despite the apparent neutrality of this conceptual schema, its practical implementation has, in effect, granted a privileged position to American users. The Electronic Frontier Foundation's *Everybody's Guide to the Internet* (Gaffin 1994) indicates this privilege without comment. "In general, American [e-mail] addresses end in an organizational suffix, such as '.edu,' which means the site is at a college or university. Other American suffixes include: .com for businesses, .org for non-profit organizations, .gov and .mil for government and military agencies, and .net for companies or organizations that run large networks. Sites in the rest of the world tend to use a two-letter code that represents their country" (pp. 28–29).

Top-level domain designations for users in the United States have not, in practice, incorporated suffixes indicating their nation of origin. Although some U.S. institutions (most notably federal offices and state agencies) do employ the .us suffix specified in ISO 3166, this application constitutes the exception rather than the rule. In general, only addresses belonging to netizens of "foreign countries" have consistently employed explicit designations of nationality. This nomenclature is informed by and legitimizes U.S. domination. On the one hand, the almost exclusive employment of generic domain names by U.S. users virtually universalizes American netizens. Whereas non-American sites are almost always identified by specific indications of nationality and geophysical position, U.S. users and institutions are denoted by the seemingly universal and generic category of functionality. Virtually disengaged from the particulars of geography and specific sociopolitical circumstances, U.S. sites occupy a unique position that appears to be coextensive with the international scope of the Net itself. On the other hand, the absence of a nationally distinguished suffix, although implying nationality by exclusion, "normalizes American users" (Poster 1995, 28). It positions Americans at the center of the virtual world and literally designates everything else as "foreign" or "alien."

In both universalizing and normalizing American users, the Internet, which is celebrated for its decentralized systems architecture, actually situates Americans at the virtual center of the digital world. The Net, therefore, does not necessarily oppose or escape U.S. domination. Rather, its architecture is originally supported and continually informed by U.S. hegemony. Despite the decentralized structure of the Net, the United States has occupied and continues to occupy a privileged position within the digital infrastructure.

SPEAKING OF PLURALISM

"The language of the Internet, and not just its structure, is specific to the Western World."

Interrogate the Internet (1996, 126)

The Internet, although supposedly global in scope and decentralized in structure, has situated American users in a privileged position. This privilege extends beyond the structure of cyberspace into the very mode of on-line interaction. From the beginning, English has been the unofficial official language of the Internet. James Powell (1997) has even suggested that the World Wide Web be renamed the English Wide Web, for "everything from browser menus, to the markup elements, right down to the normally invisible hypertext transfer protocol commands are in English" (p. 188). This privileging of one specific idiom is usually justified on the basis of utility. According to Negroponte's (1996) assessment, the privileged status of English should not be confused with cultural identity. For English "is a utilitarian language that lands planes safely and keeps the Net's infrastructure running" (p. 216). This appeal to utility, which is animated and legitimated by a distinctly American ethos (namely, utilitarianism), not only effaces its own history but remains ignorant of the cultural violence that it continues to perpetrate and justify.

The privileged status of English has not been decided by a global congress or international consortium. Its position is the direct result of colonial expansion and economic power. As Britain extended her empire throughout the globe between the seventeenth and nineteenth centuries, English gradually achieved the status of an international idiom. It was not only the official language of the colonies, but, through the workings of various British cultural initiatives, most notably education, it was eventually imposed upon the indigenous, colonized peoples.[5] More recently, the economic and political dominance of the United States directly after World War II has had a similar linguistic effect. As American products and ideologies flooded the global market, the dominant language of the United States came to occupy a central position in international business and industry. The use and utility of English as a lingua franca cannot simply be disengaged from the history that has formed and substantiated it.[6] The privileging of this idiom, although currently useful for running network infrastructure and facilitating intercultural dialogue, has come at a substantial expense—one that we should not be too quick to forget. As David Crystal (1997) summarizes in his chronicle, *English as a Global Language*, "The present-day world status of English is primarily the result of two factors: the expansion of British colonial power, which peaked towards the end of the nineteenth century, and the emergence of the United States as the leading economic power of the twentieth century" (p. 53).

The utility of English as an international language has been secured through considerable cultural violence. This violence, however, is not limited to a particular time in history. It is not something that is either over and done or easily surpassed. Rather, traces of linguistic imperialism are currently manifest in the very texture of on-line interaction. Currently the only Internet working protocol for encoding computer-generated text is ASCII, the American Standard Code for Information Interchange. In a multiplatform environment like the Internet, ASCII has a definite utility. It ensures that text information produced in one operating system or text editor will be able to communicate with and be manipulated by users employing a number of different and often incompatible systems. But ASCII has serious limitations, which Tor Galaasen (1996) has explicated in his epistolary reply to Negroponte (1996):

Much could be said in response to Nicholas Negroponte's "Pluralistic, Not Imperialistic" (*Wired* 4.03: 216), in which the main issue is elegantly avoided. I am talking about the binary representation of the characters I am writing right now—the seven-bit American Standard Code for Information Interchange, also known as ASCII. Sending Internet Email in Norwegian is like having a speech impediment forced upon oneself. Characters considered "special" by Anglo-Americans are essential to the freedom of expression of non-English-speakers. The telephone system does not require its users to speak only English, nor does the postal system require us to write only English. Was someone talking about pluralism on the Net? (p. 26)

The Internet, which according to Negroponte (1996) is supposed to provide the best chance for obscure languages, imposes a rather debilitating "speech impediment" on anyone who does not speak English or write in its rather limited alphabetic script. In its basic form, ASCII is limited to the 128 characters (letters, numbers, symbols) found on a standard English-language keyboard. Although there have been several enhancements of the standard (i.e., 8-bit ASCII, which allows for 128 additional characters, and the ISO Latin-1 enhanced character set), it "cannot support every language spoken on the earth" (Powell 1997, 189). In particular, it cannot accommodate anything other than basic Indo-European, alphabetic script. It can only encode a limited number of diacritical marks and is absolutely unable to accommodate other alphabets (i.e., Cyrillic, Hebrew, Arabic) or nonalphabetic script (i.e., Kanji). Non-ASCII characters can be incorporated either through the employment of graphical character entities (images of the character encoded as a graphic file) or by installing a specially designed international character set. Although these two techniques provide a means by which to mitigate the limitations of ASCII, they not only constitute special cases that are considered deviations from the norm but exhibit specific technical restrictions not encountered by ASCII users. Employing graphical characters, for example, is a time-consuming process not only for the writer/programmer, who must encode each character or word as a separate graphic file, but also for the reader/user, who is required to wait for his or her system to display each graphic individually. International character sets, although more convenient, must still be procured or purchased and installed on each individual machine. Finally, even if one takes the time to encode graphical characters or is adequately equipped with the proper international character sets, the substructure of the Internet is still mediated and supported by ASCII. In an HTML document, for example, the URLs, the document tags, and hypertext transfer commands must be encoded in ASCII characters despite the idiom of the document's content. In all cases, the subtext of on-line interaction is inscribed in English.

Internetworking standards like ASCII, which have become the standard for global information exchange and communication, have actually privileged American and Western European users. This privilege is not the result of some global "conspiracy." Rather, it is a by-product of the genesis and evolution of the Internet. Because the Net was initially developed by and for the U.S. Department of Defense, it incorporated protocols and standards derived from the dominant idiom of the U.S. federal government. However, in the process of international expansion these protocols and standards have come into conflict with the global scope and multicultural context of what is now known as the Internet. These standards, although no less useful for operating and maintaining the system, were not designed for nor are they easily adapted to global applicability. Contrary to Negroponte's (1996) assurances, the international employment of ARPANET technology and protocols has not escaped nationalism. Consequently, the internationalizing of the Internet will remain illusory and incomplete as long as this situation is not explicitly addressed.

CONCLUSION: THE DIGITAL IMPERIUM

"Just when we thought that the age of European colonialism has finally come to an end, suddenly we are copied into the second age of virtual colonialism."

Kroker and Weinstein (1997, 11)

In opposition to the imperialist legacy that had accompanied the mechanical era, the Information Age has been described as providing global liberation and multicultural empowerment. According to assessments like those offered by Nicholas Negroponte (1995, 1996), the Net a priori resists any form of cultural imperialism. These messianic proclamations, however, remain rather naïve. In the first place, statements that locate sociocultural emancipation in the very material of technology efface history by actively disengaging technology from its cultural context and genealogy. Technologies are never neutral; they are always, as Simon Penny (1994) reminds us, products of a specific culture. Consequently, technologies are always informed and animated by distinct ideologies and teleologies. The Internet, in particular, is a product of the U.S. Department of Defense, and its architecture and protocols were developed for purposes other than multicultural empowerment and cooperation. This is not to say that the Net could not eventually begin to disentangle itself from the web of its own genealogy. This disentanglement, however, would need to take this complicated paternity and its consequences seriously.

Second, blanket assertions like those made by Negroponte ignore the changing features of cultural hegemony in the digital era. If "being digital" entails the general transition from an economy of material atoms to one of immaterial information bits (cf. Negroponte 1995, 11–12), then we should expect the very matter of imperialism to be subjected to a similar dematerialization. The current forces of cultural domination are no longer centered in the corporeal elements most readily associated with European colonialism and Americanization. Imperialism, for example, no longer takes the form of a battalion of occupation forces coordinated by a central bureaucracy. In the Information Age, cultural imperialism is itself digitized and recoded in the very form and content of the electrically mediated world. Again, this revelation does not preclude the possibility of eventually developing a truly multicultural environment within the fabric of the Net. This project, however, would need to learn to take the new digital forms of cultural imperialism into account, rather than discounting them *tout court* as the detritus of a bygone era.

Finally, the future evolution of the Internet will require not only new international standards and protocols but a self-reflective critical perspective, one that recognizes that any technological innovation or new administrative procedure will also be informed by specific ideologies and teleologies. For example, on February 4, 1997, the IAHC approved the creation of seven new generic domains, which are expected to be available by the end of the decade. These new, supposedly international designations appear to provide a means by which to address and eventually alleviate the nominal discrepancy that has effectively privileged American users. The new domain names, however, reinscribe privilege, for they employ a nomenclature derived from one specific idiom, the English language. The development of new standards and protocols, therefore, do not take place in a vacuum and are never value neutral. They are always and already informed and biased by specific sociocultural perspectives and preconceptions, often reiterating and reinscribing the very problem they appear to address. New technologies and administrative standards do not simply escape the complications of this system, and it would be naïve to believe otherwise. As postcolonial theory has demonstrated, there are no easy answers or solutions in this arena, only an interminable struggle that continually questions the implications of its own movement and innovation.

NOTES

1. "Telematics" is the English spelling of *télématique*. The word was originally coined by Simon Nora and Alain Minc in their 1978 report commissioned by French president Giscard d'Estaing, *L'informatisation de la société*. Nora and Minc employed this neologism to name the convergence of computer technology (*informatique*) with telecommunications systems. Other nominations for this new technological object

include "informatics" (Haraway 1991), "computer mediated communication" (Jones 1995), and "new media" (see *New Media* magazine).

2. Similar proclamations have been disseminated in, for example, the Progress and Freedom Foundation's "Cyberspace and the American Dream: A Magna Carta for the Knowledge Age" (Dyson et al. 1996), Bruce Schuman's (1988) *Utopian Computer Networking*, and Mitch Kapor's (1996) "Where is the Digital Highway Really Heading? The Case for a Jeffersonian Information Policy."

3. For an account of the history and development of the Internet, see Negroponte (1995), Sterling (1993), and Gromov (1995).

4. Earlier this year, the Internet Ad Hoc Committee (IAHC) approved the creation of seven new generic domains (.store, .firm, .web, .info, .arts, .rec and .nom). An analysis of this proposal is in the conclusion.

5. For an analysis of the mechanisms and logic of colonialism, see Ashcroft, Griffiths, and Tiffin (1995).

6. The status of English as the international language of the Net has been explicitly marked, on the Internet, by individuals for whom English is not the primary language: "Internet es la consagración final del inglés como idioma de intercambio entre todas las lenguas del mundo [Internet signifies the consagration of English as the language that acts as a bridge between all the other languages in the world]" (Fernandez Hermana 1996, 1). "The universal language on Internet is English, or more exactly a vague collection of languages called 'English' because their common origin is the national language spoken in England by the English" (Korpella 1996, 1). On the historical and cultural complications of international exchange languages, see Eco (1996).

REFERENCES

Ashcroft, B., G. Griffiths, and H. Tiffin. 1995. *The Postcolonial Studies Reader*. New York: Routledge.

Critical Art Ensemble. 1998. *Flesh Machine: Cyborgs, Designer Babies, and New Eugenic Consciousness*. New York: Autonomedia. Also available at <http://www.well.com/user/hlr/texts/utopiancrit.html>.

Crystal, D. 1997. *English as a Global Language*. Cambridge: Cambridge University Press.

Dyson, E., G. Gilder, G. Keyworth, and A. Toffler. 1996. Cyberspace and the American Dream: A Magna Carta for the Knowledge Age. *The Information Society* 12: 295–308. Also available at <http://www.pff.org>.

Eco, U. 1996. *The Search for the Perfect Language*. Cambridge: Blackwell.

Fernandez Hermana, L. A. 1996. *The Intelligible Tower of Babel*. <http://www.partal.com/luisangel/enredeng2.html>.

Gaffin, A. 1994. *Everybody's Guide to the Internet*. Cambridge: MIT Press. Also available at <http://www.eff.org>.

Galaasen, T. 1996. A Global Village, Huh? Letter to the editor. *Wired* 4 (7): 26.

Gromov, G. R. 1995. *The Roads and Crossroads of the Internet's History*. <http://www.intervalley.com/intval.html>.

Haraway, D. 1991. *Simians, Cyborgs, Women: The Reinvention of Nature*. New York: Routledge.

Interrogate the Internet. 1996. Contradictions in Cyberspace: Collective Response. In *Cultures of Internet*, edited by R. Shields. London: Sage.

Jones, S. 1995. *Cybersociety: Computer-Mediated Communication and Community*. London: Sage.

Kapor, M. 1996. Where Is the Digital Highway Really Heading? The Case for a Jeffersonian Information Policy. *Wired* 1 (3): 163–174. Also available at <http://www.nlc-bnc.ca/documents/rfcs/rfc1259.txt>.

Korpella, J. 1996. *English—The Universal Language on Internet?* <http://www.hut.fi/~jkorpela/lingua-franca.html>.

Kroker, A., and M. A. Weinstein. 1997. *Data Trash: The Theory of the Virtual Class*. New York: St. Martin's Press. Also available at <http://www.ctheory.com/a-political_economy.html>.

Negroponte, N. 1995. *Being Digital*. New York: Vintage.

———. 1996. Pluralistic, Not Imperialistic. *Wired* 4 (3): 216.

Nora, S., and A. Minc. 1978. *L'Informatisation de la société*. Paris: La Documentation Française.

Penny, S. 1994. Virtual Reality as the Completion of the Enlightenment Project. In *Cultures on the Brink: Ideologies of Technology*, edited by G. Bender and T. Druckrey. Seattle: Bay Press.

Poster, M. 1995. *The Second Media Age*. Cambridge: Polity Press. Also available at <http://www.hnet.uci.edu/mposter/writings/Internet.html>.

Powell, J. E. 1997. *HTML Plus!* Belmont, Calif.: Wadsworth.

Sardar, Z. 1996. Alt.civilization.faq: Cyberspace as the Darker Side of the West. In *Cyberfutures: Culture and Politics on the Information Superhighway*, edited by Z. Sardar and J. R. Ravetz. New York: New York University Press.

Schuman, B. 1988. *Utopian Computer Networking*. <http://www.rain.org/~origin/ucs.html>.

Sterling, B. 1993. *Short History of the Internet*. <http://w3.aces.uiuc.edu/aim/scale/nethistory.html>.

7

Creating New Relations: The Internet in Central and Eastern Europe

Margot Emery and Benjamin J. Bates

The political, social, and economic environment in Central and Eastern Europe is in the midst of a not-so-quiet revolution. The profound changes that have occurred in the region since 1989 have followed, if not been aided and abetted by, the growth of new telecommunications systems epitomized by the Internet spreading throughout Central Europe, Russia, the new independent states of the former Soviet Union, and the nation-states of former Yugoslavia. This chapter seeks to examine how the Internet in particular is helping to transform and create social, economic, and political relationships throughout post-communist Europe.

The impact of information and of more open information systems on the once closed political and social structures of the former Second World were not totally unanticipated. Information is power, and emerging media and information systems threatened to shift power relationships by changing information flows. The presumption of impact and influence can be seen in the coopting, control, and utilization of media by the state and Communist party in Marxist states, in the Voice of America and Radio Free Europe efforts at reaching Second World populations, and in the more recent political debates over the free flow of information. All presume that control of information is key to fostering the "right kind" of political and economic relationships.

As new communications systems began developing in the 1960s, concerns did not remain abstract. Several studies of emerging information systems focused on their potential for changing economic relationships and promoting democratization and the promulgation of personal liberty and political independence (Masuda 1981; Nora and Minc 1980; Pool 1990; Sackman and Nie 1970; Salvaggio 1989; Westin 1971). This was a transformation reinforced by the increasing role of information in modern economies (Dordick and Wang 1993; Machlup 1962; Nora and Minc 1980; Porat 1978) and the concurrent need for improved communication systems. An EEC conference in 1981 (Bannon, Barry, and Holst 1982) examined changing patterns of work and economic relationships. A UNESCO commission examining the "free flow of information" issue concluded that the rise of new communications systems had, and should, foster greater independence and democratization (MacBride 1980). Stonier (1983) focused on the impacts of new information technologies on the Soviet Union and the Eastern bloc, suggesting specifically that the rise of "an extensive, powerful, yet leaky communication network" (p. 144) was driving democratization and leading to social upheaval.

A plethora of other scholars have suggested that the rise of new information systems is a central factor in the rise of what is generally called the Information Age. Many of these (Bell 1973; Beniger 1986; Dizard 1982; Ito 1980; Masuda 1981; Nora and Minc 1980) saw the transformation as social as well as economic. The social transformations foreseen often included shifts in guiding social values and, in particular, shifts in social relationships and the rise of new communities (i.e., new patterns of social relationships) caused by the rise and development of new communication systems (Bates 1989).

More recent critical considerations (Gerbner, Mowlana, and Schiller 1996; Sussman 1997; Tehranian 1990) have tended to focus on the "transnationalizing" and commodifying aspects of the new information systems, as well as the democratizing effects. Oddly enough, the Internet has been held to increase both the integration and the fragmentation of societies around the world, facilitating a global emphasis even as it supports the rise of provincial and special interests. Staple (1997) describes this dynamic as a dialectic of universalism and particularism, cyberspace and tribal space, and others have noted its existence is evident in the rise of cultural-specific uses and applications of the Internet and related technologies (Kalin 1997; Keogh and Cook 1997). Growth in these areas is predicted by some to be the second wave of Internet development, occurring as the strongly Western-dominated conventions and structures of the technology are adapted for non-Western uses (Somogyi 1996).

The rise of computers and information systems such as the Internet has not been the sole factor driving the new media environment. VCRs (Ganley and Ganley 1987; Levy 1989), copiers, cellular and satellite phones, video cameras, and fax machines have all been said to contribute to the changing social and political environment, particularly in formerly authoritarian regimes, and many can recall how citizens used such technologies to communicate with the West during the fall of the Soviet Union. Builder and Bankes (1992) contend the roots of the current information revolution stretch back even further, to the development of solid-state electronics in the early 1950s, which spawned the worldwide spread of cheap, reliable, and powerful information systems. First radio, then television, computers, and the "small" technologies that followed all helped to transform global patterns of communication and the processing, storage, and use of information, contributing to an environment of broader change and evolution throughout the world.

The social change engendered by the information revolution has, in significant ways, been greatest in Central and Eastern Europe. Several factors contribute to this. First, the new telecommunications system's basic structure is so distinctive from that of the previously dominant postal, telegraph, and telephone (PTT) systems, print, and broadcast media, which were traditionally state run, centralized, and tightly controlled. Shifting to the newer technologies has also enabled Central and Eastern Europe to leapfrog over some of the limitations of existing telecom systems (Lewis 1995; Technology Leap-Frogging 1996) into an inherently more open and decentralized set of information systems. Second, the opportunities for expansion, adoption, and utilization of these new systems have been relatively high. An educated, largely urban populace has allowed Central and Eastern Europe to take greater and more immediate advantage of the developing information economy/society. Third, social and economic factors have also spurred integration of the systems, driven by the region's growing international ambitions and lack of reliable alternative communications in remote areas. Finally, there is the liberating change that heightened information flow itself helped drive in the region, a flow that was apparent even before 1989 in *samizdat*, the distribution of self-published, uncensored writings (Skilling 1989), and in transnational spillover of media broadcasts. These earlier streams and today's wide-ranging flow of information delivered by the Internet, transborder satellite television networks and accelerating international contacts and alliances have all facilitated the networking and reconnection of the region, both domestically and internationally. Information is the fiber that is reweaving the fabric of the societies, their transitional systems, and their relations to others, both in the region and around the world.

This chapter begins by developing a context for examining the growth of the Internet and the World Wide Web in Central and Eastern Europe as one example of emerging new information systems. We open with a theoretical overview of how information systems can change macrosocial patterns and behaviors. We then consider how the rise of the Internet is helping to create and redefine social, economic, and political relationships in the region during a period of profound cultural transformation.

THE INFLUENCE OF COMMUNICATIONS STRUCTURES

The general idea that the structure of communications systems can have both individual and social impacts is hardly new. From the basic assumption of Marxist and criticalist theories that the ruling class constructs media structures to help maintain social control, to McLuhan's famous line that "the medium is the message," there has been an indirect acknowledgment that the structure of media systems can have broad social impacts. Perhaps the most direct statement of that relationship can be found in Innis's (1972) *Empires and Communication*. In that work, Innis argued that the development and utilization of new media could be linked to the rise and fall of empires. Specifically, Innis (1964, 1972) argued that the structure of communications systems contained certain "biases," that they promoted certain patterns of use and control by dominant groups. As new media systems came to predominate within a culture, their rise undermined previous power relationships and brought forth the potential for new groups of users to come to power through their ability to use and control the new medium, and their ability to take advantage of the changing social and information structures and relationships. With new media came new structures, new patterns of use and control, and, perhaps, new dominant groups.

A clearer statement of the mechanisms of how communications system structures can have broad social impacts can be found in Bates's (1993) "access, bias, control" model. The Bates model argues, based on a synthesis of critical and social-scientific theories of social effects, that the structure and operations of communications systems can have broad social effects through the operation of one or more of three basic mechanisms. The *access* mechanism is based on the notion that some social impacts come from a structure's inherent capacity to limit access to the communications system. The *bias* mechanism argues that structural factors can exert influence by favoring certain types of content or certain uses of the communications system. The *control* mechanism examines the structural factors allowing or regulating the ability of outside groups to exert control of all types on the communications system, and through that control have influence.

These influences work, in essence, by helping to define and delimit relationships between various sets of users of the communications system. The approach is neither determinative nor definitive; rather, it attempts to provide a mechanism for examining patterns and relationships, both in the communications systems and within the social systems that utilize them. Let's examine what this approach suggests about the basic structure of the Internet.

The Internet was designed and developed as a test system for a cooperative, multisystem, fault-tolerant, multiply redundant digital communications system; a system through which any one computer system connected to the network could communicate with any other connected computer system, using a variety of routings. The network topology followed none of the standard design templates; rather, it incorporated them all. The rules for network operations were developed cooperatively, and the technical standards are still developed and implemented on a cooperative basis. The digital nature of the system permits a wide range of communications uses. At its heart, the Internet is a heavily decentralized, cooperative, relatively small-scale system of networks incorporating a wide range of communications uses.

Initially, access to the Internet was somewhat restricted. The original network, ARPANET, was limited to military, government, and selected academic and private research centers. Only users of those systems were allowed access to this precursor of the Internet, and thus, to the communications and information the network provided. However, the advantages of the open Internet structure over proprietary networks were quickly realized, and other networks in the United States and Europe quickly adopted the Internet approach and began interconnecting. Each new connection further opened access, contributing to the building of a critical mass of users and content that continues to drive growth.

The commercialization of the Internet in the United States and other countries arguably added some access restrictions (based on ability to pay), while removing others (being associated with academia or the government). And the open nature of the Internet system has meant that while access may be somewhat limited by commercial fees, the ability of new service providers to enter the business has kept prices fairly low. More serious access restrictions within the structure of the Internet are the need for computer access and computer and Internet literacy. Initially, the computer literacy requirement was high, although with the rise of World Wide Web protocols, it has dropped tremendously. In addition, the Internet, while accommodating multiple languages, remains heavily dominated by English-language content, users, and conventions.

Thus, while access is generally open, and the basic Internet system structure is essentially open, local access to users can be limited by four basic factors: availability of basic telecommunications and electrical infrastructure to support electronic communications, availability of local access providers and network connections, the availability of terminals or personal computers to users, and the level of computer and Internet literacy. This would seem to be reflected by diffusion patterns, highest among industrialized countries and among the more educated and better-off. Still, the Internet provides greater potential for access to content providers than any other medium of mass distribution, and thus holds forth a tremendous potential for empowering individuals and groups by allowing them to make their messages available to others.

The digital, widely distributed structure of the Internet does have some implications for the "bias" mechanism of macrosocial influence. In theory, the digital nature means that any kind of information or communication can be accommodated within the system. There is, however, an element of structural bias in that bandwidth limitations currently favor asynchronous (other than in real time) communications and those forms of content that digitize/compress easily into smaller digital files. Therefore, with limited-bandwidth Internet structures there is a bias toward text and still images and store-and-forward forms of communication, although other forms can be, and are, accommodated. One implication of this current bandwidth bias is that it actually enhances the opportunity for creating content. Those interested in creating content do not have to acquire or master expensive technical equipment or invest heavily in professional quality production techniques in order to make content widely available.

Bates (1990) suggested that one shifting factor in the emergence of cooperative information systems such as the Internet was that the more open structure limited the ability to exert the old hierarchical patterns of control. In a similar vein, Mulgan (1990) noted that the rise of information systems such as the Internet facilitated not only older patterns of social control, but opened the way for new patterns of control and new social relationships. The Internet was designed to be a cooperative, "survivable," communications system, one without a central fixed base or fixed structure. It is very difficult for any single outside source to effectively control content or information flow on the Internet. The differential patterns of use and control offered by the newer cooperative structures were confirmed in a later study of the FidoNet computer network (Bates and Lansing 1993).

Thus, for the "control" mechanism, the open, cooperative nature of the Internet makes it inherently difficult for groups to exert control over the system. The rise of ubiquitous interconnected telecommunications systems has also contributed to this limit on the ability to control communincations, providing numerous ways for users to bypass local control efforts. The growth of the ubiquitous telecommunications system and of the Internet as an international phenomenon has made it difficult for single local groups or states to exert coercive control over the use of Internet systems or restrict access to its content. Despite a variety of attempts in several countries to place restrictions on content or access, the ability to control the Internet remains elusive. This inability to control and thus limit access and content further empowers individuals and previously disadvantaged groups and their ability to seek out and create new relationships.

The rise of a decentralized communications system has created a technology that gives voice to large numbers of people, enabling them to speak for themselves in public. This, Weston (1996) notes, is "an ironical reversal of the historical social patterning of asymmetrical, centralizing communicating technologies that have molded all of the social relations of modern society" (p. 195). These structural factors, enhancing the ability of individuals and groups to seek out and/or provide a wide range of information and content on the Internet and to bypass old controlled communication structures and form new relations and social structures, are at the heart of the arguments about the democratizing influence of the Internet. In few regions has that voice been so eagerly embraced as in Central and Eastern Europe, where the Internet and the freedom to use it have unfolded in simultaneous fashion.

THE DEVELOPMENT OF THE INTERNET AND INFORMATION SYSTEMS IN CENTRAL AND EASTERN EUROPE

For a region plunged into economic, social, and political restructuring, wrestling with legacy issues of bankrupt economies and fractured infrastructure, Internet access in Central and Eastern Europe arrived surprisingly early and spread fairly quickly. As with the West, access came first to academic and research institutions, arriving at many institutions as early as 1991, a period that mirrored the technology's spread beyond the pure and applied sciences at Western universities.

Several factors led to a rapid diffusion of the technology. First, the long-standing emphasis on producing scientists and technicians had created a substantial technically oriented population able to understand and make use of the technology. Second, monetary support, while always tight in the region, was generally available for academic and scientific institutions to purchase computer technology in support of their need for experimentation and its significance for industrial development. Fairly liberal policies existed in many of the countries during the 1980s that allowed the importation of computer technology from the West, as well as local assembler operations that created homegrown computers, among them the Optimus in Poland and Pravetz in Bulgaria (Bennahum 1997b). These efforts supported early diffusion of stand-alone PCs and the rise of regional networks for research institutions, as well as spin-off bulletin-board systems that both broadened access and awareness of networking. International connectivity, however, remained scarce and make-shift until the arrival of Internet-protocol-based networked computing in the early 1990s.

By 1991 backbone connections to the Internet for academic and research networks were in operation in Poland through a connection with the Austria-based EARN network, and independently in Yugoslavia and Croatia. By the following year, access through Poland's Austrian connection had expanded to include Hungary and Czechoslovakia, and networking was underway in Romania, Bulgaria, Lithuania, and elsewhere. These efforts made international networking more widely accessible, which in turn stimulated further development. In Russia a group of computer programmers developed a private network, called Relcom, that connected to EUnet through Helsinki, Finland, in 1990, expanding to more than 100 cities in Russia by 1994 (Voiskounsky 1998).

Recognizing the region's compelling need for modernization, a number of sources stepped forward to offer equipment, services, and connectivity. Private foundations, government agencies, computer manufacturers, telecommunications firms, and European Commission initiatives all offered assistance in one form or another. A number of these early initiatives, among them from the Soros Foundation, included provisions for training and the integration of community organizations, including nongovernment organizations, into the information-technology projects. These initiatives spread Internet training and access from the university base into other segments of society, reaching social organizations and activists.

The variety of assistance offered had another consequence: It helped spark cooperation among the nations in network construction. In contrast to Western Europe and the United States, where the push for connectivity initially led to individual networking solutions that were immediately available, Central and Eastern Europe's simultaneous needs for telecommunications infrastructure improvement and low-cost, efficient network solutions prompted many of the countries in the region to coordinate efforts. As Rastl (1995) notes, they did so in part because the biases and conditions inherent in some of the forms of assistance offered to them were conflicting and threatened to guide development in competing, sometimes less-than-optimal, directions. Pressure from these competing offers coupled with the desire for efficient development compelled the countries to join together to coordinate development. The result was the use of the Austrian-based EARN network for early connectivity and, in 1994, the creation of CEENet, the Central and Eastern European Networking Association, which coordinated the efforts of fourteen nations of the region to promote a consistent and optimized network infrastructure. Complementary initiatives by a variety of new European networks, as well as outreach efforts by NATO, the U.S.–based International Research and Exchanges Board, and the Soros Foundation's telecommunications program and efforts of other philanthropists, helped accelerate and expand diffusion throughout the region.

Backbone networks mean little without the means to make use of them. Information technology and telecommunications infrastructure are both required, and the growing economies of Central and Eastern Europe created a climate conducive to addressing both needs. The opening of domestic markets to privatization and investments from outside led to a rapid spread of information technology. By the mid-1990s PC dealers, system integrators, and third-party software development all had expanded rapidly in the region, and PC sales in Central Europe were doubling annually.

Upgrading the telecom infrastructure has proved more problematic. With some of the lowest telephone penetration rates in the world—generally hovering between 15 percent and 25 percent compared to a West European average of 50 percent—and technology consisting of overburdened and unreliable analog technology, much work was, and continues to be, needed. Privatization of state-run telecom monopolies again has been the key, although development by country has been uneven, reflecting differences in sector-policy evolution, investment generation, and national economic development. Interest among Western telecom giants has been intense and has made for a chaotic, quickly changing landscape of investments and partnerships, requiring telecom officials to be agile and to capitalize on opportunities when they present themselves (EU Telecoms Policy 1998).

In general, Hungary and the Czech Republic have led in telecom development to the point that their degrees of modernization now rival some European Community members. A middle tier of countries follow, including Poland, Slovakia, and Estonia, with development trailing behind in Romania, Albania, and former Soviet states such as Belarus and Moldova (Telecommunications 1996). The situation has been most acute in the former Soviet Union, where waits to download a simple Web page can take as long as two hours and where spatial and geographical obstacles outside of Moscow and St. Petersburg are leading some regions to pursue wireless satellite and cellular solutions.

The progress the region has made during the 1990s is reflected in the growth of Internet hosts. According to a domain survey conducted in October 1990 by Réseaux IP Européens (RIPE), only Yugoslavia had Internet hosts, two of them. A year later Bulgaria, Hungary, Poland, and the Soviet Union each had hosts up, Poland having four and Yugoslavia's increasing to nine. By 1992 Albania, Estonia, Lithuania, Latvia, and Slovenia had hosts running. While RIPE figures are not available for more recent years, a domain survey by Network Wizards in January 1998 found the following number of hosts per country in the region: Albania, 70; Bosnia and Herzegovina, 93; Bulgaria, 4,140; the Czech Republic, 52,498; Estonia, 14,299; Croatia, 6,509; Hungary, 46,082; Lithuania, 3,647; Latvia, 6,108; Macedonia, 179; Poland, 77,594; Romania, 9,335; the Russian Federation, 94,137; Slovenia, 15,432; Slovakia, 11,836; domains still registered as Soviet Union, 20,027; Ukraine, 9,179; and Yugoslavia, 4,020 (RIPE 1998).

Network connections and computer servers only provide the backbone of the system, however. There is still the issue of individual access. Here, again, a combination of factors have contributed to the fairly rapid diffusion and adoption of this new medium. The heavy academic diffusion continues to introduce new generations to the Net and through libraries and other public spaces can often offer even wider opportunities to their communities. Many of the international and foundation initiatives include efforts to widen access by connecting libraries and other public spaces, and through the support of local Internet service provider efforts. Access has also been furthered by the rise and spread of cybercafés, offering patrons relatively cheap access to the Internet and other information systems (Bulder and Kazari 1997).

The region's rapid progress in getting people linked up, improving telecom networks, and aiding in the spread of computer technology has reached the point that some of the best-connected Central European countries now rank with their Western neighbors in terms of per capita Internet use. By 1997 Slovenia had proportionally more Internet servers than Belgium, France, or Italy, while as a whole Central Europe was more wired than other developing markets such as Latin America and East Asia. While connectivity in areas of Russia and the NIS lags behind, substantial investments are underway, aided by innovative government–private sector partnerships. Throughout the region there has clearly been a rapid diffusion and utilization of the Internet and other new media.

NEW STRUCTURES AND NEW SOCIAL RELATIONSHIPS IN CENTRAL AND EASTERN EUROPE

The rise of the Internet and related information systems in Central and Eastern Europe has certainly opened the door for the rise of new media structures, the empowerment of individuals and groups, and the building of new social relationships. Some of these new relationships are emerging from purposely developed structures designed to meet certain needs or foster specific goals. Other structures and relationships are evolving from the new patterns of use emerging from the Internet itself and its community of users. We will start this section by considering some of those intentional structures and the relationships they are attempting to construct.

East–West partnerships often aim at aiding in technology diffusion, but many include broader efforts to support understanding, wider communication, and adoption of technology. Examples include the following:

- The Soros Foundation—Open Society Institute (www.soros.org). Ambitious and extensive initiatives funded by philanthropist George Soros have taken a variety of tactics to aid connectivity, from small grants to provide e-mail access to the use of national foundation offices as ISPs for area NGOs. Soros's initiatives share the aim to support open societies. Specific programs include an Internet academy in Romania, human-rights initiatives, and children and youth networks.

- Friends & Partners (www.friends-partners.org/friends/). A chance meeting on the Internet between a Russian and a U.S. computer specialist led to one of the first information systems jointly developed by citizens of the two nations. In four years Friends & Partners has grown into a wide-ranging virtual community that has had extensive economic and social impacts, including civic networking listservs and chatrooms, mutually created databases, a system of model civic networks in Russian cities, spin-off Friends & Partners initiatives in China and Romania, and MIRnet, a $5-million grant-funded use of the Internet 2 for scientific and civic experiments using high-speed networking between Russia and the United States. Reflective of its significance, Friends & Partners was used as a key informational resource during the Dayton Peace Accords.

- Network of East–West Women (NEWW) (http://neww.org). An international communications and resource network supporting dialogue, informational exchange, and activism related to women's rapidly changing status in Central and Eastern Europe, NEWW links over 2,000 women's advocates in more than forty countries. Impacts include developing connectivity between seventy-five women's NGOs, providing daily news updates about women's activism to more than 600 subscribers of English- and Russian-language listservs, and establishing a "Kosova/Kosovo" on-line resource for information sharing on Kosovar–Serbian conflicts.

- The Virtual Foundation (http://www.virtualfoundation.org). The foundation posts proposals for environmental and human health projects from small grassroots organizations at its Web site and matches needs with on-line donors. Successes include restoration of wetland habitat in Lithuania and funding participation by Model United Nations Club students.

- The New School's East and Central Europe Program (http://www.newschool.edu/centers/ecep) initially sought to assist scholars trying to reestablish credibility for the social sciences in post-communist countries after decades of constraint by ideology and isolation. Its Internet programs have expanded to focus both on educational restructuring and democratization efforts. Similar efforts are conducted by the 100-member Alliance of Universities for Democracy (http://www.friends-partners.org/friends/audem/).

- The Corvallis, Illinois Sister Cities Association with Uzhgorod, Ukraine (http://www.orst.edu/~corvuzh/) illustrates a smaller-scale effort that effectively uses e-mail to communicate, create understanding, and explore collaborations.

Through their focus on expanding basic infrastructure and access, these efforts tend to reinforce the basic Internet structure with its emphasis on empowerment and open communication.

East–East partnerships usually involve more limited, practical goals:

- CANGOnet (http://CANGO.net.kg) has focused on aiding local NGOs and community-based individuals and groups with Internet use in each of the Central Asian Republics, while expanding linkages between them.
- The Local Government Information Network of Estonia (http://www.ibs.ee) aims to speed up the development of on-line resources representing local governments in the Baltic states. Its underlying goal is to enable citizens to communicate with local government and access information in an easy and more flexible and customized way. Its projects include use of an on-line comprehensive site of Estonian legislation on the national level (http://seadus.ibs.ee/), managed by the Institute of Baltic Studies and the republic's Supreme Court system.
- Initiative for Social Action and Renewal in Eurasia (http://www.isar.org) began linking environmental groups across Russia by e-mail in 1990 and today focuses on both civil society and environmental activism using a network of seven cities. The Regional Environmental Center (http://www.rec.org) in Hungary also has extensive experience developing e-mail networks in Eastern Europe.
- Internews (http://www.internews.ru) is a server in Moscow that serves the new independent states' independent media through e-mail, file transfer protocol, Web-based material, and related services. Its majordomo supports about sixty lists from across the region, aiding in media networking. The power of such collaboration was evident in 1996, when weeks before critical national parliamentary elections an independent station was knocked off the air due to a fire. Other stations quickly contributed spare equipment, and the station was able to resume broadcasts within a week, even though it was nearly a month before its new transmitters arrived from Italy.

Many of these efforts are, in fact, designed to promote change in social relationships, often by seeking to give a voice to previously ignored or oppressed groups and by providing them access to the larger world community. Establishing connections between groups with similar interests and facilitating alliance building and future cooperative efforts are often specific goals.

Internally focused efforts normally address specific local needs or goals and are designed to create change. These include the following:

- The Polish Multiple Sclerosis Society (http://ciuw.warman.net.pl/alf/ptsr) is a telematics application project by a computer scientist at Warsaw University and a member of the Polish Multiple Sclerosis Society, designed to develop centralized information resources on treatments, resources, and other issues of concern to the MS community. Development includes improving access in branch offices throughout Poland, as well as maintaining links to other international resources of information.

- CARNet in Croatia (http://www.CARNet.hr) is a government-established Internet network that, until the first commercial ISP appeared, provided network connectivity free to individuals, institutions, foreign visitors, and international organizations throughout Croatia. In this way it facilitated the spread and implementation of information technologies in the new state and abroad, operating as a national test bed for gaining experience on Internet technologies as well as a strong impulse for other potential Internet providers to appear.
- Center for Economic Initiatives (http://www.ukrainebiz.com) is a Ukraine-based center that provides "yellow pages" for businesses in the area, building an on-line informational resource for partnerships and networking.

Internally created mixtures of internal and external focuses are efforts that differ from those discussed earlier in that they emerge more from within Central and Eastern European communities, thus reflecting more local concerns with increasing communications and other outreach efforts. Examples of these efforts and structures include the following:

- WWW Irkutsk (http://www.irkutsk.com). This volunteer-run Web server facilitates local communication in the region of East Siberia, functioning as the largest Internet provider in its region while it develops and manages English-language resources about the city of Irkutsk, the region, and Lake Baikal. Through grants, an array of local NGOs have achieved connectivity, user stats indicate 3,000 hits per month to WWW Irkutsk's main Web page, and the on-line information has been found to attract an average of one visitor per week to the isolated region.
- Britske Listy in Czech Republic (http://blisty.Internet.cz) is an independent Czech-language electronic newspaper in existence since 1996. According to research by a Prague-based polling agency, the "British Times," as the name translates, is read by some 24,000 people per week. Its open, direct approach to reporting makes for a distinctive voice in the nation, where media continue to conform to old controlled standards. Britske Listy has "broken" a number of stories, including the rising economic problems that led to the prime minister's ouster in 1997. The e-paper's approach is said to be paving the way for a greater measure of Western-style adversarial reporting by its print counterparts.

Partly as a result of the efforts of Britske Listy and other on-line media, new patterns of information and media use are emerging. Surveys in the West are beginning to show an increasing use of the Internet and its sources for news and information. Indeed, use of such resources seems heaviest for Central and East European nations, fueled in part by the many hundreds of citizens who live in other countries and are increasingly turning to the Internet to keep up with events back home (Bennahum 1997a; Machlis 1998). One study of reference use in the soc.culture.yugoslavia newsgroup (Jones 1998) showed heavy reliance on electronic media sources, particularly those available on-line and those whose views were consistent with user attitudes. Many of these sources bypass traditional media and their gate-keeping functions, reducing their power to influence.

Internet-based news and information sources can also bypass other powers as well, and nowhere has this been more evident than in former Yugoslavia. In the Balkans the Internet has become an instrument of war. In 1991, as Croatia began its split from Yugoslavia, computer technology arrived at the same time the Serbs began their assault on the fledgling state. The first use the technology was put to was to create a national news service to communicate information about the war from the Croatian point of view (Chapman 1998). This effort grew into the CARNet Internet backbone, which today is used to diffuse Internet technology to all sectors of the state.

The Internet's role in political conflict expanded again during the winter of 1996–1997, when thousands of students and other civil protesters filled the streets of Belgrade to protest the government's annulment of municipal elections won by the opposition. The Milosevic administration responded by jamming broadcasts by independent radio station B92 (http://www.opennet.org), first sporadically, then, as protests expanded, with a total shutdown. The station responded by shifting its broadcasts to the Internet using RealAudio to send on-line broadcasts to an Internet service provider in Amsterdam.

The collaboration that followed made clear the decentralized power of the network. When the U.S. manufacturer of RealAudio learned of developments in the region, it donated a more powerful server to the station to allow greater numbers of users to log on simultaneously. As jamming of broadcasts escalated, Radio Free Europe/Radio Liberty, the Voice of America, and the German radio station Deutsche Welle quickly entered into agreements with B92 to pick up the station's Internet feed and rebroadcast it on their frequencies. Other broadcasters around the world used B92's around-the-clock Web postings as a source to report breaking news of the protests to their own audiences (N. Radic, personal communication, 26 June 1998). Recognizing the failure of its media crackdown, the Milosevic administration abandoned its jamming effort after only two days and, after several more weeks, eventually conceded the opposition wins in the election. Protestors called their victory "The Internet Revolution" (Bennahum 1997a; Borchanin and Moffett 1997). Months later, at a U.S. Institute of Peace–sponsored conference in Washington, D.C., the editor in chief of B92 described the Internet as a model of self-defense and a new key of resistance to totalitarian regimes (Borchanin and Moffett 1997).

A more interesting pattern from the perspective of this book is the potential offered by the Internet for community building (Rheingold 1993; Schuler 1996). Through listservs and newsgroups, individuals can seek out and find others who share interests. E-mail, chatrooms, and similar technologies provide opportunities for interaction and relation building, and the continuing development of Internet telephony and videotelephony would seem to offer the potential to bypass most traditional limits on human interaction. As virtual communities emerge, they will develop their own relations, both internally and with external communities and constituencies. As the Internet diffuses, the impact of these new communities and relationships will drive the creation of the Information Age.

REFLECTIONS: CENTRAL AND EASTERN EUROPE IN AN INFORMATION AGE

There have been innumerable speculations on the impact of new technologies and new information systems such as the Internet, ranging from the direst of dystopias to the most Disneylike of utopian visions (Bates 1989). While the future remains indeterminate, two trends seem clear: one is the growth of information and global information systems such as the Internet, and the other is the growing freedom of movement and the attendant global migrations of individuals and families. These trends suggest that society and the information technologies that serve it will continue to change to meet the changing needs of people and communities. Further, these trends suggest a decline in the ability to exert authoritarian control and an increase in the empowerment of individuals and self-defined social communities.

Perhaps the strongest long-term impact will come from the redefinition of community and the shift from externally defined communities to self-defined communities. While virtually any attribute can serve to define communities, historically the predominant attribute has been geography, often as manifested in language and national identity. Nationality is essentially an externally defined, socially constructed attribute, one that may be accepted and embraced by the individual but whose definition comes from some external authority. Increasingly, language and culture are more self-defined and are no longer synonymous with nationality. Further, people are increasingly identifying with multiple communities, each based on the aspects of life and society that they deem important. They are defining and constructing their own communities and their own identities, and are aided by new information technologies in doing so. These emerging trends in community identification fit in well with the opportunities the open structure of the Internet offers for building virtual and real communities.

What this suggests for the future of Central and Eastern Europe is a trend toward greater democratization and self-realization, which will be fed by the emergence of, adoption of, and full participation in a more globally focused society and economy.

CONCLUSION

The Internet is a communication structure designed and predisposed toward enhancing communication and the diffusion of information. After generations of highly controlled media and limited access to information, Central and Eastern Europe appear to be welcoming the Internet with open arms. As the Internet diffuses and opens up the channels of communication to their full potential, new relationships are emerging. New social, political, and economic ties are being formed, new groups are being empowered, and new influences are being felt.

Despite some states' attempts to maintain control over their citizens and economies through their control of information and communication, the genie is out of the bottle and refuses to meekly return to the "good old days." Newly empowered groups and individuals are finding new options and opportunities in a marketplace for goods and ideas that is increasingly global. The Internet, and the telecommunications infrastructure that supports it, is in the process of redefining and reconstructing relationships and creating the information society.

REFERENCES

Bannon, Liam, Ursula Barry, and Olav Holst. 1982. *Information Technology: Impact on the Way of Life*. Dublin: Tycooly.

Bates, Benjamin J. 1989. Evolving to an Information Society: Issues and Problems. In *The Information Society: Economic, Social, and Structural Issues*, edited by J. L. Salvaggio. Hillsdale, N.J.: Lawrence Erlbaum Associates.

———. 1990. Information Systems and Society: Potential Impacts of Alternative Structures. *Telecommunications Policy* 14: 151–158.

———. 1993. The Macrosocial Impact of Communication Systems: Access, Bias, Control. Paper presented at the 43rd International Communication Association annual conference, May, Washington, D.C.

Bates, Benjamin J., and K. P. Lansing. 1993. The New World of Democratic Telecommunications: FidoNet as an Example of Horizontal Information Networks. *Southwestern Mass Communication Journal* 8: 85–98.

Bell, Daniel. 1973. *The Coming of the Post-Industrial Society*. New York: Basic Books.

Beniger, James R. 1986. *The Control Revolution*. Cambridge: Harvard University Press.

Bennahum, David S. 1997a. The Internet Revolution. *Wired* 5 (4): 122–171.

———. 1997b. Heart of Darkness. *Wired* 5 (11): 226–277.

Borchanin, Natasha, and Julie Moffett. 1997. *Serbia: Internet Plays Key Role in Belgrade Politics*. Radio Free Europe/Radio Liberty. 4 April. <http://www.rferl.org/nca/features/1997/04/F.RU.970404192806.html>.

Builder, Carl H., and Steven C. Bankes. 1992. Technology Propels European Political Change. *IEEE Technology and Society Magazine*, Fall, 10–17.

Bulder, Bert, and Gyula Kazari. 1997. The Cyber Cafés of Central Europe—Hungary. *Suite101.com*. 15 July (cited 17 July 1998). <http://www.suite101.com/articles/article.cfm/2528>.

Chapman, Gary. 1998. Digital Nation: Engineer Wires a War-Torn Croatia. *The Los Angeles Times*. 13 April (cited 17 July 1998). <http://www.latimes.com>.

Dizard, Wilson. 1982. *The Coming Information Age: An Overview of Technology, Economics, and Politics*. New York: Longman.

Dordick, Herbert S., and Georgette Wang. 1993. *The Information Society: A Retrospective View*. Newbury Park, Calif.: Sage.

EU Telecoms Policy: A Market Assessment. 1998. Special Report. Telecommunications Market Research and Development (cited 26 June 1998). <http://www.intltech.com/europe/report.htm>.

Ganley, Gladys D., and Oswald H. Ganley. 1987. *Global Political Fallout: The VCR's First Decade*. Norwood, N.J.: Ablex.

Gerbner, George, Hamid Mowlana, and Herbert I. Schiller, eds. 1996. *Invisible Crises: What Conglomerate Control of Media Means for America and the World*. Boulder, Colo.: Westview Press.

Heap, Nick, Ray Thomas, Geoff Einon, Robin Mason, and Hughie Mackay, eds. 1995. *Information Technology and Society: A Reader*. London: Sage.

Innis, Harold. 1964. *The Bias of Communication*. Rev. ed. Toronto: University of Toronto Press.

————. 1972. *Empire and Communication*. Rev. ed. Toronto: University of Toronto Press.

Ito, Yoichi. 1980. The "Johoka Shakai" Approach to the Study of Communication in Japan. *Keio Communication Review* 1: 13–40.

Jones, Steve. 1998. Media Use in an Electronic Community. In *Network & Netplay: Virtual Groups on the Internet*, edited by Fay Sudweeks, Margaret McLaughlin, and Sheizaf Rafaeli. Menlo Park, Calif.: AAAI Press/ MIT Press.

Kalin, S. 1997. There's More to Taking Your Web Site Global than Translation—Factor in Local Lingo and Flavor. *Computerworld* 16. Dow Jones Publications Database, Record AN CWOR9727800086.

Keogh, Garret, and David Cook. 1997. European New-Media Design. *Print* 51: 154–161.

Levy, Mark R. 1989. *The VCR Age: Home Video and Mass Communication*. Newbury Park, Calif.: Sage.

Lewis, Jane. 1995. Eastern Europe: Raising the Iron Curtain—IT Markets. *Computing*. 20 July (cited 9 June 1997). <Dialog@Textline>. Current Global News/ 01059363.

MacBride, Sean. 1980. *Many Voices, One World*. London: Kogan Page.

Machlis, Sharon. 1998. Balkans Turn to Web for News. *Computerworld Online News*. 26 June (cited 4 July 1998). <http://www.computerworld.com/home/news.nsf/all/9806265balk>.

Machlup, Fritz. 1962. *The Production and Distribution of Knowledge in the United States*. Princeton, N.J.: Princeton University Press.

Masuda, Yoneji. 1981. *The Information Society as Post-Industrial Society*. Bethesda, Md.: World Future Society.

Mulgan, G. J. 1990. *Communication and Control*. Cambridge: Polity Press.

Nora, Simon, and Alain Minc. 1980. *Computerization and Society*. Cambridge: MIT Press.

Pool, Ithiel de Sola. 1990. *Technologies Without Boundaries: On Telecommunications in a Global Age*. Cambridge: Harvard University Press.

Porat, Marc U. 1978. Global Implications of an Information Society. *Journal of Communication* 28: 70–80.

Rastl, Peter. 1995. Coordinating Networks in Central and Eastern Europe: CEENet. Proceedings of INET '94/JENC5 (the Annual Conference of the Internet Society, held in conjunction with the 5th Joint European Networking Conference) (cited 12 July 1998). <http://ceenet.nask.org.pl/papers.html>.

Rheingold, Harold. 1993. *Virtual Communities*. Reading, Mass.: Addison-Wesley.

RIPE (Réseaux IP Européens). 1998. DNS Host Count Surveys. Survey Results (cited 4 July 1998). <http://www.ftp.ripe.net/ripe.host/hostcount/history/>.

Sackman, Harold, and Norman Nie. 1970. *The Information Utility and Social Choice.* Montvale, N.J.: AFIPS Press.

Salvaggio, Jerry L. 1989. *The Information Society: Economic, Social, and Structural Issues.* Hillsdale, N.J.: Lawrence Erlbaum Associates.

Schuler, Douglas. 1996. *New Community Networks: Wired for Change.* New York: ACM Press.

Skilling, H. Gordon. 1989. Samizdat *and an Independent Society in Central and Eastern Europe.* London: St. Anthony's/Macmillan.

Somogyi, Stephen. 1996. Nets Without Frontiers: Internet Growth by Language and Culture Rather than Geography. *Digital Media.* Dow Jones Publications Database, Record DGMD9609000005.

Staple, Gregory C. 1997. Telegeography and the Explosion of Place: Why the Network That Is Bringing the World Together Is Pulling it Apart. In *Globalism and Localism in Telecommunications,* edited by E.-M. Noam and A.-J. Wolfson. New York: Elsevier.

Stonier, Tom. 1983. The Microelectronic Revolution, Soviet Political Structure, and the Future of East/West Relations. *Political Quarterly* 54: 137–151.

Sussman, Gerald R. 1997. *Communication, Technology, and Politics in the Information Age.* Thousand Oaks, Calif.: Sage.

Technology Leap-Frogging. 1996. *Business Central Europe* 2. September (cited 7 July 1998). <http://www.bcemag.com/>.

Tehranian, Majid. 1990. *Technologies of Power: Information Machines & Democratic Power.* Norwood, N.J.: Ablex.

Telecommunications. 1996. *Business Central Europe* 4. September (cited 7 July 1998). <http://www.bcemag.com/>.

Voiskounsky, Alexander E. 1998. Investigation of Relcom Network Users. In *Network & Netplay: Virtual Groups on the Internet,* edited by Fay Sudweeks, Margaret McLaughlin, and Sheizaf Rafaeli. Menlo Park, Calif.: AAAI Press/ MIT Press.

Westin, Alan F. 1971. *Information Technology in a Democracy.* Cambridge: Harvard University Press.

Weston, Jay. 1996. Old Freedoms and New Technologies: The Evolution of Community Networking. *The Information Society* 13: 195–201.

8

A People's Electronic Democracy and an Establishment System of Government: The United Kingdom

Glen Segell

This chapter, based upon the results of the May 1997 general elections and May 1998 local elections in the United Kingdom, looks to see how the influence of the Internet has succeeded in breaking down boundaries and bringing cultures closer together. These elections have shown that the Internet is a people's democracy, as it grew from the population upward for many years prior to the elections. Political parties and governments have been late in understanding its value and in utilizing it for political purposes from government downward to the people. The 1997 general elections in the United Kingdom were a watershed in this respect. Not only were they used as a political broadcast medium, but also as a means of popular expression. Hence, this is a two-way street of communication. The 1998 local elections furthered this communication on a more local basis for more particular political purposes. Preparations for the forthcoming European Union Parliament elections show that the Internet is acting as an agent in reducing conflicts within the European Union by making people more aware and more tolerant of each other's national interests and identities. This has been on the personal level as well as within the professional work environment. The Internet as a people's democracy has redefined not only British but also European economic, social, and political empowerment. The chapter concludes by posing the question of whether the Internet has broken down such boundaries on a national level and in a process of regionalization in the context of the European Union, or if it is a wider process of globalization. The issue is whether the Internet is acting as an agent for globalization as the infant child of imperialism in generating a new British Empire in European affairs, and at the same time generating Americanization in the global sense in both cultural values and the cybermarketplace.

MODELS OF A PEOPLE'S ELECTRONIC DEMOCRACY

A people's electronic democracy can be understood as the capacity of the new communications environment to enhance the degree and quality of public participation in government. Several core issues are immediately raised by this concept. For example, the Internet will enable citizens to vote electronically in elections, referenda, and plebiscites. It will also facilitate opinion polling. Communications technology more generally will strengthen interaction between government and citizens and between political candidates and voters. These developments will have important and direct ramifications for democracy. However, the more significant implications will come as a result of a transformation of political culture. Ideally, the new communications environment will facilitate the revitalization of society by empowering citizens to voice their ideas and concerns.

To understand the role of the Internet in a traditional establishment system of government such as the United Kingdom it is first necessary to understand the basic assumptions of electronic democracy. Four models of electronic democracy can be identified. They are not mutually exclusive.

The electronic bureaucracy model refers to the electronic delivery of government services. This happens as a matter of course in the United Kingdom as in other countries with well-developed telecommunications infrastructures. Even though it is innovative, it is a purely mechanical task. The information management model refers to more effective communication between individual citizens and candidates or decision makers. This is a goal that many strive for, but few government agencies or politicians can cope with answering all the letters. Hence, a bureaucratic organization develops that defeats the purpose. The populist model would enable citizens to register their views on current issues. This is a good idea and will play an important but not executive role in the future. Finally, the civil society model is the most important model for understanding a people's democracy and how borders have been broken down by the Internet. Such a civil society model shows how the Internet would strengthen connections between citizens, thereby building a robust and autonomous site for public debate. While the first three models are useful and an ongoing process in the United Kingdom, it is this fourth model that I believe has the potential to be the most significant for evaluation in comparison to other media, such as television, radio, and newspapers.

The civil society model refers to a transformation of political culture. Hence it is the migration of the British establishment system of government, which is based upon a well-developed historical cultural heritage of centuries of government. As such, it can only be appreciated within the context of the broader transformation wrought by communications technology. For example, the quality of public debate will be influenced by changes in interpersonal relations, employment patterns, and organizational structures. The growing cultural and commercial value of information will also be relevant, as will government responses to such issues as technology, privacy, and regulation. The success all depends on careful evaluations and even more careful and well-planned implementations.

The economic impact of the new environment (for example, the possible erosion of the tax base) and the transformation of the education sector will affect political relationships in such transformations toward electronic democracy to the civil society model. The effects of the new technology on policy making will also have ramifications for democracy. While none of these issues is directly about democracy, which has to already be prevalent and well adhered to in each individual, each will have considerable bearing on the shape that democracy and the traditional establishment system of government actually takes (as opposed to its formal nature). Analysis of such areas will reveal more about the future of democracy and the system of government than an examination of the technicalities of electronic voting or managing e-mail deluges.

This civil society model approach is premised on a particular view of democracy; namely, that it is more than a mechanism for determining government. Rather, the term implies genuine opportunities for popular participation, open and accountable government, broad input into policy debate, and an informed and critical public. All these are contrary to the historic nature of the British establishment system of government, which has been behind closed doors. In this the Internet is changing the face of the establishment system of government in the United Kingdom.

THE 1997 GENERAL ELECTIONS AND 1998 LOCAL ELECTIONS

Democracy is enhanced and the system evolves when people are informed about issues, when there is a high level of public debate, when residents organize in support of their positions, and when citizens evaluate public officials and then hold them accountable for the effects of their decisions. Taking this theoretical and philosophical framework into consideration is important when looking at the 1997 general elections in the United Kingdom, held on May 1, 1997, and the local elections, held in May 1998.

The general elections in 1997 were unique in that it was the first time in twenty years that the Conservative Party (Tories) would not be in power. The Tories had taken the country through two major military conflicts, to the end of the Cold War, and into an age of global openness for the man in the street. Satellite and cable television, broadcast on a global basis to the most remote and oppressed populations, was not an accepted media in 1979. In 1997 it was as common as making a pot of tea. In 1979 the desktop computer was unheard of outside of sophisticated computer laboratories. By the 1997 elections all of these were an integral part of political party's campaign planning and implementation. Each media was conveyed over a different technological platform to a different sector of the population, but with the same political message.

These general elections were unique in that it was the first time that all major political parties used the Internet in their campaign. The winner of those elections, Tony Blair of the New Labour Party, called for government to build and use a network that academia and the people at large had already been using in varying degrees for twenty years. This was both during the campaign and after his successful victory. In doing so, he could never have imagined that over 100,000 extra voters would cast their vote by postal ballot from outside the United Kingdom after having read and heard his campaign over the Internet. Over 1 million other people, not eligible to vote, learned about the British electoral system and its democratic basis and values. The use of the Internet in the May 1997 general elections was therefore a turning point in breaking down boundaries and bringing cultures closer together.

It was recognized at the time and in hindsight that this Internet success was elitist. There was an element of inequality both then and now, one year later, because those who had Internet access were of a certain age and economic and social group. Nevertheless, the impact was significant because the Internet had until then been considered an academic network born out of a military network. It was not considered a political network or a medium for political broadcasts. It is expected that the use of computers will eventually enter the daily lives of more of the world's population, making the May 1997 success felt even further and wider.

Part of the uniqueness was the considerations of the special needs of the Internet electorate, where the public relations and media planners of the political parties attempted to ascertain the different needs of each sector of the electronic population in order to plan a more cohesive winning campaign. The same format of information, for example, that was available on television broadcasts was made available over the Internet. In some cases this was as transcripts of those broadcasts and in some cases this was as the actual audiovisual files in downloadable formats. There was an attempt to apply different marketing techniques. Lessons learned from the general elections were applied even more successfully in the local elections one year later. In May 1998 it was surprising for the first time to see that the radical elements of local elections had chosen to fight their differences on the Internet and not on the streets. For the first time in thirty years there was absolutely no street violence in local regions between disparate and ethnic parties. Marginal extreme parties also lost more seats as cultural differences were broken down by greater awareness generated out of information available from Internet sources.

So where did it all begin and why was there such a success at the political-party level to capture the growing Internet market of the electorate and to change the nature of the traditional establishment system of government? Why has the Internet been successful in the British traditional establishment system of government for election purposes, both national and local?

To start off, one needs to understand the significance of the party versus the individual constituency candidate in the United Kingdom. The United Kingdom votes on a constituency basis for the House of Commons. The other house is the House of Lords, formerly made up of hereditary peers but now consisting of peers appointed for life. General election campaigns therefore apply only to the House of Commons. The Internet has therefore no role for the House of Lords or the monarchy, other than as advertisement, because a single tabloid article against either of these can destroy years of radio, TV, and Internet good will. The difference between the two Houses of Parliament is also significant, as each have different functions on a daily basis. The House of Commons is devoted mainly to the monetary functions of the state. The House of Lords is concerned with other functions such as the judiciary. The executive of the government comes from the House of Commons and decides interalia foreign and defense policy. This is significant, for at present it is the more affluent and the white-collar votes and citizens who have access to the Internet.

This is very significant because both local and general election campaigns are very much issues of economics. Much of the twentieth century has seen British elections won and lost on issues of the allocation of the budget to health and education, and the levels of taxation and employment. It is extremely rare to have any matter of defense or foreign policy as a major campaign issue. The campaigns for the House of Commons, every five years, have a national basis of party manifestos and a local basis of individuals running for each constituency. The majority of constituencies won by a political party or coalition thereof is asked by the monarch to form the government. The winning party therefore provides the cabinet, which is the executive of the government. The prime minister is an elected member of the House of Commons from the winning party.

The traditional use of all media has therefore been diversified in election campaigns by political parties. The national media provide the party political platform, concentrating on the party leaders and the ideological basis of that party's existence. The local media concentrate on individual candidates for each constituency, sometimes with less emphasis on which party the candidate belongs to, as they do not have to be affiliated with any political party. The local election campaign is often seen as "Who is the better chap for the job?" while the national campaign is seen as "do we want socialists or capitalists and how much are beer and cigarettes going to cost us?" The Internet crosses the boundary in theoretically being able to aim both at the constituency and at the party level of campaigning. In practice the 1997 general election experience showed that its value is to concentrate on the party level, and the 1998 local elections showed it can concentrate on the individual candidate.

I feel that it is also important to note the lessons of the 1997 and 1998 elections for the future role of the Internet in a traditional system of government such as Britain compared to radio and TV in a comparison of technical terms. Radio and TV are passive forms of media for both local and national campaigning. The voter is presented with information as determined by the TV or radio program scheduler, script writer, and producer. There is subjective bias in this information. In many cases this is due to the availability of information rather than the personal opinions of the TV and radio presenters. Newspapers and the Internet are active forms of media for both local and national campaigning. They are active in that the voter has to actively seek the information and is more concentrated when reading that information. Newspapers are very politically aligned. A voter who buys the *Telegraph* will get a very Conservative Party outlook. To get all views the electorate will have to buy all newspapers, which they are normally hesitant to do. This is the value of the Internet. Each political party on the national level and each constituency candidate on the local level can provide their own views and political agendas where the voter can actively compare them without intermediate opinion and editing and for a very nominal fee that he or she is already paying for Internet access for other purposes. It is democracy at the level of people participating without regulation.

It then becomes understandable how the Internet has acted in such a dramatic manner in changing the nature of the establishment system of government in the United Kingdom. It is also understandable how this change has continued after the highpoint of the traditional establishment system of government, the general elections held every five years, to increase the lines of communication between government and the citizen between elections.

This watershed of the usage of the Internet in May 1997 also played a very important role in providing citizens, and especially citizens residing outside of Britain, with more information about the role of government agencies between elections.

This once again was a people's democracy from bottom to top. In the six weeks of permitted political advertising prior to the general elections, the senior politicians in each party were spurred by younger advisers who had become familiar with the Internet and other computer networks during university days and turned the Internet into a key consideration and implementation success for political party election purposes. This was from top to bottom. It was not a population- or electorate-generated move, though the politicians were not even aware of this. The politicians assumed many issues without full research or investigation. Before the elections and the campaign over the Internet there was no information available on who in the electorate would access the Internet.

There was no evaluation by any political party to ascertain whether Internet election campaigning as part of a civil society model was even relevant, and who could be influenced by such campaigning. It was a matter of perceptions in the minds of a few members of each of the political parties strengthened by public statements to convince themselves and each other. It was a people's democracy in action without any form of professional marketing agency or consultancy involvement.

It came as a surprise to all that over 100,000 extra voters cast their votes as a direct consequence of Internet campaigning. The 1997 elections therefore showed that political parties have succeeded in using the Internet to provide more than other media such as TV, radio, or newspapers, or door-to-door canvassing. The Internet has also duplicated these media.

This immediate success has also shown a longer-term realization of the value of the Internet for the civil society model of democracy. This has been to further the intangible goals of democracy and promoting the country and its values. The election campaign over the Internet globalized these elections to an audience outside of the national boundaries. In the traditional establishment system of government prevalent in Britain this is important, for citizens of the commonwealth, British protectorates, and the European Union are all eligible to vote after meeting certain residency and other requirements. As such, the Internet could play a major role in future elections in conveying information to this eligible electorate who do not have access to local radio, TV, and newspapers in their domicile, albeit temporary, outside of the United Kingdom.

Turning to the statistical specifics of how the Internet entered the election fray and why it succeeded finds us at the feet of Tony Blair of the Labour Party, who first tried to introduce an Americanization by bringing the information superhighway into the election campaign. It was clear from the onset that this was more than mere political election rhetoric, because he was responding to what was already happening. The established media had already set up Web sites and had e-mail access in the hope that this new form of communication would bring about an electronic democracy. At the time and in hindsight it was clear that the media was making better use of the Internet than did the political parties, in response to public demand for information and interactive participation in the democratic process.

The *Financial Times* (FT), for example, provided a different set of information and format in its printed newspaper. This was the same with the television networks, such as the BBC and ITN. Even CNN had a section of its Web site devoted to the British elections. This separation of information became a crucial consideration for the media in their coverage of the elections without distracting from the normal content of the printed newspaper. The FT, for example, provided a full Web site with letters to the editor and his editorial team's responses, where a lively debate ensued, albeit with only twelve citizens out of a population of over 50 million. The FT newspaper coverage in print was confined to a few short articles followed by election results in its normal style of financial rather than domestic political coverage. Other newspapers that were more politically allied used less Web coverage and more printed coverage, such as the *Telegraph*. It was clear that the media knew who was reading the print, watching the TV, listening to the radio, and had Internet access. The market had been well surveyed and was being catered to. The media thus made full use of the new technology.

The Internet's interactivity was also exploited to the full by the media in response to public demand: Readers were invited to vote on the key election issues and got instant gratification from dynamically updated databases that fed back the new voting picture as soon as they lodged their vote. There was an on-line audience of over a million during election night itself, of which some 80 percent were within the United Kingdom. Of these, 45.8 percent were twenty-one to thirty years old, over 50 percent were college graduates, 80 percent were male, and over 50 percent have a household income of £20,000 or more. In terms of occupations, 36 percent were in education, 31 percent were in computing, 16 percent were professionals, and 11 percent were in management. Around 47 percent have Internet access paid for by the employer (compared with the United States, which has 27 percent).

The 1997 election proved to be a watershed in the development of a people's electronic democracy in the United Kingdom. The election proved that the Internet is a medium in its own right with its own unique characteristics and strengths. What other medium has made it so easy, for example, to compare the party's policies on any given topic? What other medium is capable of providing the immediacy of television, the depth of analysis of print, and the intimacy of radio?

One year later, in May 1998, local elections were held throughout Britain. In addition, London voted whether it should have a single mayor. The lessons learned from these elections echoed those of the previous year's general elections. A people's electronic democracy had been born and in the true traditional style of English democracy had a continuity without direct government intervention. The electronic democracy started by the population was being continued by the population.

EUROPE AND BEYOND

Findings from the 1997 and 1998 elections in the United Kingdom are not unique in the European context. Elections held in other European Union countries show similar and in some cases duplicate results. Internet as a people's democracy has redefined not only British but also European economic, social, and political empowerment. What remains to be seen is whether the internal events of one country can influence the internal events of another country. The 1999 European Union parliament elections showed that the Internet is acting as an agent in reducing conflicts within the European Union by making people more aware and more tolerant of each other's national interests and identities.

It is good to talk, and communication over the Internet is helping to achieve a main goal of the European Union since its formation as the European Iron and Steel Committee in the early 1950s: reducing conflicts by making people more aware and more tolerant of each other's national interests and identities. The Internet has succeeded in doing this on the personal level as well as within the professional work environment. The Internet is acting in these spheres as an agent of regionalization. The Internet has broken down boundaries, not only on a national level but also in a process of regionalization in the context of the European Union. This is not surprising, in that the European Union is striving toward being a federal state. What is exceptional and wholly pleasing is that this is being achieved without direct government intervention. It is happening through the Internet and other electronic networks in a process of electronic democracy, initiated and continued by the average citizen.

The pattern of voting by ballot from outside the United Kingdom in the 1997 general elections shows that this is more than a process of regionalization. It is also a process of globalization. Globalization in the form of cyberglobalization is not cyberimperialism. This is because imperialism implies an active government involvement, including a governmental structure and organization for implementation. Global relations in the new electronic frontier are therefore not imperialism but a people's democracy of globalization. In this is promogating those values held sacrosanct by democracy and by the practice of democracy but not by the elected representatives of democratic states.

CONCLUSION

Lessons learned from the 1997 and 1998 British elections show that the Internet and other emerging forms of electronic communication are breaking down traditional systems of democracy and boundaries and bringing cultures closer together. The elections have shown that the Internet is a true people's electronic democracy, as it has grown from the population upward. Political parties and governments have been late in understanding its value and in utilizing it for political purposes. Political parties and governments have little influence across national boundaries via the Internet. The average citizen and more frequently the average company has the sway in influence.

With reference to the all-important civil society model, this people's electronic democracy is more than an agent of the process of regionalization. It is also an agent of the process of globalization. This then is teledemocracy in the style of the Greek polis, which encourages a participatory style of government by accommodating the voters' personal concerns in much the same way the personal views of Athenians were addressed. Global relations in the new electronic frontier are a people's democracy.

NOTE

This chapter has been written as the findings of five years of statistical research. The first findings were presented at a conference convened at the National Audiovisual Archive of The Netherlands, Amsterdam, October 24, 1997, in a paper entitled "The Role of the Internet in a Traditional Establishment System of Government: The United Kingdom." All the statistical data referred to in this chapter are available in both written and electronic forms from the Institute of Security Policy, P.O. Box 108, 37 Store Street, London, WC1E 7BS, United Kingdom. Arrangements are underway to deposit the data with the British Library.

PART **III**

GLOBAL ECONOMIC
ISSUES IN CYBERSPACE

9

Prospects of Small Countries in the Age of the Internet

Vasja Vehovar

The Internet introduces specific features into the globalization process. Small economies are particularly challenged by this for two reasons. First, it is increasingly difficult to maintain a presence on the international virtual market. Second, it is even harder to establish a profitable domestic virtual market. However, the Internet also provides important advantages, such as global visibility and simplified communication. In addition, due to their flexibility, small countries may adapt faster than larger ones to a changing environment. The overall advantages and disadvantages of this process are complex, with the future relatively unclear.

Of course, globalization is not a new process. It began with the first exchange of goods and it evolved with the growth of market production. International trade and cooperation are increasing steadily, with many economic activities being affected by global competition. Globalization has inadvertently created an economy of scale with various forms of economic concentration and monopolies. Today a growing amount of world production belongs to markets controlled by a few global corporations.

The effects of globalization have been relatively ambiguous for small countries. Despite centuries of well-documented international cooperation, there is no theory dealing with the relation between the size of a country and globalization. This lack of an elaborated theory can be observed in the definition of a small country. The United States can be viewed as the only large country in the Internet Age, because even Germany falls behind it in creating a virtual reality (Fritz and Kerner 1997). Some authors similarly treat Japan as a small state (Momose 1997). The other extreme is the concept that all countries are small in a global world. However, here and in the following sections the upper limit of 10 million inhabitants (Senjur 1992) will define a small country. (The words "country" and "economy" are used interchangeably to denote an internationally recognized state.) With this definition, one cannot ignore the fact that some of the most developed countries are small (e.g., Switzerland, Sweden, Austria, and Norway).

In a literature review (Svetlicic 1997) it appears that many authors discovered that globalization removes the disadvantages of small countries (i.e., communication barriers) and reinforces their advantages (i.e., flexibility). It is also strongly believed that the economic position of a small country depends, in large part, on its own strategy and behavior. Most authors somehow support the notion that globalization is advantageous for small economies (p. 20). However, in an empirical study the comparisons of income per capita, economic growth rates, and other sociodemographic indicators within three groups of countries (according to the level of development) show a slight disadvantage for small economies (Salvatore 1997). Similarly, the models of economic efficiency impart a certain disadvantage to small countries, although size is not an important factor in these models (Damijan 1997). On the other hand, an analysis of twelve indicators of socioeconomic development in 102 countries shows that small economies do have an advantageous position (Kropivnik and Jesovnik 1995). Of course, there is no causality here due to the nonexperimental nature of the data. Any interpretation is sensitive to the variables that cannot be controlled, such as historical circumstances, geography, natural resources, culture, or politics. A safe conclusion would be that until now globalization has created no clear disadvantages for small economies. However, none of the literature reviewed incorporated the specific features of globalization that are emerging with the Internet.

As has been true throughout history, it is quite plausible that in the Internet Age the size of a country will continue to play only a minor role in the globalization process. A country's future is more strongly determined by its initial stage of information–communications development and its current behavior. Michael Dertouzos (1997, 241), director of the Massachusetts Institute of Technology Laboratory for Computer Science, argues that the tendency for rich countries to become richer and poor to become poorer is inherent in the contemporary globalization process. Only active aid programs can help to reduce the increasing gap of inequality between rich and poor countries.

There are two issues related to the globalization process that must be carefully separated. The first is the gap between developed countries and the rest of the world. The second is the impact of being a small country. The future of less-developed countries is complex and often viewed as relatively unfavorable. The effect of globalization on small countries is more unclear, as many are highly developed (e.g., Scandinavia) and are leaders in Internet penetration (Juliussen and Petska-Juliussen 1998, 302).

The following question may help to clarify the effects of globalization: Who is interested in the latest wave of globalization? No doubt there are general and global benefits for everyone, both producers and consumers, small and large economies, developed and underdeveloped countries. However, the interesting issue is the *relative* advantage. Who will benefit most? The fact that large countries and major corporations are the important protagonists of globalization may not bode well for the future of small economies.

The Internet, in its increasingly important role in the globalization process, introduces a very specific change into the interaction between globalization and the size of a country. In the following sections some important aspects of this change will be discussed: virtual competition, economy of scale, virtual advertising, language problems, and regulation issues.

As a case study, the results from the Research on the Internet in Slovenia (RIS; see www.ris.org) project will be discussed. The RIS surveys are performed annually (RIS 1996, 1997, 1998). The 1997 survey included 800 schools, 3,600 companies, 3,500 Web users, 5,000 households, and 500 nonprofit institutions. Slovenia, with its 2 million inhabitants, is a small country located in Central Europe, near Austria, Italy, Hungary, and Croatia. Its Internet penetration is moderate, with over 1,000 hosts per 100,000 people in 1998. One-fifth of the active population (fifteen to sixty-five years old) has accessed the Internet, and one-third are regular (weekly) users. In the commercial sector, the majority of companies with five employees or more have Internet access.

THE SPECIFIC ROLE OF THE INTERNET

Communication via the Internet is a cheap, quick method of accessing currently available electronic information, whether it is a consumer inquiry, a search for daily news, or a linkage between two companies. In addition, it can enormously simplify commercial transactions. Another important feature of the Internet is the direct delivery of products and services that can be packaged into digital form: information, consultations, text, voice, music, pictures, and video. This new communication technology removes many barriers that both protect and preserve location-specific economic activities. With these communication obstacles removed, international competitors can penetrate local markets much more easily, which leads to a new wave of international economic concentration and to new monopolies (Kropivnik and Jesovnik 1995).

However, the Internet is not only changing production, distribution, and consumption (as was the case with previous stages of globalization), but also altering the communication process itself. Due to simple and affordable communication, the international flow of information has been dramatically increased. The previous patterns of international contacts had been limited to business cooperation, the tourist industry, and, in a passive way, the entertainment industry. These patterns have been dramatically changed as more and more activities are performed in virtual reality: reading the daily news, searching for general information, carrying on research activities, making professional and business inquiries, chatting, shopping, participating in entertainment, and so forth. However, in small countries the incoming flow of data through the Internet are much larger than the outgoing flow. The Slovenian public Internet service provider, for example, reports that one-third of the network's flow is international. With commercial Internet service providers in Slovenia, the international share is 60 percent. In both cases the ratio of international import to export traffic exceeds 2 to 1 in favor of incoming data. Obviously, the users from a small country perform a large part of their Internet activities on foreign Web sites. The 1998 RIS survey confirms this fact: In a Web survey that attracted almost one-tenth of regular Slovenian users, respondents claimed they spend 53 percent of their Web time on sites located in the United States (they spend only 31 percent of this time on Slovenian Web sites). Eventually the owners of these sites will charge access, memberships, commissions, or advertisements. There are also other subtle ways of taking advantage of a virtual visit, such as building databases for future marketing activities.

These characteristics of the Internet create an important change in the relationship between the globalization process and the size of a country. Some of these changes can already be observed and others have yet to develop. In the following subsections, different aspects of these changes will be discussed in more detail.

Virtual Competition in a Consumer Market

The virtual market is reestablishing the ideal form of perfect competition described by classic economic thought: The customers are completely informed about the potential supply, and they are in a position to select the best option. Many local producers have already faced global competition on the Internet. For example, any local bookstore, virtual or classic, that sells books in English will compete with the large virtual bookstores, such as Amazon.com. Other products, such as airline tickets and professional publications, also face competition on the Internet. A certain part of consumption thus moves to large virtual suppliers, usually without a local distributor or sometimes without any distributor at all. An extreme example is software, in that users directly access the product from one virtual point. When technology enables an efficient transmission of sound and pictures, the entertainment industry will experience a similar pattern. The consumption of global products thus not only moves outside the small countries, it bypasses local distribution as well.

Electronic commerce, of course, has some limitations in the field of final consumption goods (Meeker and Pearson 1997). For example, virtual shopping lacks interactive help from the vendor. This missing physical contact can be a serious problem for certain goods (e.g., cars and clothes). Delivery lag time can also be a disadvantage, particularly when the product is perishable or instant consumption is needed (e.g., food and medicine). However, with technological improvements (i.e., speed, multimedia, and interactivity), virtual shopping will become more attractive and the spectrum of suitable products will expand. For certain products (e.g., software and hardware) the majority of purchases will be performed on the Internet, while for others virtual shopping will occur only to a limited extent. Currently, the share of virtual final consumption is still relatively small, even in the most developed countries. However, electronic commerce is increasing extremely rapidly.

Global products comprise a growing share of final consumption goods purchased on the Internet. These products, advertised and sold worldwide, are typically software, books, journals, and CDs. To a smaller extent other final consumption goods also fit into this category. The international virtual markets of these global products are fiercely competitive, and the leading suppliers already have a large advantage, particularly in terms of brand recognition and software development. It is relatively clear that, at this time, virtual shops originating from small countries cannot play a significant role in the marketplace of global products.

It is not surprising that among Slovenian Internet users who reported virtual shopping the majority shop on sites outside the country. In a household telephone survey (RIS 1998), almost one-fifth of those who used the Internet reported some virtual shopping abroad. That can be compared to 12 percent of users who reported some domestic virtual shopping. Within a few years complete domestic virtual supply may be established in small countries, and they will retain the majority of their internal electronic commerce. Sweden, for example, has already achieved this. However, an increasing amount of the final consumption of global products will still flow from small countries to the large global suppliers on the Internet.

To summarize, a portion of the final consumption market is slowly but persistently moving to the Internet. In addition, certain products have become globally available on the Internet. For these products the Internet simplifies distribution, eliminates local retailers, and, therefore, reinforces certain virtual oligopolies. In the future more and more products will follow this pattern of global production, consumption, distribution, and concentration. As a result, a growing portion of final consumption in small economies will be transferred abroad.

Compared to final consumption goods, where small countries cannot market global products in their own virtual stores, the industrial market is different. There the Internet is becoming a massive market of niches. The Internet dramatically increases the number of niche markets, improves their visibility, and removes communication and transaction obstacles that are particularly restrictive for companies in small countries.

Economy of Scale

A country's small size usually means it does not have a market of sufficient size to facilitate the development of commercial Web applications. This is especially true at the initial stages of Internet penetration. However, while the problem of low Internet penetration disappears within a few years, the small size of a country remains a permanent obstacle, particularly when new or initial investments are challenged. In addition, the costs of updating and maintaining Internet applications, as well as the costs of adapting to permanent technological changes (e.g., software and hardware), are increasing. Even for some globally known Web sites with millions of visitors, such as the *LA Times*, the *New York Times*, the *Chicago Tribune*, or *Knight-Ridder*, 1997 reports show that on-line revenue hardly covers maintenance costs (On-Line Publications on the Internet 1998). In certain quarters of 1997, losses were reported even by Amazon.com, Yahoo, and Netscape (Big Earnings for Yahoo 1998), clearly illustrating the fierce competition that exists on the Web and the large initial investments needed. Over time it is likely that sites with rich content will charge for access, or they will increase their prices for products, services, and advertising.

With low initial investment capital, it is difficult to maintain a Web site long enough to attract and keep users to the point where they will pay. In the case of a small virtual audience, the profitability of such an investment is questionable. This was not the situation in the United States, however, where only 8.4 million people, 4 percent of the Internet users among the 1995 adult population, were needed to establish the critical mass for a wide range of profitable businesses (Clemente 1998, 53). In absolute numbers, no small economy could ever attain this many users. Specifically, a small country such as Slovenia will hardly reach even one-tenth of this number.

It is true that the same population ratios have existed for centuries with no obvious disadvantages for small economies. However, with the standard production of goods a specific optimal size of production often exists. After a certain point an increase in production results in an increased cost per unit and in diminishing profits. This basic economic principle holds for the majority of goods and services, from retail shops to bakeries to automobile production lines. However, no such limit exists for the majority of products and services offered on the Internet. There, more users and more customers serve only to lower the cost per unit and increase profits. Contrary to other products and services, economy of scale has no disadvantages with commercial applications on the Internet.

The most typical example of this unrestricted feature of economy of scale is the search engine. In principle, all Internet users can be interactively served from a single virtual point of a certain search engine. There are no disadvantages arising from an increased number of customers, but there are continuing advantages of economy of scale. Such a specific production–consumption feature never existed before the Internet. It is not surprising that the oligopoly of search engines was already established a few years ago. Infoseek, Excite, Yahoo, Lycos, and Alta Vista thus control the market. Despite some attempts to develop local search engines, the majority of Web visitors from small countries use one of these global engines. At most, these global services employ translated or adapted versions in small countries, with more (e.g., Alta Vista Sverige) or less (e.g., Alta Vista Slovenia) success. Because of the specific production–consumption pattern, only one search engine, such as Microsoft's Start, may overtake this service.

A similar process has been developed in other global services. These services face no disadvantages in the economy of scale and they tend to select local partners in small countries. Economy of scale thus reinforces transfer of service or product development to large countries (where there is a critical mass to create them). If there is a need, the small country subcontractor is responsible only for implementation or distribution.

This does not mean that domestic commercial Web applications are not appearing in small countries. However, it is a fact that such applications are not yet profitable activities, though they do contribute, to a large extent, to positioning and preparation activities (EITO 1997, 195). In other words, many Internet applications in small countries carry merely a promotional cost. This is also the status of the more than fifty virtual shops in Slovenia.

Because small countries have not been able to establish profitable search engines, news agencies, advertising brokers, bookstores, or shopping malls, their populace is forced to access these virtual services abroad. Only in the most developed Scandinavian countries, those with high Internet penetration, have some of these applications become profitable, but even there global services take a considerable share.

The low profitability of Web sites in small countries is further substantiated by research done on commercial Web sites in Belgium (Belgian Business Use 1997). This research finds that no commercial sites report any significant income generated on the Web.

Slovenia provides an even more typical example, with one-fifth of its active population being Internet users in 1998. However, the number of regular (weekly) users is far below that needed to pay off the investments in sophisticated Web applications. Commercial Slovenian Web sites with more than 10,000 unique visitors per month are very rare. Specific commercial Web sites—shops, daily newspapers, bookstores, CD shops—rarely exceed a few hundred sessions per day. Even Internet yellow-page advertising is hardly a successful business in Slovenia. However, although there is such a small audience, applications continue to appear because of promotional and strategic-positioning reasons.

Sweden, with more than double the Internet penetration and a population four times larger than Slovenia's, is in a much better position because there are almost ten times more virtual customers. However, even Swedish consumers, to a large extent, use global services. For example, three U.S. sites are among the top ten most visited (Top Ten Sites 1998). In addition, its critical mass is still relatively small to create and promote a sophisticated and well-known global Web site.

The most popular Web sites in Slovenia reflect these facts. There is a clear domination of Web sites developed in the economy-of-scale environment of large, developed countries. In the 1997 RIS Web survey, Web-site visitation was recorded from answers to an open-ended question about the respondents' most frequently visited foreign sites. Responses included very few Web sites that were located outside the United States and the United Kingdom, except for some well-known brands (e.g., Mercedes, Siemens, Sony, and Ferrari), and even those ranked relatively low. There was not one single page from any small country listed among the first 250 foreign Web sites.

Small countries experience an additional technical disadvantage related to economy of scale. A large share of international Internet traffic significantly increases communications costs because international communications lines are much more expensive than local ones.

To summarize, the sale of global products that are most suitable for on-line shopping (e.g., books, CDs, software, and hardware) is already concentrated in a few large-scale global suppliers. The same is true for search engines and other Internet informational services. Small economies are almost completely excluded from becoming direct suppliers for any global product or service on the Internet. The small countries hardly provide enough domestic audience to market goods and services locally. Similarly, these economies lack the critical scale necessary to develop vital Internet services such as search engines. This argument is particularly important in the early stages of Internet penetration. Therefore, even as small countries approach the development of Internet applications, they experience a major setback. This leads to an increase in the variety of imported Internet services (i.e., intensive use of foreign Web sites) and to an increased dependence on large countries for advanced product and service developments.

Advertising

Advertising on the Internet is growing much faster than forecast just a few years ago (Hoffman and Novak 1996). By 1997 there were almost a billion dollars spent in the United States alone. Internet advertising is a very specific form of advertising; it has a relatively limited function for targeting the general population. However, the merging of personal computers with television sets can dramatically increase its role (Death of PC-Centric Era 1998).

Again, the lack of a critical mass of users in small countries postpones their development of Internet advertising. The delay particularly affects accompanying services, such as Web measurement services or Web advertising brokers. In Slovenia, for example, there are a dozen Web sites that offer advertising, but there are no accompanying services. The potential audience for

Web advertising remains small, despite the fact that companies are very prone to use it. In 1997, 25 percent of the companies in Slovenia with five or more employees planned some form of Internet advertising in the next twelve months (RIS 1997). However, the target groups of Internet users are small and the cost per thousand impressions (CPM) remains high. The most visited domestic sites are still the public sites, such as "What's New?" (1998) on the national home page or the telephone directory (both have English versions). These sites receive several hundred thousand sessions per month, with over 10,000 different visitors (unique IP numbers). However, in a telephone survey of 400 Internet users (RIS 1997) no domestic commercial site was visited regularly by more than 5 percent of the respondents. Similarly, in a Web survey no commercial Web sites were listed among the top five domestic sites. On the other hand, the foreign global sites—such as Yahoo, Alta Vista, Microsoft, CNN, and Netscape—are visited more frequently than the domestic commercial sites. This may change when more content becomes available on local Web sites. As already mentioned, even in Sweden there are three foreign sites—Geocities, Alta Vista, and Microsoft—among the ten most visited Web sites (Top Ten Sites 1998). These illustrations confirm that in small countries foreign Web sites take a significant, even a dominant, share of time spent on the Web. Therefore, these sites are very attractive to local advertisers.

The Internet is the only medium that enables the tailoring of advertisements to the characteristics of the consumer (visitor). This gives global sites an opportunity to adapt the advertisement (banner) to the visitor's country of origin. Local advertisers thus meet their local audience on foreign Web sites. Of course, these sites charge for their monopolistic position. This example clearly illustrates the principles of globalization in the Internet age. Even if competition among the global sites prevents the creation of an actual extra profit, such advertising still forms a net import of the technological services from large, developed countries. This directly supports the development of the information sector in large countries.

These disadvantages, in fact, arise as a consequence of the unfavorable principles discussed earlier. Namely, it is the nature of virtual competition and economy of scale that creates specific drawbacks for small countries in the field of advertising, too.

The Language

According to a Graphics Visualization and Usability (GVU) Center survey (Kehoe 1997), the largest global self-selected survey on the Web, 70 percent of European users would use the Web more often if there were more content in their national language. A similar result was found in the 1997 RIS Web survey. Although the English language dominates the Web, there is only a handful of countries where the majority of the population speaks English. In Slovenia, only 40 percent of the adult population can actively use the English language. This is a relatively high percentage for a non-English-speaking nation.

Knowledge of English is strongly related to Internet use. In the 1998 RIS telephone survey of the general population (ages fifteen to seventy), 5 percent of the respondents labeled their knowledge of English as fluent, 15 percent as good, and 20 percent as partial. The remainder labeled it as poor (25%) or nonexistent (35%). It should be noted that only respondents who clearly understood the meaning of the term "Internet" (85%) were asked these questions. Of the first group (fluent in English), 75 percent used the Internet, but only 1 percent have done so in the last group (non-English speakers).

Age and education are major factors determining both Internet use and knowledge of English. However, the level of familiarity with English stands as the strongest predictor of Internet use in all sociodemographic subgroups. The majority of English-speaking Slovenians are already Internet users, so the future audience will be recruited mostly from the non-English-speaking segments. This has important consequences for the coming patterns of Internet use, because non-English-speaking users are much more sensitive to language. However, the same survey shows that the English-speaking users receive Web sites in the domestic language much more favorably as well. Of course, for a Web site to become globally visible it must be in English. Two-language versions of sites have severe cost implications. In Slovenia, one-third of the Web sites are in English. In addition, some sites also have German and Italian versions.

This illustrates important disadvantages for non-English-speaking countries. These disadvantages are particularly critical for small countries, because their domestic audience cannot stimulate the creation of sufficient domestic content. Large countries, which can create enough content, are more self-sufficient: for example, France and its Minitel service. Therefore, because of the limited content in the domestic language, English-speaking users in a small non-English-speaking country visit foreign global sites relatively often. For that same reason, non-English-speaking users find the Internet much less attractive. Thus, the segment of the population that is attracted to the Internet is smaller, and the national potential for Internet absorption is lower. In addition, the majority of users will never benefit from the full potential of the Internet. Together with the increased costs of the English version of Web sites, these disadvantages create another obstacle for the spread of the Internet in small non-English-speaking countries.

The opposite is also true. Web sites in small English-speaking countries, such as Ireland, are in a much better position. The reason is obvious: Any domestic application on the Internet is automatically available to a global audience and all domestic users are automatically global users.

Issues in Regulation

The Internet is closely linked to the latest changes in information and telecommunications technologies, which are vital to the globalization process (Negroponte 1995; Gates 1995; Dertouzos 1997). An important component of this process is the removal of barriers, both in telecommunications and in customs taxes for information and telecommunications products. Establishing global technological standards and standards of industrial property are important parts of this process as well.

Globalization inherently leads to oligopolies, not only on the Internet, but also in the entire information and telecommunications industry. The most typical examples are hardware and software. Similarly, with satellite communications only a few large companies will offer complete communications service to the largest corporations (Can the Old Giants Fight Back? 1998). The difficulties of British Telecom, the most deregulated and most strategically oriented European telecom, pose the question of whether there will be a place at all for any such European company. At this point the regulation of national telecommunications becomes extremely important.

The proper regulation of the national information and telecommunications environment arises from the recognition of the importance of these technologies. The critical mass of users that created this awareness was first established in the United States. Its government responded quickly, with national information infrastructure programs, telecommunication laws, the introduction of the Internet into public schools, the use of electronic commerce in public administration, efforts for tax-free Internet commerce, and increased immigration quotas for technical workers. An illustration of the high priority of these issues can be observed on the official U.S. page on electronic commerce (*The Emerging Digital Economy* 1998).

Issues of regulation are also crucial for small countries. However, due to the lack of the critical number of Internet applications, the impetus and the vision for the necessary steps are not so strong. Even when such awareness exists, it faces severe obstacles, from historical monopolies to specific political barriers. The European Community, for example, encounters severe problems in its efforts to demonopolize the national telecommunications industry. The small countries, in particular, hesitate and postpone the liberalization process because it will dramatically alter their fragile and complicated national infrastructure. The telecommunications infrastructure, which has enjoyed a monopoly from the very beginning of its existence, is closely linked to government policy, to national political balance, and to the very real question of national sovereignty. In Slovenia, for example, the process of demonopolizing its national telecom was found to be so delicate that it was postponed until 2002. It is questionable, of course, whether this prolongation is an optimal strategic step for the future.

The costs of telecommunications services are typically higher in small countries than in large ones. A leased telephone line is approximately two times more expensive in Europe than in the United States. In small countries such as Slovenia this ratio is even higher. The reason for this is the inefficiency that arises from the monopoly of national telecommunications. However, small countries face severe obstacles in removing these monopolies. Whatever the obstacles, they produce additional drawbacks for the future of small countries.

DISCUSSION

The Internet alters the interaction between the globalization process and the size of the country. For centuries this interaction has been ambiguous and unarticulated. Today the Internet radically simplifies the communication patterns and thus reinforces the process of international economic concentration and monopolization. In addition, the Internet introduces virtual reality, which is a very specific and new phenomenon. In virtual reality, dominant suppliers and dominant Web sites are located in a few large, developed countries, particularly in the United States. It was also in the United States that an early audience of sufficient size generated at least a two-year initial advantage in Internet applications. Contrary to this, the modest audience in small economies persistently delays developments of Internet services and content. Their Internet users then access foreign services, which further stimulates the development of those services and neglects the domestic ones. After five years of development, the leading Web-site brands and other virtual oligopolies are firmly positioned in large, developed countries. It is very likely that they will remain dominant into the future.

Because of this, a portion of the consumption of global products on the virtual markets moves outside the small countries. The same is true for many vital Internet services. Consequently, Internet users from small countries concentrate their virtual visits to foreign sites, which also offers specific opportunities for advertising to these sites. The disadvantages of small countries are reinforced by the existence of a non-English-speaking majority, which obstructs Internet usage and increases the cost of presentations on the Web. The higher costs of Internet usage in these countries arise also from expensive and monopolistic telecommunications services, which are, in general, particularly difficult to deregulate.

There are many obstacles that keep small economies from obtaining their share of the emerging virtual markets of global services and global consumption products. But a considerable part of economic activity in virtual reality does remain local. The virtual economic prospects for small countries seem to be this remaining portion. Filling niche markets is another prospect for small economies.

Nevertheless, the active role of the countries themselves is extremely important in the globalization process. There are many historical examples where proper strategy resulted in strong positive effects for a country. The role of the government is particularly important in the initial stages of Internet penetration. The education system, electronic commerce in public administration, and the deregulation of telecommunications are crucial targets of government action. This action can dramatically affect the future of a small country.

With respect to the virtual oligopolies, their patterns of concentration resemble those in the entertainment industry. There, too, suppliers from a few large countries control a large portion of the global market. One example is the movie industry, where U.S. products dominate. To a certain extent, this applies to television broadcasting, music performance, video games, and CDs as well. Another parallel is the oligopoly in the software industry (e.g., Microsoft, Oracle, etc.). In both cases, certain extra profits are transferred from small to large countries. The process of concentrating and raising the oligopolies on the Internet is very similar to both the entertainment and software industries, but it is much more clear and elegant—and with unlimited possibilities.

These arguments highlight only the early development of these tendencies. It is not yet clear whether they will become dominant or remain minor. Specifically, there must be no exaggeration of the role of the Internet. Internet penetration seems to stop below 50 percent of the population. The percentage of final virtual consumption is small, below 1 percent of the total final consumption. The same is true for Internet advertising. The amount of virtual shopping that flows from small countries is still a negligible portion of international transactions. However, the described tendencies are gaining momentum rapidly and may radically affect the small economies in the very near future.

The disadvantages should not overshadow the positive changes that the Internet has introduced to the way globalization affects small economies. First, consumers from small countries benefit from the increased quality, price competition, and variety of final consumption goods. Second, for companies the market is expanded and the communication barriers reduced. The Internet also reinforces all the standard advantages of globalization: niche marketing, profile developing, and flexibility. The Internet thus brings new opportunities, stimulates economic growth, and improves the quality of life. It is not surprising that the users from small countries are very enthusiastic about these changes. In the 1998 RIS Web survey the majority of respondents disagreed that the Internet would lead to the cyberimperialism of the United States (25% agreed, 41% disagreed, with 19% undecided and 15% don't knows). They also strongly agreed that the Internet would improve the situation of small countries. (However, they disagreed that it would improve the situation of the undeveloped countries.)

Of course, the consumers and companies from large, developed countries enjoy these same advantages of globalization. In addition, they enjoy the benefits brought about by their status as the dominant suppliers in global virtual markets.

To conclude, the Internet definitely improves the position of small economies. However, these benefits are smaller than the advantages of large, developed countries. One reason is that certain extra profit flows from small economies to large ones because of global concentration and monopolies. However, as there are much larger absolute gains to be had, the only option for small countries is to recognize and properly adjust to the new globalization rules.

REFERENCES

Belgian Business Use. 1997. *Nua Internet Surveys*. 5 May. <http://www.nua.ie/surveys>.

Big Earnings for Yahoo. 1998. *Nua Internet Surveys*. 9 April. <http://www.nua.ie/surveys>.

Can the Old Giants Fight Back? 1998. *The Economist*, 4 April, 19–26.

Clemente, P. 1998. *The State of the Net: The New Frontier*. New York: McGraw-Hill.

Damijan, J. P. 1997. Main Economic Characteristics of Small Countries: Some Empirical Evidence. In Small States: New Challenges and Opportunities. Book 1, edited by M. Svetlicic. *Development & International Cooperation* 13 (24–25): 43–84.

Death of PC-Centric Era. 1998. *IDC Executive Insights*. <http://www.idc.com>.

Dertouzos, M. 1997. *What Will Be*. San Francisco: Harper Edge.

EITO. 1997. *European Information Technology Observatory 1997*. Mainz, Germany: Eggebrecht-presse.

Fritz, W., and M. Kerner. 1997. On-Line Marketing on WWW in Germany. In *COTIM-97: Proceedings of the Conference on Telecommunications and Information Markets*, Brussels, November 1997, edited by N. Dholakia, E. Cruse, and D. R. Fortin. Kingston, R.I.: Research Institute for Telecommunication and Information Technology.

Gates, B. (with Nathan Myhrvold and Peter Rinearson). 1995. *The Road Ahead*. New York: Viking Penguin.

Hoffman, D. L., and T. P. Novak. 1996. New Metrics for New Media: Toward the Development of Web Measurement Standards. *World Wide Web Journal* 2: 213–246.

Juliussen, E., and K. Petska-Juliussen. 1998. *Internet Industry Almanac*. San Jose, Calif.: Computer Industry Almanac.

Kehoe, C. M. 1997. GVU's 7th WWW User Survey. In *GVU's WWW User Surveys*. <http://www.cc.gatech.edu/gvu/user_surveys/survey-1997-04>.

Kropivnik, S., and P. Jesovnik. 1995. Small Countries in the Global Economy: Slovenia, An Exception or the Rule? *Journal of International Relations* 2: 66–95.

Meeker, M., and S. Pearson. 1997. *The Internet Retailing Report*. Morgan Stanley. <http://www.ms.com>.

Momose, H. 1997. Japanese Perception of Small States in Transition. In Small States: New Challenges and Opportunities. Book 2, edited by M. Svetlicic. *Development & International Cooperation* 13 (24–25): 327–348.

Negroponte, N. 1995. *Being Digital*. New York: Vintage.

On-Line Publications on the Internet. 1998. *Nua Internet Surveys*. 5 March. <http://www.nua.ie/surveys>.

RIS. 1996. *Raba Interneta v Sloveniji 1996* (Research on Internet in Slovenia 1996). Ljubljana, Slovenia: University of Ljubljana, Faculty of Social Sciences, Center for Methodology and Informatics.

———. 1997. *Raba Interneta v Sloveniji 1997* (Research on Internet in Slovenia 1997). Ljubljana, Slovenia: University of Ljubljana, Faculty of Social Sciences, Center for Methodology and Informatics.

————. 1998. *Raba Interneta v Sloveniji 1998* (Research on Internet in Slovenia 1998). Unpublished raw data. University of Ljubljana, Faculty of Social Sciences, Center for Methodology and Informatics.

Salvatore, D. 1997. The Economic Performance of Small Versus Large Nations. In Small States: New Challenges and Opportunities. Book 1, edited by M. Svetlicic. *Development & International Cooperation* 13 (24–25): 21–42.

Senjur, M. 1992. The Viability of Economic Development of a Small State Separating from a Larger One. *Development & International Cooperation* 8 (14–15): 5–20.

Svetlicic, M. 1997. Small Countries in a Globalised World: Their Honeymoon or Twilight. In Small States: New Challenges and Opportunities. Book 1, edited by M. Svetlicic. *Development & International Cooperation* 13 (24–25): 5–20.

The Emerging Digital Economy. 1998. <http://www.ecommerce.gov>.

Top Ten Sites. 1998. *RelevantKnowledge Sweden.* <http://www.relevantknowledge.se>.

What's New? 1998. *Guide to Virtual Slovenia.* <http://www.ijs.si/slo>.

10

Counterhegemonic Media: Can Cyberspace Resist Corporate Colonization?

Jeffrey Layne Blevins

The mass media are the primary products and tools of ideology in society, and thus how these systems are controlled and influenced is a significant consideration. Through integration of different types of media, corporate conglomerations can produce a preponderance of the information and entertainment that circulates through the media. As conglomerated communications empires claim more of the sources that transmit information and entertainment, their influence over ideology becomes more inordinate. The nature of this threat is by no means a grand conspiracy, but rather is one that has developed in a free-market capitalist society. This chapter explores the implications of this influence by surveying Marxist and Gramscian theories that have already explored elite domination over ideology in capitalist societies. Neo-Marxist perspectives on political economy will also be considered, as they express how organizing and financing media systems through commercial means structures messages. Finally, the new communications technology of the Internet will be discussed, as it may be used to counteract this locus of control. Considering the overbearing structure of corporate conglomerations within the world's media industries, can the veins of cyberspace effectively function as a conduit for news, information, entertainment, ideas, and culture without their hegemonic influence?

THEORETICAL PERSPECTIVES ON EMPIRES AND IDEOLOGY:
A MARXIST VIEW OF MASS MEDIA

Mass media have advanced along many technological and sociological lines since the life of Karl Marx. The printing press was the primary mode of communication during his lifetime, while today communications may travel through a vast array of media, including books, magazines, radio, television, video, film, and cyberspace. Making their way through these outlets are pictures and words that human beings use to make sense of the world around them. Undoubtedly, then, any control over the means or production of communications is significant. Considering that Marx was largely concerned with how elite control over material production conditions the consciousness of society, it is useful to examine the current state of mass media ownership in terms of his views. It could be said that today a bourgeois class controls the mass-media industry and disseminates an ideological view of the world that is consistent with its interests. So few corporate entities control information to the masses that their feudal-like ownership of the media industry suggests that elite interests can exert a preponderant influence over the consciousness of society. Keeping in mind the constant message of ideology that is now possible, Marxist concepts developed over a hundred years ago of how modes of production relate to class consciousness are highly applicable to the current state of media ownership today.

When writing *The German Ideology* in 1845–1846, Marx (1978a) recognized that "the production of ideas, of conceptions, of consciousness, is at first directly interwoven with the material activity and the material intercourse of men, the language of real life" (p. 154). Marx goes on to say that "life is not determined by consciousness, but consciousness by life" (p. 155). At the time Marx was concerned with the processes of industrialization and urbanization and their relations to social problems. He believed that the bourgeoisie (the ruling class) was able to influence and manipulate the proletariat (the majority subordinate class) through its control over "modes of production," and understood that the production of ideas, conceptions and consciousness was directly related to the material activity of real life (p. 154).

In 1859 Marx developed this insight further, when he wrote in his preface to *A Contribution to the Critique of Political Economy* (1978b):

In the social production of their life, men enter into definite relations that are indispensable and independent of their will, relations of production which correspond to a definite stage of development of their material productive forces. The sum total of these relations of production constitutes the economic structure of society, the real foundation, on which rises a legal and political superstructure and to which correspond definite forms of social consciousness. The mode of production of material life conditions the social, political and intellectual life process in general. It is not the consciousness of men that determines their being, but, on the contrary, their social being that determines their consciousness. (pp. 4–5)

Marx posits that the economic reality of society determines the relationships and consciousness of its people. It seems Marx was concerned with showing how elites dominate society through direct control over the means of production (labor, factories, land, etc.) and maintain their power ideologically. This kind of influence still poses a threat to present-day society.

Even though television and other media technologies did not exist during Marx's life, they disseminate and sustain "conceptions of life" today much in the same manner he was describing 150 years ago. "As a matter of general theory it is useful to recognize that means of communication are themselves means of production" (Williams 1980, 50). Use of the mass media, which is now ever-present in society, can heavily impact the shaping of individual consciousness or shared meanings of a society. "The pen is mightier that the sword," may be an overworked cliché, but whoever controls the dissemination of ideas has an excellent mechanism for gaining and maintaining social, political, and economic control without ever having to use force. Herein lies the type of influence that Marx foreshadowed in his recognition that elite control over the means of production conditions the consciousness of society.

The term "hegemony" has traditionally been used to imply preponderant influence or authority, especially of one nation over others. "Marxism extended the definition of rule or domination to relations between social classes, and especially to definitions of a ruling class" (Williams 1977, 108). In *The Eighteenth Brumaire of Louis Napoleon*, Marx (1977) explained this dynamic relationship in society.

Upon the several forms of property, upon the social conditions of existence, a whole superstructure is reared of various and peculiarly shaped feelings . . . illusions, habits of thought and conceptions of life. The whole class produces and shapes these out of its material foundation and out of the corresponding social conditions. The individual unit to whom they flow through tradition and education may fancy that they constitute the true reasons for and premises of [their] conduct. (p. 76)

Here it seems that Marx is defining superstructure to encompass all ideology, all "conceptions of life." This ideology can be expressed not only in legal and political practices (institutions), but in forms of culture and consciousness that express a particular view of the world. Of course, Marx was concerned primarily with a hierarchical class system between the bourgeois and the proletariat during his time, which he considered to be the root of all social problems. Nonetheless, Marx foretold hegemony in the sense of a system of meanings and values that is the expression or projection of the ruling class interest.

Antonio Gramsci defined this type of hegemony as ideology that consistently favors the elite in a way that subordinate groups may not realize. "For Gramsci this is . . . characterized by ideological struggle which attempts to forge unity between economic, political and intellectual objectives, placing all the questions around which the struggle rages on a 'universal,' not a corporate level, thereby creating the hegemony of a fundamental social group over a series of subordinate ones" (Moueffe 1979, 180). Gramsci's work is considered one of the major turning points in Marxist cultural theory (Williams 1977). For Gramsci hegemony was "bourgeois domination of the thought, the common sense, the life-ways and everyday assumptions of the working class" (Gitlin 1979, 384). This notion of ideological hegemony gave particular attention to how "routine structures of everyday thought . . . worked to sustain class domination" (p. 385). This form of influence may seem more subtle, but is actually more insidious. Perhaps Chantal Moueffe (1979) describes best how this notion of hegemony works in her writing on Gramsci and Marxist theory: "A successful hegemony is one which manages to create a 'collective national-popular will,' and for this to happen the dominant class must have been capable of articulating to its hegemonic principle all the national–popular ideological elements, since it is only if this happens that it (the class) appears as the representative of the general interest" (p. 194).

What is important to consider here is that hegemony includes formal meanings, values, and beliefs that a corporate elite can develop and propagate. This system of meanings and values constitutes a reality for most people in a society. "A subordinate class has . . . *nothing but* this ideology as its consciousness" (Williams 1977, 109), since the production of all ideas is in the hands of those who control the primary means of production. This could never be more possible than in the late twentieth century, where control over the means of communications production is becoming increasingly concentrated.

Though Marx could not conceive of such concentrated conglomerate rule as today's communications industry, its hegemonic influence resonates with his original proposition that material means condition the whole process of social, political, and intellectual life. Therefore, it is useful to apply Marxist notions of hegemony in relation to today's commercial media system, where the media elite seem to exploit the massive audiences for self-serving interests.

As Marxist notions have been used to examine the relationship between ideology and the social structure of society, political economy studies in communications investigate how the mass media influence society. Moreover, the political economy of communications is concerned with how "ownership, support mechanisms (e.g. advertising), and government policies influence media behavior and content" (McChesney 1998, 3), especially in capitalist societies. While many economists may see the marketplace as unquestionably benevolent, political economists do not automatically make this assumption.

To engage Marxist conceptions further and more directly in the study of mass media, scholarship under the heading of "critical political economy" has sought to examine "the interplay between the symbolic and economic dimensions of public communications" in a comprehensive and dynamic manner (Golding and Murdock 1996, 11). This investigative orientation reveals how different means of financing and organizing media (cultural) productions structure the contours of representation and meaning. As a neo-Marxist approach, critical political economy draws attention to the way mass media operate ideologically to sustain and support prevailing relations of domination.

It is worth mentioning that critical political economy differs significantly from two other similar perspectives: liberal political economy and classical political economy. It is important to make the distinctions clear, as do Golding and Murdock (1996). Liberal political economists are attentive to the market exchange between consumers and competing commodities. They would assert that the greater play in market forces means greater "freedom" of consumer choice (p. 14). Therefore, liberal political economists believe privatization of public services would be "good" because it would increase consumer choice or "freedom" in the marketplace of ideas. This notion is diminished, however, in light of evidence that the marketplace of ideas is constrained in the choices it offers consumers because of privatization of the media industries. Classical political economists would also assert that government intervention should be minimized so that market forces can have the widest freedom of operation (p. 17). Doing so, however, would likely result in more conglomeration and subsequent constriction of the marketplace of ideas. Therefore, critical political economists diverge from both of these perspectives by seeing beyond this supposed freedom to the actual distortion and inequalities of the market system, and wish to engage in questions of justice, equity and the "actual" public good, which may not simply be the sum of individual choices in the marketplace. Critical political economy also seeks to explain how the economic dynamics of media production would structure public discourse by promoting certain cultural forms over others.

Marxism and critical political economy are two perspectives that have illustrated the problem presented by corporate conglomeration of the communications industries in a dynamic way and will help guide our understanding of them. Marxist notions have explained how bourgeoisie domination of production "by the immensely facilitated means of communication" (Marx 1991, 739) allows them preponderant influence over ideology. Gramsci provided the term "hegemony" to describe this type of preponderant influence. Hegemony exemplifies how the mass media today operate ideologically to sustain and support prevailing relations of domination. The merging together of mass-media entities not only means fewer conduits for communications, but also compresses the range of information, entertainment, ideas, and opinions that circulate through the public arena. Critical political economists attribute the exacerbation of this problem here to the organization and financing of media systems through commercial means. This type of system allows the media elite to support their position of privilege by setting the agenda for the masses in the realms of information and entertainment. Thus, how society understands the issues and events presented in the media and their perceptions of reality may be profoundly influenced by the few controlling media empires.

CORPORATE CONTROL OVER MASS MEDIA SYSTEMS

By the very nature of information dissemination, whoever selects the media's messages must have substantial control over what people consider. Mass media both transmit and transmute ideology by selecting "the images, topics, and styles that circulate through living rooms" (Gitlin 1993), and thus shape how we understand ourselves and the world around us. As media have grown throughout the history of the United States, corporate control of them has equally grown. Corporate presence in the communications industry has increasingly been characterized by conglomeration and hegemonic influence over ideology.

At a rapid pace, corporate conglomerates are swallowing up the communications industries, and with them the power to articulate issues and events in the media. Since the "Golden Age" of television ABC, CBS, and NBC controlled all prime-time programming in American homes, and there were many complaints about the sameness among the three broadcast networks. In 1970 the Federal Communications Commission (FCC) established a "prime-time access" rule that limited the programming these networks could provide to their affiliates to just three hours between 7 and 11 P.M. The rule was "designed to release some prime television time from network control" so programming from independent producers and local stations could develop (Barron 1973, 188–189). To no avail, network affiliates often used off-network syndicated reruns to fill the extra hour because there was still pressure to select programming that would draw the largest audience possible. Even though cable television has added more channels, there is still little diversity among producers.

Today "the preponderance of U.S. mass communication is controlled by less than two dozen enormous profit-maximizing corporations" (McChesney 1997, 6). Three of the most prominent of these conglomerates are Time-Warner, Walt Disney Company, and News Corporation (Fox). Time-Warner's holdings include an imposing number of cable channels, production companies, home video and entertainment services, magazines, music companies, and book publishers. To mention just a few, Time-Warner owns HBO, Cinemax, CNN, TNT, Warner Brothers television, Castle Rock Entertainment, Time–Life Video, Warner Home Video, Turner Home Satellite, *Sports Illustrated*, *People, Time, Money, Entertainment Weekly, Parenting,* and *Life,* Elektra, Columbia House records, Time–Life Books, and Book-of-the-Month Club. The Walt Disney Company now owns ABC television and radio and operates many of the local stations in nearly every U.S. market. Disney also owns ESPN, A&E, and Lifetime cable channels, Touchstone, Hollywood, Miramax, and Buena Vista motion picture companies, and several magazines and newspapers (Bishop 1996, 8–9). News Corporation owns Fox Broadcasting Co., including twenty-three U.S. television stations, several television production companies, and a host of motion picture companies, publications, and music labels (Top 25 Media Groups 1997, 3). Even with these type of conglomerated media structures, newsstands still hold rows and rows of newspapers and magazines on a variety of subjects, while cable television channels continue to multiply, as do movies and records. They are likely, however, to be variations of the same themes and messages (Golding and Murdock 1996, 20). Thus, while the wide array of media may imply a rich variety of entertainment and information, it in fact represents an increasingly narrow range of ideology.

Film studios, television networks, cable networks, music studios, record distributors, publishing companies, magazines, and various commercial outlets under blanket ownership can help the market value of each other. For instance, company newspapers can give publicity to their television stations, and television shows can give publicity to the movies that their film studios are producing. It may not exactly be "free" publicity, but the profits and expenditures seem to keep circulating via the same corporate ties, which suggests more than a little advantage. Disney, for example, is able to promote its films by selling soundtracks on its record labels, broadcasting on its television network, printing a book version, delivering rave magazine reviews, and offering merchandising to boot (not to mention Saturday morning cartoons). Now Disney also has an Internet Web site to further promote and sell its wares.

The current rate of consolidated communications activity over an increasingly larger consumer class may seem troublesome in the United States, where these networks of media dominate, but its is perhaps even more problematic that these media empires are now becoming prevalent around the globe. Today's business community is a global one, and just like McDonalds and Pizza Hut exist in Russia, so too does CNN. The difference here is that information, not hamburgers, is the commodity, and that is troublesome. If an oligopolistic class of corporate media conglomerates dominates the circulation of ideas and images around the entire planet, then they can assert a preponderant influence over world cultures. As Bagdikian (1989) has suggested,

All resist economic changes that do not support their own financial interests. Together, they exert a homogenizing power over ideas, culture and commerce that affects populations larger than any in history. Neither Caesar nor Hitler, Franklin Roosevelt nor any Pope, has commanded as much power to shape the information on which so many people depend to make decisions about everything from whom to vote for to what to eat. (p. 809)

As international media empires spawn from the United States, we are likely to see more U.S. television programming, movies, and cultural objects become more pervasive abroad. Several American companies produce first-run television shows for overseas markets. Syndicated shows like the ever-popular *Baywatch* may or may not cover production costs after being sold in the United States, but they make pure profit on the international market. This form of deficit financing leads to the creation of programs that there is already a market for in foreign countries. Although new communications technologies such as DBS (direct broadcast satellite) have increased the number of television channels in many Second and Third World countries, it has also increased the demand for U.S. productions, rather than more diverse programming. U.S. producers no longer consider just the "U.S. markets" while in production. Instead, "The ideas that actually make it into production are those that have mass appeal, can be broadcast in many areas of the world, and can be shown as reruns many times" (Schafer-Gross 1995, 10). The United States has always been the leading program exporter, accounting for most of the television shows worldwide.

Via satellite, Time-Warner's broadcast now transcends U.S. borders, as does programming of media mogul Rupert Murdoch, chairman and CEO of News Corporation. Each conglomerate can disseminate their programming literally around the planet. Not only do industrialized countries (i.e., the United States, Canada, England, France, Japan) receive their satellite signals, but also newly industrialized (Brazil, Mexico, Turkey) and developing regions (Central America, Africa, India). Korea and even communist China, despite considerable debate, have authorized transmission of Murdoch's STAR satellite. Moreover, both Time-Warner and News Corporation have recently set designs on entering Russian and other Eastern European countries to bolster their audience (Schafer-Gross 1995, 153). As the reach of their programming increases, so does U.S. advertising. In China, "Parents complain that their children are humming tunes from Coca-Cola commercials," and in Argentina, "Parents try to cope with their children's desires for *Simpsons* tee shirts" (p. 15). It seems evident that U.S. corporate ideology is expanding its influence abroad, mainly through various forms of mass media.

The concern that arises through each of these examples is that private commercial interests are influencing culture through their monopolization of information and entertainment, not just in the United States, but increasingly around the world. Furthermore, the notion that information and entertainment are shaped, selected, and disseminated according to profitability is significant. Considering this priority, McChesney (1997) suggests that the "commercial basis of U.S. media has negative implications for the exercise of political democracy. . . . It permits the business and commercial interests that actually rule U.S. society to have inordinate influence over media content" (p. 7). Because television, newspapers, and many other forms of media are already subject to corporate manipulation and commercialization, there seems to be little hope for public sovereignty in communications, where everyone could have access to receive and disseminate messages across the world along channels that are not convoluted with commercials and advertisements.

The Internet is one possible means of eluding the corporate influence because of its unique dynamics. Due to the suffusion of telephone lines the Internet can connect individuals from all around the globe, and thus diminish the significance of mainstream forms of communication such as television. With instant Internet access stemming from all corners of the world it could prove to be a revolutionary force for democratic communication and culture. Since the Internet came into being it has mainly functioned as an unfettered and unregulated conduit. The Internet seemed to be outside the control of traditional corporate and governmental authorities "due to its direct form of communication combining the immediacy of telephone, the intimacy of mail, the graphics of television, and the social interaction of a community bulletin board" (Foerstel 1997, 118). Everyone could have access to receive and disseminate messages across the world. In an information society, this is important. As Halloran (1997) has said, "It will not be possible to achieve the goals of citizenship in the absence of information and communication systems which provide the information base and the opportunities for access and participation for all citizens" (p. 47). Since corporate interests already dominate mainstream forms of mass communication (television, radio, films, newspapers, magazines, etc.), can the Internet resist their influence?

MASS MEDIA AND TELECOMMUNICATION REFORM

As McChesney (1996) has noted, the current Internet revolution is parallel to the emergence of broadcasting in the 1920s and 1930s, when legislators debated "who should control the technology and for what purposes" (p. 3). This dilemma has emerged once again as a concern for legislators in the 1990s. It would be for the betterment of political democracy if the Internet could function as a mass media to be used by and for all citizens, rather than the case of U.S. broadcast television, which is essentially monopolized by a handful of large conglomerates who utilize the medium to maximize profits (through selling ad space). It seems that commercial broadcasting has resulted in a narrower range of expression. What the Internet offers, however, is a decentralized, pluralistic service for all of society.

In 1994 the Clinton–Gore administration seemed to recognize some of the concerns presented by corporate conglomeration. Gore remarked that the most pressing issues in telecommunications reform were providing open access to the Internet and avoiding a society of information "haves" and "have-nots" (Gore 1994). When the Telecommunications Act was signed into law in 1996, President Clinton remarked at the signing ceremony that "this bill protects consumers against monopolies. It guarantees the diversity of voices our democracy depends upon" (Clinton 1996). Gore added that "also, in the interest of promoting diversity of voices and viewpoints that are so important to our democracy, this legislation will prevent undue concentration in television and radio ownership" (Gore 1996). The Telecommunications Act also called for public libraries and schools to provide Internet access.

The actual language of the act, however, had more to say about promoting big business, rather than guarding against undue concentration of ownership.

The new law seems to strengthen monopolies, as it eliminated any provisions limiting the number of AM and FM broadcast stations that may be controlled by any one entity, eliminated the same provisions for broadcast television, and wiped away restraints against a single entity controlling a network of broadcast stations and cable systems. The only limits placed on broadcast ownership was a 35-percent cap on the total national audience. Prior to the 1996 act broadcast ownership was limited to just twelve stations and 25 percent of the national market for television. Radio ownership was limited to just forty stations and 25 percent of the national market. Local ownership combinations of radio and television, television and newspaper, radio and newspaper, and television and cable were also prohibited. All these restrictions were stripped away by the 1996 act, and presidential rhetoric about preventing undue concentration of television and radio ownership appears to be an empty promise. We are, however, still left with the possibilities of the Internet.

INTERNET AND COMMUNICATIONS DEMOCRACY

Through the Internet people can suffuse their messages across the globe in a matter of minutes. This unprecedented communications technology can connect individuals around the planet and prove to be a revolutionary force for democratic communication and culture. Everyone could have access to receive and disseminate messages everywhere. Individuals could have more voice in the information and entertainment that circulates through society.

On the surface it certainly seems possible that the Internet could function as counterhegemonic media by empowering the individual with an infinite amount of information from innumerable sources. It is relatively easy to navigate cyberspace by pointing and clicking with a computer mouse. It is also hard to censor content. In the United States students have on-line access through their schools, and public libraries provide access to the public. If one is not a U.S. student or able to travel to U.S. public libraries, though, Internet access is limited by the ability to pay for its services.

The Internet has functioned mainly as a resource for the socioeconomic privileged since its popularity began to rise in the 1990s. One of the most prominent early studies on Internet usage was conducted in 1995 by Nielsen Media Research. That study revealed that only 8 percent of the U.S. and Canadian population over the age of sixteen use the World Wide Web: "Web users were found to be more upscale than the typical population of the U.S. and Canada. For instance, 25 percent of the web users have an income of more than $80,000 per year compared to 10 percent of the general population (that makes that much). In addition, 64 percent of web users have a college degree, while only 28 percent of the population has completed a four-year program" (p. 3). It seemed evident here that the Internet was more likely to empower the elite rather than the public as a whole. The most recent Nielsen Internet demographic study (Nielsen 1997), however, showed that 46 percent of users have annual incomes of over $50,000 per year and 49 percent have college degrees. Although Internet usage has become slightly less elitist over the past two years, it still appears to favor corporate interests more and more.

The primacy of corporate control still reigns supreme in practically every industry, including the media industry, and the Internet is no exception. Access is already beginning to be dominated by large commercial providers such as Yahoo, Netscape, and America On-line (Relevant Knowledge 1998). These large commercial providers also help popularize Internet versions of other mainstream media. For instance, ABC, Disney, and ESPN were among the ten most popular Internet sites in 1997 (Relevant Knowledge 1998). Although ABC, Disney, and ESPN appear as three separate entities on the top-ten list, they all stem from the corporate headquarters of Disney. Although the Internet is a relatively young medium, a few major players appear to have dominant positions. "From month to month," one or two companies may trade places on the top ten, "but the list is relatively stable for a medium as volatile as the web is supposed to be" (Dodge 1998).

Corporate firms that control U.S. journalism are also major players in "jockeying for the inside lane on the information highway" (McChesney 1996, 5). The most popular news conglomerates in television, radio, and newspapers already are also the most prominent sources for news in cyberspace. For example, NBC has MSNBC, CNN has CNN on-line, *Sports Illustrated* (owned by the same company as CNN) has a Web site, ESPN (owned by Disney) has the SportsZone on-line, Fox Sports has a Web site, as does *USA Today*, and the list goes on and on. The point is that corporations have already begun colonizing cyberspace. As a result, Web sites are becoming littered with advertisements and the flow of junk e-mail is beginning to increase. As Jerry Young, head of Yahoo, has stated, "We are driven off of advertising and promotions. We are a full-service marketplace and a media company" (Dodge 1998). This dreary evidence lessens some of the possibilities that the Internet will empower the individual. It will rather help the few who dominate the marketplace.

The digitization of words, pictures, audio, and video via such a pervasive medium as the Internet should empower every person to be a highly individualized producer and consumer of media. Every person from Switzerland to New Zealand should be able to circumvent mainstream television and magazines by being able to distribute media materials around the world themselves, and to receive an infinite amount of other information from a vast array of sources—a real "marketplace of ideas," if you will.

Thus, we ought to be witnessing at the end of the twentieth century a transformation of media industries into hundreds and hundreds of small companies. That, anyway, is what was predicted at the start of the computer revolution. We are supposed to be living at the end of "mass" society. This is the age of media individualism, infinite free choice, consumer sovereignty. Deregulation, espoused by politicians in country after country, should be guaranteeing this great opening of the information and entertainment market. (Smith 1991, 3)

Examples from recent history, however, are far from any prediction about consumer sovereignty and empowering citizenry. In the United States, at least, privatization has meant commercialization, not democratization. Deregulation in the name of competition has meant conglomeration and oligopoly in practice. The messages of advertisers and corporate hegemony proliferates at an ever-increasing rate, and cyberspace will likely not diffuse them, but rather echo them.

Marx (1991) seemed to anticipate this possibility as well when he wrote that the "bourgeoisie cannot exist without constantly revolutionizing the instruments of production, and thereby the relations of production, and with them the whole relations of society" (p. 739). In particular, Marx notes the bourgeoisie will utilize the "immensely facilitated means of communication" to further their purposes (p. 739). It is important for Marx's perspective to be considered here, since the concentration of media control in a handful of commercial interests challenges the social capacity to generate a less-centralized public sphere. It seems likely that the Internet will function as another means of production dominated by the corporate bourgeoisie, rather than a counterhegemonic instrument for society.

REFERENCES

Bagdikian, B. H. 1989. The Lords of the Global Village. *The Nation* 248 (23): 805–820.

Barron, J. A. 1973. *Freedom of the Press for Whom? The Right of Access to Mass Media.* Bloomington: Indiana University Press.

Bishop, E. 1996. Giant Conglomerates Devour News Media—Limit Scope of American Journalism. *St. Louis Journalism Review* 26 (187): 8–9.

Clinton, W. J. 1996. Remarks by the president in signing ceremony for the Telecommunications Act, 8 February, Washington, D.C. <http://www1.whitehouse.gov/WH/EOP/OP/telecom/release.html>.

Dodge, J. 1998. Traffic Leaders Emerge as the Web Matures. *PC Week Online*, 11 May. <http://www5.zdnet.com/zdnn/content/pcwo /0511/315245.html>.

Foerstel, H. N. 1997. *Free Expression and Censorship in America: An Encyclopedia.* Westport, Conn.: Greenwood Press.

Gitlin, T. 1979. Prime Time Ideology: The Hegemonic Process in Television Entertainment. *Social Problems* 26 (3): 251–266.

———. 1993. Flat and Happy. *Wilson Quarterly*, Autumn, 47–55.

Golding, P., and G. Murdock. 1996. Culture, Communications, and Political Economy. In *Mass Media & Society.* 2d ed., edited by J. Curran and M. Gurevitch. London: Arnold.

Gore, A. 1994. Remarks delivered by vice president to the Superhighway Summit, 11 January, Royce Hall, UCLA, Los Angeles.

———. 1996. Statement of the vice president on passage of telecommunications reform legislation, 1 February, Washington, D.C. <http://www1.whitehouse. gov/WH/EOP/OP/telecom/VP-stmt-bill-passage.html>.

Halloran, J. 1997. International Communication Research: Opportunities and Obstacles. In *International Communication and Globalization*, edited by A. Mohammadi. London: Sage.

Marx, K. 1977. The Eighteenth Brumaire of Louis Napoleon. In *Marxism & Literature*, edited by R. Williams. Oxford: Oxford University Press.

———. 1978a. The German Ideology: Part I. In *The Marx–Engels Reader*, 2d ed., edited by R. C. Tucker. New York: W. W. Norton.

———. 1978b. A Contribution to the Critique of Political Economy. In *The Marx–Engels Reader*, 2d ed., edited by R. C. Tucker. New York: W. W. Norton.

———. 1991. The Communist Manifesto. In *Great Political Thinkers: Plato to the Present*, 5th ed., edited by W. Ebenstein and A. Ebenstein. Fort Worth: Harcourt Brace Jovanovich College Publishers.

McChesney, R. W. 1996. *The Internet and U.S. Communication Policymaking in Historical and Critical Perspective.* <http://www.usc.edu/dept/annenberg/vol1/issue4/mcchesney.html>.

———. 1997. *Corporate Media and the Threat to Democracy*. New York: Seven Stories Press.

———. 1998. What Is the Political Economy of Communication? *Communique* 16 (1): 3–15.

Moueffe, C. 1979. Hegemony and Ideology in Gramsci. In *Gramsci & Marxist Theory*, edited by C. Moueffe. London and Boston: Routledge and Kegan Paul.

Nielsen Media Research. 1995. *CommerceNet/Nielsen Announce Internet Study Results.* <http://www.nielsenmedia.com/news/cnet-pr.htm>.

———. 1997. *Internet Demographic Study Fall 1997 Release.* <http://www.nielsen media.cdm/interactive/commercenet/F97/>.

Relevant Knowledge. 1998. April's Top 10 Web Sites. <http://www.relevant knowledge.com>.

Top 25 Media Groups. 1997. *Broadcasting & Cable*, 7 July, 23.

Schafer-Gross, L., ed. 1995. *The International World of Electronic Media*. New York: McGraw-Hill.

Smith, A. 1991. *The Age of Behemoths: The Globalization of Mass Media Firms*. New York: Priority Press.

Williams, R., ed. 1977. *Marxism & Literature*. Oxford, England: Oxford University Press.

———. 1980. *Problems in Materialism and Culture*. London: Verso.

11

The Information Revolution, Transnational Relations, and Sustainable Development in the Global South

Rodger A. Payne

Sociologists have produced a voluminous theoretical and empirical literature on social movements.[1] This research mostly addresses the formation, organization, and operation of a wide array of social movements that have aimed to elicit societal change within various countries. These efforts have, for instance, at least incrementally improved the status of women, secured environmental protection, and assured civil liberties for ethnic minorities. An important common research thread is the examination of how ordinary people join together, or mobilize, to confront elites and authorities so as to achieve economic, political, and social objectives. Indeed, the proven ability of some movements to achieve remarkable social change explains why scholars have been so interested in their activities. Unfortunately, given the great need for a dramatically improved quality of life for residents of the developing world, most collaborative activity of this type has historically occurred in wealthy Western democracies (Falk 1987, 364). Indeed, empirical findings suggest that societal prosperity seems to be a precondition to social movement activity and that "the most deprived appear unlikely to sustain more than momentary insurgency" (McAdam, McCarthy, and Zald 1988, 702).[2] For anyone interested in the prospects for "sustainable development" in the global South, this is quite a discouraging finding.

By contrast, much recent research within the field of international relations explores the often successful transnational activity of so-called nongovernmental organizations. Like social movements, a large number of NGOs serve the interests of the relatively poor and powerless against elites and authorities, including on the global level versus states, transnational corporations, and multilateral development banks (see Payne 1995b; Wapner 1996; Weiss and Gordenker 1996; Willetts 1996).[3] Though NGOs are often headquartered in Western democracies, they are networked with likeminded peoples and groups all over the world, including in the global South. NGOs have achieved important successes by influencing various national and international policies and practices, albeit not always with mass support of people living in poverty and affected by their actions. Keck and Sikkink (1998a) and Lipschutz (1996, 19), among many others, argue that information and persuasion have been central to these global advocacy efforts, explicitly providing NGOs with a powerful means to challenge the status quo.

Keck and Sikkink (1998a, 21) and many others also specifically note that the spread and use of various advanced communications technologies has "had an enormous impact on moving information to and from third world countries" and has thereby helped create "a dense web of north–south exchange" in global campaigns for social progress. This chapter examines how the proliferation of advanced information technologies might help NGOs link with entrepreneurs in the global South to construct lasting social movements. Technologies like personal computers, fax machines, telephone modems, and other devices connecting these systems can facilitate transnational cooperation among socially minded actors. New global bonds then make it possible for movements to tap internal and external stocks of both material and ideational resources.

Before these claims are investigated more thoroughly, specifically in the context of sustainable development, the following section presents two reasons to be skeptical about whether NGOs and social movements in the global South might use advanced information technologies to facilitate social change.

IMPEDIMENTS TO GLOBAL ACTION

The first subsection to follow looks very briefly at social movement theory to explain the constraints on cooperative social interaction. The next subsection looks at the arguably gloomy data on the proliferation of new communications technologies.

Social Movement Theory: Barriers to Collective Action

A central research issue for scholars of social movements concerns the so-called resource mobilization problem. Put simply, how can individuals unite in active social movements, especially given the relative powerlessness of potential participants and individual disincentives for participating in any cooperative endeavor. Even when large numbers of people agree with the goals of a budding social movement, individuals might prefer to "free ride" on a group's potential achievements. This "logic of collective action" (Olson 1965) apparently serves as an important barrier to accumulating necessary resources, such as information, time, money, personnel, and leadership. As noted, some scholars find that these obstacles to collective action are virtually insurmountable in the context of extreme poverty.[4] Since per capita incomes in the global South are minuscule (UNDP 1997), individuals there have little to offer a burgeoning movement.

Not all social movement scholars worry about Olson's collective action problem, which is grounded in economic rationality. Many (see Kitschelt 1986; Kriesi et al. 1992), for example, stress the central role of "political opportunity structures" in making social movements necessary and/or possible. In addition to the obvious "pull" of potential benefits from collective success (balanced against the costs), Tarrow (1994, 189), for example, stresses the "push" of collective identity formation. This means that movements are constituted and sustained by people building solidarity and consensus around "common meanings and values." Still, resource-related difficulties are acknowledged. As Tarrow argues, the central task for movement organizers is the creation of "focal points for people who have no sources of compulsory coordination, who often lack direct connections with one another and have few, if any internal resources" (p. 189). Movements identify and utilize resources "external to the group—unlike money or power—that can be taken advantage of even by weak or disorganized challengers" (p. 18). This means organizers solve so-called transaction cost problems by using external resources grounded perhaps in cultural frames or "mobile social capital" (Meyer and Tarrow 1998, 15). The latter refers, in part, to the availability of influential societal allies, whose availability seems "closely related to whether the groups succeeded or not" (Tarrow 1994, 88). Unfortunately, as evidence in the next section highlights, residents of the developing world are in many ways isolated from potentially powerful global allies, like those in sympathetic Northern NGOs.

The Information Revolution: The Case for Skepticism

Over twenty years ago Nye and Keohane (1972) argued that new information technologies benefit the affluent nations of the North at the expense of the world's poor. Development problems are therefore potentially compounded, rather than resolved. Many of the authors in the Nye and Keohane volume on transnationalism argued that international connections might "enrich and strengthen the strong and rich—in short, the most modernized, technologically adept segments of the world—because only these elements are able to take full advantage of its network of intersocietal linkages" (p. xxv). Recently compiled evidence suggests that those warnings were quite prescient. In 1995, for example, most of the world's computers connected to the Internet were in the United States (Holderness 1996–1997, 40). In the world's most affluent countries, there are one or more computers for every ten people, while in China and India there is only one computer per 1,000 people (Young 1993, 11–12). Within the global South as a whole only about 15 percent of people have access even to telephones, and roughly only 5 percent, almost exclusively male elites, have computers (Monahan 1996; Garcia 1996, 49). Overwhelmingly, computer transmissions are in English and most software is written in English. Computer accounts and phone connections cost relatively more in real terms in the global South and basic illiteracy serves as a major barrier to any use of advanced information technologies.

In all, because of Northern elite monopolization of the latest information revolution, Hall (1994) concludes that "the new technologies may ironically reinforce center–periphery relationships" (p. 111), not help overcome the root dependency.[5] Holderness (1996–1997) similarly reports that a "new information elitism may arise to further disenfranchise the majority of the world's people" (p. 40). Not surprisingly, then, Falk (1987) is quite skeptical that social movements can form advantageous global connections. He points out that success "requires contact and communication, which in turn depends upon adequate resources. Many social movements operate on tiny budgets and cannot possibly afford to create transnational networks of like-minded groups and individuals" (p. 366).

This evidence and analysis obviously clashes sharply with some of the data noted being accumulated by those who study NGOs and a burgeoning "global civil society." Which empirical observations are correct? Can information technologies facilitate global social interaction or not? Who will benefit from the "wiring" of the world? The following sections explore answers, beginning with a brief discussion of the challenges and opportunities presented by the idea of "sustainable development." In the concluding section future prospects are briefly assessed in light of the global activities of social movements.

THE CASE OF SUSTAINABLE DEVELOPMENT

The subsistence lifestyle shared by most residents of the global South is a reflection of the great resource-use disparities between rich and poor nations. The world's wealthiest states consume three-quarters or more of many important material resources, while the poorest states barely survive on the remainder despite having about three-fourths of the world's population (UNDP 1997). Moreover, the overwhelming majority of new population growth occurs in these poorest states, where hundreds of millions of people already live in abject poverty. In addition to their indigence, some of the least-affluent states are now also suffering virtual ecological collapse as important forests or fisheries have disappeared after years of unsustainable economic activity. Ironically, overexploitation of these so-called renewable resources makes them particularly susceptible to exhaustion and/or irreversible contamination (Mathews 1989). In short, poverty leads the poor to overexploit their natural resources, which then worsens their condition in the long run. Scholars find that resource scarcities compounded by environmental degradation can trigger violent intranational conflict and even interstate war (Homer-Dixon 1991; Kennedy 1993). Researchers have linked ecological scarcities to numerous conflicts in troubled areas like El Salvador, India, Mexico, the Middle East, and the Philippines (see Bronkema, Lumsdaine, and Payne 1998).

It seems clear that the global South will need much greater external assistance in order to achieve what the seminal World Commission on Environment and Development (WCED) called "sustainable development."[6] Impoverished states whose needs are not currently being met must simply gain long-term access to global material and economic resources. Unfortunately, because redistributional politics are inherently contentious, the poorest states are apparently pitted against the globe's richer states in a struggle over wealth and resources. At the same time, de facto global ecological interdependence means that wealthy states cannot afford to allow the world's poor to pursue unsustainable development. Conca (1993) goes as far as to note that "the South appears to hold an effective veto over . . . international environmental protection—merely by staying on its current course of growth and development" (p. 319). The WCED (1987, 23) concluded that "the security, well-being, and very survival of the planet" are potentially at stake in these battles. The North apparently needs the cooperation of the South every bit as much as the South needs the North.

Though the phrase "sustainable development" is fairly fresh terminology that brings important points about ecology into global economic discourses, the underlying problems of economic underdevelopment are not new. North–South links are historically characterized by the latter's dependence on the former. To move toward mutually beneficial interdependence, states of the global South have long argued for increased foreign assistance, preferential terms of trade, higher (and stable) prices for their exportable commodities, debt relief, and greater direct foreign investment. A few modest redistributive reforms have been achieved, involving limited trade preferences and some debt relief, but nothing like a "new international economic order" has been secured (South Commission 1990). The North remains understandably wary of any extensive redistributive economic agenda.

The environmental dimensions of sustainable development do provide a relatively new item for North–South dialogue (Payne 1998). In fact, arguably the WCED's greatest contribution was pointing out that everyone shares an interest in sustainable development. For example, all states must worry about the collective use of energy and other nonrenewable resources and about controversial ecological issues like biodiversity and the so-called greenhouse effect. Experts warn that economic prosperity cannot long be maintained in a global context of ecological destruction and unsustainable exhaustion of world resources. Of course, any limits placed on the poorest states whose needs are not currently met would be potentially quite onerous. Indeed, given the redistributive argument, the North might need to make more energy and other resources available to the poorest states.

The coupling of economic and ecological goals nonetheless opens the possibility for a coalition between Northern environmentalists and development activists of the global South. The next section explains how the linking of objectives can make it possible for movements to become truly transnational efforts. Put simply, since organizers in the South share substantive goals with numerous individuals and groups in the rich states, the former can gain access to external material and ideational resources to organize and mobilize their movements. New information technologies arguably play a vital role in facilitating these connections, thereby helping overcome the many crises plaguing the world's poorest nations.

TRANSNATIONAL MOBILIZATION

Global movements seeking sustainable development goals must not only mobilize sufficient resources to propel their collective activity. In the end they must also seek redistribution of global wealth and resources to achieve their broader social and political objectives. It is almost as if the movements need to succeed substantively before they can hope to organize and mobilize. They need wealth and other resources in order to form and act. Yet, of course, they apparently cannot elicit such wealth without first mobilizing resources to sustain collective activity. The cart needs to come before the horse to stimulate motion, but the cart will not budge without horsepower.

More narrowly, social-movement organizers in developing states may well need to depend upon acquiring resources from sympathetic individuals and groups in the North. Because of their poverty they simply cannot hope to sustain an active movement without an external resource infusion, whether material or ideational. However, organizers and participants likely do not have easy access to these resources. They are separated from potential wealthy donors by distance and time, and their own impoverishment might reduce their ability to share information or act in a concerted fashion. Moreover, interested parties in the North likely lack detailed information about where their resources could best be applied. If Northern actors wish to encourage sustainable practices in the South, they need to have closer contact with the agents of development.

Pursuit of global connections should provide active members of social movements in the global South with a link to sympathetic individuals and NGOs in the North and vice versa. The actors in the resulting coalition can share information, garner attention for their causes, and, most important, gain greater leverage to alter the distributive policies of states and international institutions.

North–South Coalitions

It is much easier to hypothesize about the formation of transnational social-movement connections than it is to document them. Logically, as argued, there is a great incentive for North–South collaboration. It is unclear whether practice matches the theory.

In their review of Third World environmental movements, Taylor and colleagues (1993) find that social-movement survival and likelihood of success already "are greatly enhanced through the strategic building of coalitions" (p. 71). The authors particularly note a number of examples of transnational alliances linking social movements in developing states with environmental activists in affluent countries. These alliances connect activist citizens of troubled impoverished societies to sympathetic counterparts in the more-affluent world. The extent of such partnerships is difficult to document. In a recent annual report, the World Resources Institute (1992, 230) cited a "notable trend" to create "network organizations," sometimes involving hundreds of organizations from dozens of countries. These networks involve both South–South and North–South collaboration and encompass a variety of issue areas, including human rights (Brysk 1993; Sikkink 1993).

Case studies of transnational social-movement activity perhaps best document the extent of these connections, though many of the authors acknowledge that such ties did not exist prior to the 1980s. Bramble and Porter (1992, 348–351), for example, studied NGO attempts to influence policies of Multilateral Development Banks (MDBs) to protect the atmospheric ozone layer and establish the Montreal Protocol, and to slow deforestation and create an International Tropical Timber Organization (ITTO). They conclude that "flexible groupings of NGOs . . . were crucial prerequisites for progress in each of these cases" (p. 348). Regarding the MDB reforms, organizations from developing states actually took a leading role in directing the global campaign, and a strong North–South alliance is seen as critical for any potential ITTO success.

Consider the work of international coalitions to change World Bank lending practices and to halt large development projects, such as the Sardar Sarovar Dam in India (Payne 1995b, 1996). The Narmada Bachoa Andolan coalition within India was critical in the transnational effort to halt construction and reform World Bank procedures, but the local movement could not have reached any of these goals without external support from groups like the U.S. Environmental Defense Fund and the Japanese chapter of Friends of the Earth. In this case, the local and global groups also formed coalitions with human-rights organizations, who were concerned about the displacement of thousands of indigenous peoples. Mutual interests in environment and development were behind the collaborations.

In both these cases the two goals of sustainable development had to be acknowledged. MDBs are a mechanism to transfer resources from North to South, but the transnational movement argued that funded projects are often not environmentally sustainable. International efforts to alter loan standards and processes have resulted in some important policy changes that have been institutionalized in the MDBs. Indeed, significant new monies have been secured explicitly for funding "green" projects through the new global Environmental Facility (Payne 1998). Bramble and Porter (1992, 342–343) point out that the relative failure of efforts to preserve biodiversity in the ITTO has resulted from divergent objectives. Ironically, however, the split is not so much North–South as South–South, since Asian NGOs have sought bans on logging while Latin America NGOs sought new management practices. Their differing goals are apparently a consequence of their societal experiences; many Asian forests have already virtually disappeared.

In sum, connecting with sympathetic and relatively well-heeled groups in affluent societies is a promising means for social-movement organizers in developing states to mobilize resources. In the last decade this strategy has become increasingly prevalent and might now be considered fairly typical for some movements (Taylor et al. 1993, 85)—especially those interested in halting large, centralized development projects funded by MDBs. So far, of course, the question has been skirted as to how these groups connect with one another.

The Role of Technology

Technological change, particularly involving global communications, has played an integral role in the mobilization of resources by social movements in the global South. Some futurists and international-relations theorists have long argued that technology is making the world smaller. For these observers, modern communications and transportation have created a "global village" (McLuhan and Fiore 1968) featuring "complex interdependence" (Keohane and Nye 1989). Put simply, if certain technologies are available to organizers in the South, they can more readily link to sympathetic individuals and groups within the North. As shall be explained, this provides a format for both making original connections and sustaining them. It also means that groups with even very modest material resources can gain maximum benefit from them because of the efficiencies of these technologies and because of their obvious potential for transmitting ideas.

Annis (1991) and others have documented the widespread proliferation of advanced information technologies throughout the developing world. The technologies are increasingly becoming affordable and available, thereby rendering them usable for more and more residents of the South. Especially in Latin America, argues Annis, there are "so many entry points" that these new information technologies "can be described as 'poor accessible'" (p. 94). A high-ranking World Bank official (Rischard 1996, 94) has forecast that within the next two decades telecommunications could become "a virtually free commodity," since costs will be so low. For Rischard the key statistic is not telephones per capita, but rather "how many people live within walking distance of a public phone" (p. 101). The combination of declining costs, full digitalization of information, and new data compression techniques leads Rischard to conclude that "near-universal networks [will] serve the planet some 20 years from now" (p. 96). Movement toward expanded access for the developing world is being fostered by the World Bank, which has, for example, made "Internet connectivity programs for Africa . . . a priority item" (p. 102). Private companies like AT&T and Motorola are also investing in optic cable and satellite technology, respectively, in order to bring the information revolution to the world's poorest areas.

Anyone who has shared the experience of communicating almost instantly with another individual somewhere on the planet can recognize how these technologies might benefit mobilization efforts. First, the technologies can allow for contacts that would not otherwise occur. EcoNet, for instance, literally connects over 10,000 activists and NGOs in over ninety countries around the world (Garcia 1996, 46; WRI 1992, 231). The Internet now permeates over 110 states with literally thousands of systems and countless more users being added each month. The volume of activity on the Internet doubles every five months (Young 1994, 106), and an estimated 40 million (or more) people now use it (Holderness 1996–1997, 40; Browning 1995, 1,337; Penn 1996, 135). In China alone about 4,000 new PCs are sold daily, half outfitted to link with the Internet (Dobson 1998, 20).

As with other computer networks, Econet or Internet can be used to transmit documents instantly and cheaply, or they can serve as forums for live electronic conferences. These virtual meetings can facilitate sharing of information, technical assistance, fundraising ideas, and action alerts. In other words, just about any goal that can be accomplished in face-to-face settings at traditional meetings can be achieved over the global communications network. Of course, in the case of South–South or North–South contacts the computer networks facilitate connections that would likely not otherwise occur face to face.

Clearly, modern information technologies have helped social movements and NGOs in the South mobilize scarce resources and create global ties with influential allies. A fair amount of empirical research now documents these efforts. In broad summary terms, Annis (1991) describes the "web upon web of interpenetrating grassroots groups [forming] new social networks [and empowered by] even newer electronic connections" (p. 106). Rosenau (1997) points out that new microelectronic channels of communication, by providing resources from NGOs in the industrialized world, are "a major reason why hundreds of thousands of environmental NGOs in the developing countries alone have obtained the support necessary to get started and subsequently to flourish" (pp. 332–333).

North–South resource transfer is not the only benefit provided by the new connections. Information moves in both directions and does not stop. Social movements and NGOs in the South are now the originating sources for many new data about development practices, alerting the world about day-to-day practical matters by using their access to modern technologies. If even one grassroots activist has access to modern technology, the world can soon know about his or her development experiences. This is because information can be disseminated to supportive individuals and groups throughout the world in a matter of minutes. Receivers can become senders and provide the additional resources needed to make important information known worldwide. When the Narmada Bachoa Andolan, for instance, faxed updated messages to NGOs in Washington, D.C., recipients created "fax chains" and forwarded the fresh information to interested organizations and activists around the world. Groups also utilized relatively cheap desktop-publishing techniques, photocopying, and mass mailing to disseminate inexpensive newsletters to thousands and even millions of concerned members. They could also "scan" new paper copies into digital form and send the information out through Econet or other electronic networks, where it could be read by thousands of interested persons within just a few days (Browning 1995, 1,338). Information could be used in support of action alerts, fundraising campaigns, or policy debates. In any event, the communication chain often begins with the activists in the South, who become "their own message-makers [and integral parts of] a new global civil society" (Mowlana 1993, 67).

Could all this information have been circulated without the new information technologies? Various scholars (Annis 1991, 99; Hall 1994, 111) have documented cases where the electronic web of global information dispersed important details about development days before the traditional mass media picked up on the stories. Scholars argue that information of this type might have been overlooked by the conventional media had developing-country sources not had access to new communication tools. Hunger strikes in India, marches in Latin America, civil violence in Mexico (Halleck 1994), or protests in any location where someone has an electronic "link" can now attract far more attention and be used quickly and efficiently to secure material resources and ideational support. Acting locally to energize support now truly has global implications for mobilizing.[7]

In sum, new information technologies help overcome resource-mobilization barriers and foster global contacts between activists from the North and South. The new technologies encourage instant and relatively inexpensive communication, which fosters greater equality and participation. In the words of one activist involved in establishing e-mail networks for women's groups throughout Central and Eastern Europe, new information technologies can help dispersed participants "organize for conferences, determine which common problems to resolve, define an efficient strategy and organize workshops" (Penn 1996, 137). Experience from NGO preparation and participation in the Earth Summit seems to confirm this point. The level of NGO involvement in the Rio conference was unprecedented, and networked activists played a significant role in shaping the debates and documents of that meeting (Hall 1994, 119–122).

CONCLUSION: PROSPECTS FOR THE FUTURE

By using transnational connections facilitated extensively by new communications technologies, creators of social movements and NGOs in impoverished societies can mobilize sufficient material and ideational resources to organize and act. They can even gain additional global attention for their causes by providing new information for modern communications resources. As noted, the needs of the poor and the expectations of change in the North are quite high. How much of a difference can even transnational collective action make?

Given the strong obstacles confronted by social movements in the developing world, and the great distance they need to travel, Taylor and colleagues (1993) argue that "it appears naive to anticipate enduring success, or even to hope for the long term survival of the peoples, and the places, at stake in these struggles" (p. 71).[8] The change and cooperation required to achieve genuinely sustainable development would be extraordinary in human history and cannot be overstated.

Empirical studies of transnational social-movement activities are only now being conducted and completed. Those who have studied similar NGO activity, such as Bramble and Porter (1992, 346–347) find that leverage is a key ingredient in success. As is documented in the various studies of MDB campaigns, transnational actors attempted to influence staff members and executive directors of the MDBs, finance officials and legislators in powerful contributing nations, and development officials in project host nations. In the case of the Indian dam, the most important leverage seemed to come from pressure applied by the U.S. Congress on the U.S. executive director of the World Bank. Yet the legislative pressure was fueled by personal testimony of Indian activists.

In addition to leverage, the ability of transnational social movements to provide information will continue to be important. Rucht (1993) notes, for example, that as environmental choices increasingly become centered around expertise rather than moral authority, "the relevance of collecting and distributing information and expertise becomes crucial in environmental policy" (p. 90). Put simply, ideas can be powerfully decisive; therefore, actors providing relevant and timely information can be powerful as well. In the electronic age, assuming some reasonable level of dispersal, even social movements in impoverished societies can mobilize their resources sufficiently to gain notoriety and policy success.[9] Therein lies much of the hope for achieving sustainable development early in the twenty-first century.

NOTES

The author extends his gratitude to David Imbroscio, Marie Kleiner, John McCarthy, and Brett O'Bannon for their thoughtful comments and research guidance, and to Sophie Maier and Jason Renzelmann for research assistance.

1. This is not an appropriate venue to review this literature, but McAdam, McCarthy, and Zald (1988), Tarrow (1994), and Meyer and Tarrow (1998) are good places for the reader to start.

2. India is an important exception, a developing country with a rich tradition of social movements.

3. Some scholars link these research fields by considering the activity of transnational social movements (TSMs) in their work (Dorsey 1993; Tarrow 1994 193–198). Nonetheless, Keck and Sikkink (1998b) explicitly argue that transnational advocacy networks should not be "understood as transnational social movements" (p. 236). They acknowledge that NGO advocacy networks "may contribute eventually to the evolution" (p. 237) of TSMs.

4. Recent work in political science (Lichbach 1994) on the rationality of peasant revolt addresses a similar theoretical problem of collective action by the impoverished.

5. An additional barrier may be domestic political structure. While democracies are permeable to global environmental activism (Payne 1995a), nondemocratic regimes are relatively closed to transnational connections (Payne 1995b). Even fairly Westernized states like Turkey provide only limited access to communications technologies by political foes (Price 1994, 673).

6. According to the WCED (1987), this means "development that meets the needs of the present without compromising the ability of future generations to meet their own needs" (p. 43).

7. Ganley (1992) documents a variety of ways "personal media" have affected mass political behavior.

8. Falk (1987, 364) refers to movements in India and Latin America as notable exceptions.

9. Widespread participation in global debate is a prerequisite for what some scholars call "deliberation." For an application to global environmental politics, see Payne (1996).

REFERENCES

Annis, S. 1991. Giving Voice to the Poor. *Foreign Policy* (84): 93–106.

Bramble, B. J., and G. Porter. 1992. Non-Governmental Organizations and the Making of US International Environmental Policy. In *The International Politics of the Environment*, edited by A. Hurrell and B. Kingsbury. New York: Oxford University Press.

Bronkema, D., D. Lumsdaine, and R. A. Payne. 1998. Foster Just and Sustainable Economic Development. In *Just Peacemaking: Ten Practices for Abolishing War*, edited by G. Stassen. Cleveland: Pilgrim.

Browning, G. 1995. Net Effects. *National Journal* 27: 1336–1340.

Brysk, A. 1993. From Above and Below, Social Movements, the International System, and Human Rights in Argentina. *Comparative Political Studies* 26: 259–285.

Conca, K. 1993. Environmental Change and the Deep Structure of World Politics. In *The State and Social Power in Global Environmental Politics*, edited by R. D. Lipschutz and K. Conca. New York: Columbia University Press.

Dobson, W. J. 1998. Protest.Org. *The New Republic* 219 (1): 18–21.

Dorsey, E. 1993. Expanding the Foreign Policy Discourse, Transnational Social Movements and the Globalization of Citizenship. In *The Limits of State Autonomy, Societal Groups and Foreign Policy Formulation*, edited by D. Skidmore and V. M. Hudson. Boulder, Colo.: Westview.

Falk, R. A. 1987. The Global Promise of Social Movements: Explorations at the Edge of Time. In *Towards a Just World Peace: Perspectives from Social Movements*, edited by S. H. Mendlovitz and R.B.J. Walker. Boston: Butterworths.

Ganley, G. D. 1992. *The Exploding Political Power of Personal Media*. Norwood, N.J.: Ablex.

Garcia, D. L. 1996. Global Communications: Opportunities for Trade and Aid. *SAIS Review* 16 (1): 35–66.

Hall, B. W. 1994. Information Technology and Global Learning for Sustainable Development: Promise and Problems. *Alternatives* 19 (1): 99–132.

Halleck, D. 1994. Zapatistas On-Line. *NACLA Report on the Americas* 28 (2): 30–32.

Holderness, M. 1996–1997. The Internet and the South. *Earth Island Journal* 12 (1): 40–42.

Homer-Dixon, T. F. 1991. On the Threshold: Environmental Changes as Causes of Acute Conflict. *International Security* 16 (2): 76–116.

Keck, M., and K. Sikkink. 1998a. *Activists Beyond Borders, Advocacy Networks in International Politics*. Ithaca, N.Y.: Cornell University Press.

———. 1998b. Transnational Advocacy Networks in the Movement Society. In *The Social Movement Society: Contentious Politics for a New Century*, edited by D. S. Meyer and S. Tarrow. New York: Rowman and Littlefield.

Kennedy, P. 1993. *Preparing for the Twenty-First Century*. New York: Vintage.

Keohane, R. O., and J. S. Nye. 1989. *Power and Interdependence*. 2d ed. Boston: Scott, Foresman and Company.

Kitschelt, H. P. 1986. Political Opportunity Structure and Political Protest: Anti-Nuclear Movements in Four Democracies. *British Journal of Political Science* 16: 57–85.

Kriesi, H., R. Koopmans, J. W. Duyvendak, and M. G. Giugni. 1992. New Social Movements and Political Opportunities in Western Europe. *European Journal of Political Research* 22: 219–244.

Lichbach, M. I. 1994. What Makes Rational Peasants Revolutionary? Dilemma, Paradox, and Irony in Peasant Collective Action. *World Politics* 46: 383–418.

Lipschutz, R. D. (with J. Mayer). 1996. *Global Civil Society and Global Environmental Governance: The Politics of Nature from Place to Planet*. Albany: State University of New York Press.

Mathews, J. T. 1989. Redefining Security. *Foreign Affairs* 68: 162–177.

McAdam, D., J. D. McCarthy, and M. N. Zald. 1988. Social Movements. In *Handbook of Sociology*, edited by N. Smelser. Newbury Park, Calif.: Sage.

McLuhan, M., and Q. Fiore. 1968. *War and Peace in the Global Village*. New York: Bantam.

Meyer, D. S., and S. Tarrow. 1998. A Movement Society: Contentious Politics for a New Century. In *The Social Movement Society: Contentious Politics for a New Century*, edited by D. S. Meyer and S. Tarrow. New York: Rowman and Littlefield.

Monahan, L. F. 1996. Third World Finds Internet Can Open Doors to Better Life. *Louisville Courier Journal*, 29 December, E5.

Mowlana, H. 1993. Toward a NWICO for the Twenty-First Century? *Journal of International Affairs* 47: 59–72.

Nye, J. S., Jr., and R. O. Keohane. 1972. Transnational Relations and World Politics: An Introduction. In *Transnational Relations and World Politics*, edited by R. O. Keohane and J. S. Nye, Jr. Cambridge: Harvard University Press.

Olson, M. 1965. *The Logic of Collective Action*. Cambridge: Harvard University Press.

Payne, R. A. 1995a. Freedom and the Environment. *Journal of Democracy* 6 (3): 41–55.

———. 1995b. Non-Profit Environmental Organizations in World Politics; Domestic Political Structure and Transnational Relations. *Policy Studies Review* 14: 171–182.

———. 1996. Deliberating Global Environmental Politics. *Journal of Peace Research* 33: 129–136.

———. 1998. The Limits and Promise of Environmental Conflict Prevention: The Case of the GEF. *Journal of Peace Research* 35: 363–380.

Penn, S. 1996. Women's Movements On-Line: The New Post-Socialist Revolution. *SAIS Review* 16: 125–143.

Price, M. E. 1994. The Market for Loyalties: Electronic Media and the Global Competition for Allegiances. *Yale Law Journal* 104: 667–705.

Rischard, J.-F. 1996. Connecting Developing Countries to the Information Technology Revolution. *SAIS Review* 16: 93–107.

Rosenau, J. N. 1997. *Along the Domestic–Foreign Frontier: Exploring Governance in a Turbulent World*. New York: Cambridge University Press.

Rucht, D. 1993. "Think Globally, Act Locally"? Needs, Forms and Problems of Cross-National Cooperation Among Environmental Groups. In *European Integration and Environmental Policy*, edited by J. D. Liefferink, P. D. Lowe, and A.P.J. Mol. New York: Belhaven.

Sikkink, K. 1993. Human Rights, Principled Issue-Networks, and Sovereignty in Latin America. *International Organization* 47: 411–441.

South Commission. 1990. *The Challenge to the South*. New York: Oxford University Press.

Tarrow, S. 1994. *Power in Movement: Social Movements, Collective Action and Politics*. Cambridge: Cambridge University Press.

Taylor, B., H. Hadsell, L. Lorentzen, and R. Scarce. 1993. Grass-Roots Resistance: The Emergence of Popular Environmental Movements in Less Affluent Countries. In *Environmental Movements in the International Arena*, edited by S. Kamieniecki. Albany: State University of New York Press.

United Nations Development Program (UNDP). 1997. *Human Development Report 1997*. New York: Oxford University Press.

Wapner, P. 1996. *Environmental Activism and World Civic Politics*. Albany: State University of New York Press.

Weiss, T. G., and L. Gordenker, eds. 1996. *NGOs, the UN, and Global Governance*. Boulder, Colo.: Lynne Rienner.

Willetts, P., ed. 1996. *"The Conscience of the World": The Influence of Non-Governmental Organizations in the UN System*. Washington, D.C.: The Brookings Institution.

World Commission on Environment and Development (WCED). 1987. *Our Common Future*. New York: Oxford University Press.

World Resources Institute (WRI) (in collaboration with United Nations Environmental Program and United Nations Development Program). 1992. *World Resources 1992–93*. New York: Oxford University Press.

Young, J. E. 1993. *Global Network: Computers in a Sustainable Society*. Paper #115. Washington, D.C.: Worldwatch Institute.

———. 1994. Using Computers for the Environment. In *State of the World 1994*, edited by L. Brown. New York: W. W. Norton.

————————————12

Global Information Infrastructure in the Eastern and Southeastern Asian Countries: Emerging Regulatory Implications and Models

Chung-Chuan Yang

The vision of the future global information infrastructure (GII) was first brought up by U.S. Vice President Al Gore in March 1994 at the first World Telecommunication Development Conference at Kyoto, Japan. Later, in his keynote address to the 1995 G-7 Conference, Gore clearly defined that the purposes of global communication are "about protecting and enlarging freedom of expression for all our citizens and giving individual citizens the power to create the information they need and want from the abundant flow of data they encounter moment to moment" (*The Global Information Infrastructure: Agenda for Cooperation* 1994).

The construction of the GII is aimed to achieve the following objectives:

1. Encouraging private-sector investment.
2. Promoting competition.
3. Providing open access to the network for all information providers and users.
4. Creating a flexible regulatory environment that can keep pace with rapid technological and market changes.
5. Ensuring universal service.

Leaders from the world telecommunications community have incorporated these five principles into the International Telecommunications Union's *Buenos Aires*

Declaration on Global Telecommunication Development for the 21st Century (*The Global Information Infrastructure: Agenda for Cooperation* 1994).

Despite all these acclaimed benefits and lofty objectives that the GII is predicted to bring, an emerging but rarely discussed issue is what kinds of cultural, political, and social impacts a global communication network will have for less-developed and developing countries in East and Southeast Asia. This chapter examines regulatory implications and emerging regulatory models that the global information superhighway has brought to countries in East and Southeast Asia.

THE INTERNET PHENOMENON IN EAST AND SOUTHEAST ASIA

Deriving directly from the Internet as a worldwide network, the GII is an open, self-organizing, interactive, and interconnected system that gives its users a dynamic and democratic means for sharing information and ideas (*Communication Study: Biannual Report* 1995). The GII is conceptualized as the following models: (1) a high-performance computer network that will facilitate high-speed data access and retrieval; (2) a multimedia network for which the primary use will be conveying video data streams in conjunction with data, text, and voice; or (3) a medium for interactive television and videophone (Jipguep 1995). The GII will also be made up of local, national, and regional networks that will facilitate the global sharing of information, interconnection, and communication, creating a global information marketplace.

The Internet is the prototype of the GII of the future. The Internet is now functioning as a nascent GII and can be viewed as a rudimentary predecessor of a global GII. A superior GII will exist when higher capacity, full interactivity, higher speed, and more versatility are incorporated into the existing communication networks. As the GII is only a vision, the Internet is the closest thing to a global network at this moment. Therefore, this chapter will use the GII and the Internet interchangeably in the following discussions.

According to Cerf (1995), the Internet now encompasses an estimated 50,000 networks worldwide. An estimated 20 to 40 million people in ninety countries are involved with the Internet (December 1996). Williamson (1996) reported the number of Internet hosts by the end of the century will reach 100 million. The Internet tidal wave has also swept over most parts of Asia. Many countries in East and Southeast Asia began to offer direct access to the Internet as early as 1990.

Current development of the Internet in this region can be generalized into the following trends.

Shifting from Government-Controlled to Commercially Operated Internet Access

Most countries in this region have gradually deregulated their telecom markets. As a result, more and more telecommunications service providers are allowed to provide Internet access services to their subscribers.

In the more liberalized markets, such as Singapore, most of the Internet access services are already provided by commercial information service providers. Over twenty information service providers are now offering Internet connections. In Hong Kong there are over forty Internet service providers and 40,000 users (Asian Communications 1996c).

Countries where telecommunications deregulation has just begun are taking the heat from fiercer competition in the marketplace. In Taiwan access to the Internet was originally provided solely by three government network operators: TANet, SEEDNET, and HINET. In recent years new access providers are offering low-cost alternatives to interested Internet users. These include WOWNET, GlobalNET Communications Services, Golden Gate Technology, and TranSend Internet Company. In Indonesia the first commercial on-line information service, Indonesia Online Access (Idola), began service in 1995 and is now offering Internet access to thirteen cities. Also operating are four new commercial Internet service providers: Rahajasa Media Internet (RADnet), Visionindo Network Perdana, Prominodo Global Internet, and Sistelindo Mitralintas (Asian Communications 1996c).

Even in countries where governments still have monopolies over their telecommunications markets, lesser control is exerted over the Internet service market. In China the first commercial on-line service provider, ChinaNet, now has over 4,000 subscribers in Beijing and Shanghai and the service will be expanded to over thirty cities (Asian Communications 1996a). Japan has the largest network in Asia. Around 100 Internet service providers offer services to 5 million Japanese subscribers (Asian Communications 1996c).

Rapid Growth of the Internet Population

Across Asia the number of Internet host computers rocketed to 62 percent of the total number of host computers in Asia in the first seven months of 1994 (Internet Developments Around the Asian Region 1995). As of July 1995 the number of computer hosts in East and Southeast Asia has reached 164,437 (Asian Communications 1996a). The Four Tigers also enjoyed a rapid increase in the number of host computers connected to the Internet. At end of the same period South Korea had 12,109 host computers, Taiwan had 10,314, Hong Kong had 9,141, and Singapore had 4,014. In the newly industrialized nations in this region (such as Thailand and Malaysia), the increase rate also reached three digits (see Table 12.1).

In the Four Tigers countries, where economic and technological developments have been booming in the past decades, Internet penetration is very high. Among Singapore's 3 million people, 100,000 already have Internet accounts. According to the National Computer Board, 5 to 10 percent of Singaporeans regularly use the Internet (McCullagh 1996d). By the end of the century the Singapore government hopes to reach its goal of transforming this island state into an "intelligent island," with at least 95 percent of homes cabled for services like the Internet and interactive television (Asia and the

Table 12.1
The Growth of the Internet in Asian Countries as of July 31, 1994

Country	Number of Internet Host Computers	Change since January 1, 1994	Percentage of Total Worldwide Hosts
Japan	72,409	+69%	2.000%
South Korea	12,109	+35%	0.400%
Taiwan	10,314	+29%	0.300%
Hong Kong	9,141	+60%	0.300%
Singapore	4,014	+45%	0.100%
Malaysia	1,322	+204%	0.040%
Thailand	1,197	+334%	0.040%
China	325	N/A	0.010%
Philippines	65	N/A	0.002%
Indonesia	54	N/A	0.002%
Asian Total	110,950	+62%	3.400%
U.S. Total	2,044,401	+38%	63.000%

Source: Adapted from "Tapping the Business Potential of Internet in Asia." *Asian Wall Street Journal*, 18 November 1994, 45, and Internet Society, "Internet Global Backbone Connectivity," 1996, at <ftp://ftp.isoc.org/isoc/charts2/connectivity/country.gif>.

Internet 1996). In Korea there are an estimated 200,000 to 300,000 subscribers to Internet access services (see Table 12.2).

In newly industrialized countries in Asia the Internet has also become very popular in recent years. Malaysia's state-owned Internet service provider, Jaring, has nearly quadrupled the number of its subscribers in 1994. In just under four years subscription to Jaring has grown to some 30,000 users at a monthly rate of 20 percent (Rao 1996c). In Thailand 50,000 subscribers had access to the Internet by the end of 1996 (Asian Communications 1996c).

Dynamics Between Local Telecoms Deregulation and the Internet Boom

Due to the capital- and technology-intensive nature of network construction and management, less-developed nations in this region have depended heavily on the Western countries. In China the Post and Telecommunications Administration of Shanghai cooperated with the U.S.–based AsiaInfo Group to build its first large-scale commercial on-line information service in China, Shanghai On-line. The first phase was completed in July 1996 (Asian Communications 1996b).

With increasing dependence on foreign capital and technologies, as well as gradual integration into the world economy, the pressure to deregulate telecoms

Table 12.2
East and Southeast Asia Computer Host
Distribution by Top-Level Domain Name as
of July 1995

Country	Domain	Hosts
Taiwan	.tw	16,166
Singapore	.sg	8,208
Thailand	.th	2,481
Malaysia	.my	1,087
China	.cn	1,023
Indonesia	.id	848
Japan	.jp	159,776
South Korea	.kr	23,791
Total		164,437

Source: Adapted from "The Internet Impacts," 1996d,
Asian Communications 18 (3): 32.

market in these countries has become increasingly insurmountable. Often, the Internet service is categorized and included in the services for the early phase of privatization. Consequently, competition in the marketplace lowers the price of the service and contributes to a further boom of the Internet population.

For example, the Internet began to boom after the passage of the Public Telecommunications Act in the Philippines, which deregulated its computer-networking market. Since then the number of Internet access providers and users has grown dramatically. There are about 20,000 Internet users and over thirty Internet service providers in the Philippines. In Korea, nine Internet service providers, including KSC Comnet and Loxley Information, were granted licenses by the Ministry of Information and Communication (MIC) to provide Internet access. By the end of 1996, 50,000 subscribers had access to the Internet. In Taiwan the deregulation of the advanced value-added tele-communications service market has triggered a wave of new private Internet service providers in the market. In Indonesia, MIMIOS, which runs state-operated Jaring, was privatized in 1996. Information service providers, such as AsiaConnect and the Network Connection (TNC), began providing Internet access (Asian Communications 1996c).

Integration of the Internet into National Development Plans

Many countries in this region have realized the importance of the information superhighway in a growing converged information-based world. The role of information in an information-based service economy is also acknowledged.

As a result, many countries have followed the United States in building their version of a national information infrastructure (NII). Nations such as Singapore, Japan, Taiwan, and China have aggressively stipulated national development plans to be ahead of other nations in this region. According to *The Economist*, Asian governments are estimated to invest over $363.2 billion on telecommunications projects in the next several years (Asia and the Internet 1996).

China also plans to offer two Internet gateways and will link as many as 25,000 computers to the Internet in the future. China plans to link over 1,000 universities and over 200,000 primary and secondary schools (Kinoshita 1995). In addition, universities in China engaged Sprint in 1994 to provide gateways, initially in Beijing and Shanghai, but later to more than twenty cities (Internet Developments Around the Asian Region 1995). Taiwan's NII plan will cost US$50 billion of government money, investment incentives, and private-sector funds. Taiwan's government has been actively promoting the use of the NII and computer literacy programs. The special NII task force is also undertaking aggressive promotion to increase the Internet population to 3 million by the year 2000. Government-supported activities such as e-mail to elementary and junior high schools, public kiosks, and promotions (such as TV campaigns, conferences, and free workshops) have been implemented in the past years.

ISSUES RELATED TO A GLOBAL COMMUNICATIONS NETWORK

The availability of a global communications network is perceived as critical for expediting the realization of cultural, social, and economic benefits as well as for enhancing nations' competitive advantages. As a result, many countries in this region included a modern high-speed communications infrastructure to leap-frog to the next century. However, the borderless nature of a global communications network will open these countries to massive information flow over the Internet. More and more nations in this region as well as in Western countries have discovered that information sent over the Internet can be every bit as threatening to a country's laws or culture as the armies of the past. As the information flow between nations becomes a trend, it will create tremendous social, cultural, and political impacts on nations connected to the GII. These issues include an increasing information gap among networked and nonnetworked nations, copyrights, privacy, censorship, intellectual property rights, tariffs, data protection, criminal liability, human rights, the distinction between trade in goods and services, and so forth. Consequently, economic benefits will certainly accompany ensuing political, cultural, and social upheavals.

This scenario was envisioned by Herbert Schiller (1981) long before the Internet become as popular as it has become nowadays. Schiller warned "a combination of modern communication technologies have been developed, installed, and are operating, which ignore and bypass national decision making" (p. 112). With the development of the global communications network, geographic barriers will not impede how information will be distributed. Furthermore, the globalization of computer networks has raised new questions of whether the network will increase centralization of cultural, economic, political and social forces to reconfigure new developments in these dimensions (Harasim 1993).

The decentralized architecture of the Internet also conceals the democratic value of Western societies. Despite the trend of democratization in this region, many countries are still ruled by political leaders who either totally reject the idea of democracy or prefer a democracy with the "Occidental values." With the proliferation of the Internet, not only massive Western-produced information (over 70% from the United States), but also the values embodied in the information and the technology will flow into countries in East and Southeastern Asia. Singapore's minister of information warned that "the influx of objectionable materials via the new electronic media, if left unchecked, will undermine our values and traditions" (Asia and the Internet 1996).

However, many Asian governments are now confronting an old dilemma in a new form. All governments have set their goal to become so-called modern countries. But many reject the notion that modernity encompasses the sort of political pluralism seen in the West. In cyberspace modernity and pluralism go hand in hand. Since most Internet content remains dominated by Westerners, the Internet can be seen as part of such an attempt. As a result, we see the recent flurry of efforts by governments in the region to exert control over the Internet and overturn what they see as the American colonization of cyberspace.

H. A. Innis, one of the seminal thinkers on communications, proposed in *Bias of Communications* that civilizations are characterized by preoccupation with either time or space and this focus on one or the other reflects the dominant medium. Innis contrasted the long lasting but difficult-to-transport clay tablets of the Babylonians with the shorter-lived but readily portable papyrus of Egyptian and Greek civilizations. The Internet and the evolving global communication network are probably the first media to dominate both space and time. This new capability of universally sharing historical memory and current knowledge will be the factor which qualitatively distinguishes the civilization of the GII from preceding ones (Jipguep 1995).

Given the pattern of Internet adoption, the situation of unequal distribution can be worsened. Despite the exponential growth of the Internet, 97 percent of 27 million Internet users are in the high-income countries, which only account for 15 percent of the world's population. Tarjanne (1996) found that the distribution of Internet access is less equitable than that of telephones or television. Although there has been an amazing increase in Asian Internet users, computers in this region account for less than 4 percent of computers worldwide with access to the Internet (Tapping the Business 1994). Even in

Europe the penetration of domestic PCs will rise from 8 percent of households today to 50 percent by the year 2000 (Williamson 1996).

The globalization of computer network has raised new questions on whether the network will increase centralization of cultural, economic, political, and social forces to reconfigure new developments in these dimensions (Harasim 1993). Worrying about the massive influx of "culturally and politically offensive materials," China has implemented regulations to prevent "spiritual pollution" from entering the country (Cortese, Cary, and Woodruff 1996). However, Nicholas Negroponte from MIT's Media Lab argued that it is simply absurd to suggest that the Internet is another form of Americanization and a threat to local culture. More than 50 percent of Internet users today are outside the United States; by the end of the decade fewer than 20 percent of users will be in the United States. Thanks to the relatively low cost of tools like the Web, the Internet will actually restore cultural identities (Rao 1996c). Kumon and Aizu (1993) echoed that economic and cultural forces may preserve some of their diversity and uniqueness while participating in and contributing to a global network. Walls (1993) states that global communication can help facilitate global networking for local development.

Despite many issues that may arise from the introduction of a global communication network, what is showing the greatest effect at this moment is the massive communications flow through the Net. Transborder communications flow, defined by Branscomb (1986) as the cross-the-border movement of data from which information and knowledge will be derived, has become a daily event for most Internet users around the world. As the number of Internet users increases, so will the importance of transborder communications flow.

The effect of transborder communications flow on nations in this region comes partly from the network infrastructures among traditional nation-states. These countries are more and more interconnected, either by means of the physical connection of undersea cables, the invisible connection of satellites and discs, or the international political and economic relations. Physical borders of nations are no longer insurmountable as jurisdictional limits as soon as domestic communications networks are connected to the Internet. In the past government could exercise its control over the flow of information by "guarding" its borders. However, with the arrival of digital and encrypted transmission of information through the Internet, the control over the export and import of information is nearly impossible. Nicholas Negroponte once said that "the Internet is not something that can be regulated. It is not a controllable phenomenon" (quoted in Mikkelsen 1996). Gilmore also pointed out that "the Net interprets censorship as damage and routes around it" (quoted in Barlow 1996, 76).

Some have claimed that new measures to secure the free flow of information over the Internet can be seen as a new wave of Western imperialism. "Neo-colonialism," though deemed a politicization of the issue by some Western nations, reflects a fundamental problem in the process of stipulating international laws to regulate the Internet. In the past the bickering over regulating direct satellite broadcasting circled around disagreements over national uniqueness in law-making procedures and different readings of the concepts regarding the issues of freedom of expression (as stipulated in Article 19 of the Universal Declaration of Human Rights), cultural imperialism (television programs or movies from the United States), and national sovereignty.

DISCUSSION

Regulating the Internet in East and Southeast Asia

Many Asian countries have developed various forms of regulation to control Internet access and use. Due to poor infrastructure, usage by elites, the international political economy, and pressure from telecom deregulation, these restrictions are minimal. However, scholars (McGurn 1995; Arnold 1996) have argued that regulatory control of the Internet is almost impossible at this stage of technological developments. McGurn had said, "The Net may be changing the whole debate from whether government *ought* to control the Net to whether they *can*" (p. 72).

From a regulatory perspective the issue of whether the content of the Internet should be controlled stems from a growing sentiment that the traditional separation of responsibility for conduits (i.e., Internet access providers) and contents (information providers) is no longer appropriate on a wired globe. Traditional regulatory methods, though still applied nowadays by most nations, will have little or no effect under a modern converging telecommunications environment. As Branscomb (1993) pointed out, "Established laws governing communications transport apply specifically to mail, telephones, newspapers, cable, and radio and television broadcasting. In an electronic bits stream it may be impossible to distinguish into which of these legal categories they fall. Indeed, there may be categories of services such as computer bulletin boards or computer conferences that do not resemble any of the established legal regimes" (p. 95).

Emerging Models of Internet Regulations

Current debates over regulatory control of the Internet in South and Southeastern Asia originate from two sources: the Western threat to the morals and values of these Asian countries and the desire to prevent antigovernment, antisociety, or antireligion speeches. In Malaysia those making libelous and disparaging remarks about the country via the Internet will be penalized under new regulations being studied by the government. Information Minister Datuk Mohamed Rahmat said such action would be taken based on reports by a proposed regulatory body to be set up to monitor Internet usage here (Asia and the Internet 1996). Vietnam and China also worry that antigovernment rhetoric can be funneled into their countries by dissidents overseas through the Internet (Schwarz 1995).

Content-Based Model

In terms of content control the governments' control over information dissemination by limiting the transborder movement of persons, books, films, or radio and television programs has had little effect. Currently, the regulation of content over the Internet is practiced, but in a very obscure way. Only China and Singapore are now implementing formal processes of registration to regulate what contents should be accessed and by whom (Rao 1996a, 1996b). However, difficulties with such a mode of regulation abound, as the content is transmitted in digital as well as encrypted or compressed forms, and governments cannot easily censor information by its classification and categorization and by granting permission for certain kinds of information to circulate nationally or internationally.

Some countries have tried to extend their laws to cover content-controlled issues in cyberspace. For example, in South Korea access to North Korean information on David Burgess's World Wide Web site is deemed illegal. The Korean government invoked Chapter 2, Article 7, of the National Security Law, which bans the admiration of antistate groups and forbids unauthorized contacts with North Korea. It has ordered fourteen local computer networks with Internet links to block public access to this site (McCullagh 1996b).

Others have tried to limit the services available on the Internet. For instance, in Vietnam, under the directive issued by the general directorate of posts and telecommunications, subscribers will only be allowed access via companies that restrict information in accordance with state regulations. The rules make Internet users legally responsible for any information they provide or receive (Lappin 1996).

In some cases governments have required that Internet service providers take the responsibility of controlling undesirable materials via the Internet. In the Philippines the special committee for children has issued a memorandum requesting all registered value-added service providers to bar or block entry of pornographic materials through the Internet. The committee has raised the concern of the Internet being used as a very convenient medium for advertising sex tourism in the Philippines. The special committee for children aims to ensure the special protection of children from all forms of neglect, abuse, cruelty, exploitation, discrimination, and other conditions prejudicial to their development.

Conduit-Based Model

Because of the monopoly of the telecommunications industries and facilities in most Eastern and Southeastern Asian countries, governments in this region have tried to exert control over transmission channels or conduits. The most common method of regulating access is to restrict the number of Internet service providers intentionally. Not until early 1995 did China allow any commercial Internet service operators. In China Internet users are required to register with local computer security and supervision departments in an effort "to ban transmission of state secrets, information harmful to state security, and pornography" (Net Users Told to Register 1996, 8). Furthermore, the construction of the national fiber-optic automatic surveillance network has been going smoothly. The three surveillance stations located from Beijing to Tianjin are operating normally. It is estimated that the construction of another twenty-three surveillance stations will be completed soon. The construction of the national fiber-optic automatic surveillance network, with 500 surveillance stations, will be completed within three years (McCullagh 1996a).

Vietnam's directorate general of post and telecommunications has reportedly issued a "temporary regulation" allowing Vietnamese enterprises to apply for licenses to provide Internet connections and services. But the temporary regulation only allows for Internet services to be provided on a "trial basis" due to concerns about national security and cultural purity. In the meantime the government seeks to acquire the ability "to manage and control the network" and to filter out pornography and "other taboo subjects" (Rao 1996c).

Singapore's government has already decided to regulate Internet service providers as traditional broadcasting entities and impose numerous regulatory burdens and content controls on ISPs. Legislation will be written to make sure all Internet providers are licensed under the Singapore Broadcasting Authority (SBA). Under the regulations those who run Internet home pages discussing politics or religion will have to register with the SBA in addition to coming under a blanket license. Network content regulations will soon be published to ban providers in Singapore from offering materials considered offensive to the culture. ISPs will be also required to block international URLs that lead to sites that contain such offensive information (McCullagh 1996c). Since the start of Internet use in Singapore the government has blocked some traffic by ordering access services not to connect to some sites, including those with "alt.sex" in the address (McCullagh 1996b). Violations will result in licenses being revoked. Furthermore, about ten SBA officials will surf the Net daily for objectionable materials (Rao 1996b).

In Taiwan restriction and penalty have been set for the government-operated TANet to control improper uses of the network. Violators will be suspended from using the network. Libel laws have been applied to distribution of damaging comments through the bulletin boards (BBS). Legal responsibilities are given to BBS system operators and Internet service providers. Commercial ISPs are not regulated at this moment.

CONCLUSION

In spite of the good intentions of governments to deter the flow of undesirable information, the regulatory actions taken by individual governments in this region can have lasting legal and economic ramifications. As Branscomb

(1993) argued, in an interdependent global economy the ability to access data stored in computers is critical to the normal operations of this type of economy. Although telecommunications systems and laws are national in scope and operation, it is essential that governments come together to reach a consensus and sign a treaty that can solve the difficulties in Internet regulations.

Current regulatory models applied in this region create rather than solve problems generated from the transborder communication flow via the Internet. Imposition of broadcastlike regulations on the Internet would be a fundamental impediment to the free flow of information on-line. Regulations that may have been appropriate and easily applied in the broadcast context simply make no sense when applied to the Internet. Moreover, extension of broadcast regulations gives governments a great degree of censorship authority over Internet content (McCullagh 1996c).

As the global thrust of global communications networks is to serve people, not nations, it is necessary that new international regulatory models are figured out to take advantage of these communications tools. The author thus recommends the following policy directions.

Redefined Role of the Government

The various approaches governments have taken in response to the technological convergence of the telecommunications and information industries have resulted in the development of asymmetric markets and regulatory environments around the world (Noam and Pogorel 1994). Governments should create flexible regulatory environments through regulatory and/or legislative reform to establish procompetitive, technology-neutral regulatory environments in order to maximize consumer choice, provide fair access to networks, and stimulate infrastructure development, the introduction of new services, and the wider dissemination of information. Specifically, independent national regulatory authorities for telecommunications should be created to promote the interests of consumers and ensure effective and efficient competition. Such authorities should have sufficient powers to carry out their missions and should operate with transparent decision-making processes as crucial elements of the GII.

Enhanced Role of International Organizations

Cable and Distler (Global Regulator Needed for Information Highway 1995) said, in a report published by the Royal Institute of International Telecommunications Policy, that the growth of telecommunications is outstripping the ability of national authorities to coordinate a suitable international regulatory regime. A "global regulator" is needed to open up closed markets and establish compatibility between different national and regional systems of regulations. From their view, the global regulator can be included within the structure of the new World Trade Organization (WTO).

Other multilateral organizations can play a vital role in this effort. These include the International Telecommunications Union, the Organization for Economic Cooperation and Development (OECD), the International Organization for Standardization (ISO), and the World Intellectual Property Organization.

Regional organizations also have important roles in achieving regional consensus on issues pertaining to telecommunications and information markets. Organizations such as the Inter-American Telecommunication Commission (CITEL) of the Organization of American States (OAS), the Asia Pacific Economic Cooperation (APEC), the Association of South East Asian Nations (ASEAN), the Southern Africa Transportation and Communications Commission (SATCC), and the European Conference on Postal and Telecommunications Administration (CEPT). These bodies can also serve as effective vehicles for improving and enhancing network development and technical cooperation among participants on a regional basis.

International Cooperation on Internet Regulation

The global nature of the Internet requires nations around the world to cooperate closely with each other. Internet regulations, unlike those for traditional media, cannot be regulated within a national context. Consequently, only international laws can have regulatory power over international actors. However, whether an international Internet regulatory regime can succeed will depend on many factors.

First, the fundamental weakness of international regulatory collaboration over the Internet is its lack of enforceability due to conflicts over different cultural and political values among individual nations. As the Internet is mostly viewed as a Western technology, caution and disagreement among the Eastern and Southeastern Asian countries will undoubtedly be strong, as these nations were invaded or ruled by the West in the nineteenth and twentieth centuries.

Second, as actors in the international arena differ in their patterns of economy, socioeconomic ideology, and structure of society, international Internet regulation is, in practice or in concept, a compromise all the participating nations must reach. If not, ideological and societal differences, combined with differences in legal traditions, will hamper the proper functioning of international law, especially as the line between domestic and international regulation is obscured by the introduction of the Internet.

Third, legal traditions of different nations will affect how the Internet will be regulated. Despite the fact that international law was historically developed from the Western legal tradition, the differences among civil law, common law, and Nordic law systems in the Western nations constitute a discrepancy, "not only [in] the substantive provisions of law but also [in] the approach to the law-making process" (Ploman 1982, 164). The controversy about the formulation of laws before or after the action is likely to be carried over to the negotiation table among nation-states in dealing with regulating the Internet.

In conclusion, the establishment of a global communications network only increases the importance of transborder communications flow. The recognition of this significance will require increasing coordination between nations as the capital- and technology-intensive nature of this global communications network grows. The enhancement of this capacity will be on the agenda of national policy around the world.

The Internet today is characterized by these characteristics (Jipguep 1995):

1. Freedom to connect.
2. Freedom to disseminate information and ideas.
3. Freedom to extend and develop the network.
4. Freedom for entrepreneurial opportunities.
5. Freedom to initiate new services and new ways of doing business.
6. Freedom for educating and for learning.

These freedoms may alleviate some of the worries about the Western colonization of cyberspace.

The difficulties that the global communications network has encountered can be overcome, in part through the work of market forces and technological developments, but also in part through collective agreement among all countries to adopt, advance, and apply the core principles of the global communications infrastructure.

REFERENCES

Arnold, W. 1996. Asia's Internet Censorship Will Be Easy to Circumvent. *Wall Street Journal Interactive Edition.* September. <http://www.wsj.com>.

Asia and the Internet: Not Too Modern, Please. 1996. *The Economist*, 16 March, 42–43.

Asian Communications. 1996a. *China/Internet*, March, News in brief section, 7.

Asian Communications. 1996b. *China/Internet*, June, News in brief section, 7.

Asian Communications. 1996c. *The Internet Impacts*, March, 28–32.

Barlow, J. P. 1996. Thinking Locally, Acting Globally. *Time*, 5 January, 147.

Branscomb, A. W. 1993. Jurisdictional Quandaries for Global Networks. In *Global Networks: Computers and International Communication*, edited by L. M. Harasim. Cambridge: MIT Press.

———., ed. 1986. *Toward a Law of Global Communication Network*. New York: Longman.

Cerf, V. G. 1995. *Computer Networking: Global Infrastructure for the 21st Century*. <http://crg.org/research/impact>.

Cortese, A., J. Cary, and D. Woodruff. 1996. Alt.sex Bondage Is Closed. Should We Be Scared? *Business Week*, 15 January, 39.

Communication Study: Biannual Report. 1995. London: Ablex, Guilford, and LEA Publishing.

December, J. 1996. Units of Analysis for Internet Communication. *Journal of Communication* 46: 14–38.

Global Regulator Needed for Information Highway. 1995. *The Financial Times*, 29 November, 6.

Harasim, L. M. 1993. Global Networks: An Introduction. In *Global Networks: Computer and International Communication*, edited by L. M. Harasim. Cambridge: MIT Press.

Innis, H. 1965. *The Bias of Communication.* Toronto: University of Toronto Press.

Internet Developments Around the Asian Region. 1995. *International Herald Tribune*, 8 March, 5.

Jipguep, J. 1995. *The Global Telecommunication Infrastructure and the Information Society.* <http://www.itu.ch/INET95/inet95.paper.html>.

Kinoshita, J. 1995. Scientists Hope Competition Will Improve Internet Access. *Science*, 17 November, 1141.

Kumon, S., and I. Aizu. 1993. Co-Emulation: The Case for a Global Hypernetwork Society. In *Global Networks: Computers and International Communication*, edited by L. M. Harasim. Cambridge: MIT Press.

Lappin, T. 1996. *Vietnam Announces Internet Controls.* 6 June. <http://fight-censorship.dementia.org/top/>.

McCullagh, D. B. 1996a. *China's Surveillance Network Under Construction.* 18 June. <http://fight-censorship.dementia.org/top/>.

———. 1996b. *Re: Seoul Battles Pyongyang in Cyberspace.* 16 June. <http://fight-censorship.dementia.org/top/>.

———. 1996c. *Singapore About to Block "Offensive" URLs, Reports Dave Farber.* 19 June. <http://fight-censorship.dementia.org/top/>.

———. 1996d. *Re: Singapore Leader Condemns Net as Porn, Bomb-Building Haven.* 10 March. <http://fightcensorship.dementia.org/top/>.

McGurn, W. 1995. Wired Singapore: Island State Finds the Net a Two-Edged Sword. *Far Eastern Economic Review* 158: 72.

Mikkelsen, R. 1996. Government Alarmed Over Sex, Politics and Internet. *Reuters World News Service*, 18 February.

Negroponte, N. 1996. *Being Digital.* Cambridge: MIT Press.

Net Users Told to Register. 1996. *South China Morning Post*, 26 February, 8.

Noam, E. M., and G. Pogorel. 1994. *Asymmetric Deregulation: The Dynamics of Telecommunications Policy in Europe and the United States.* Norwood, N.J.: Ablex.

Ploman, E. W. 1982. *International Law Governing Communications and Information: A Collection of Basic Documents.* Westport, Conn.: Greenwood Press.

Rao, M. 1996a. *Internet Offers Opportunities—Not Threats—To Local Cultures.* 3 March. <http://www.iworld.com/ netday/NATW.html>.

———. 1996b. *Singapore to Block Anti-State Views, Pornography on Internet.* 16 July. <http://netday.iworld.com/business/NATW.html>.

———. 1996c. *Vietnam Allows Access to Internet on a "Trial Basis."* 17 June. <http://netday.iworld.com/business/NATW.html>.

Schiller, H. 1981. *Who Knows: Information in the Age of the Fortune 500.* Norwood, N.J.: Ablex.

Schwarz, A. 1995. For Better or Worse: Vietnam Gives Wary Welcome to the Internet. *Far Eastern Economic Review* 158: 61–62.

Tapping the Business. 1994. *Asian Wall Street Journal*, 18 November, 45.

Tarjanne, P. 1996. The Internet and the Information Infrastructure: What Is the Difference? *ITU News*, May, 6–7.

The Global Information Infrastructure: Agenda for Cooperation. 1994. <gopher://ntiaunix1.ntia.doc.gov/00/papers/documents/giiagend.txt>.

Walls, J. 1993. Global Networking for Local Development: Task Focus and Relationship Focus on Cross-Cultural Communication. In *Global Networks: Computers and International Communication*, edited by L. M. Harasim. Cambridge: MIT Press.

Williamson, J. 1996. Caught up in the Net: Will the Internet One Day Ensnare the Networking World? *Global Telephony*, January, 18–26.

PART IV

NATIONAL IDENTITIES
AND GRASSROOTS
MOVEMENTS
IN CYBERSPACE

13

Cultural Identity and Cyberimperialism: Computer-Mediated Explorations of Ethnicity, Nation, and Citizenship

Laura B. Lengel and Patrick D. Murphy

The Internet is dramatically redefining the nature of social relationships between nations and challenging cultural sovereignty by creating an increased sense of borderlessness. This process has been constituted through the growth of cybermarketplaces and the flow of ideas and information across and between cultures, societies, and political systems. But many observers, too often high-tech wizards, policy makers, and researchers alike, embody broad assumptions about the prosocial value of the technology, its facilitation of a "global village," and how the Internet affords an opportunity for open and equal dialogue between West and East, North and South. In the East and the South, however, the global village is not necessarily the concept that McLuhan envisioned. On the contrary, rather than facilitating democracy, universal understanding, and a cosmic consciousness, the integration of the Internet has been marked by concerns of control over content and the potential disenfranchising effect of technology that is available only to elite segments of a society. In addition, how does the Internet's increasingly consumer-oriented delivery of information reflect a world colored by politicized ethnic communities, postcolonial migration, and the reinvestment in traditional cultural practices? Such questions place the ambiguities of the global village and its requisite new media technologies deeply into question.

To address these complex and problematic questions, this chapter explores the impact of the Internet on ethnicity, nation, and citizenship. It problematizes questions of access and user opportunity, primarily in regions outside the industrialized world, as well as the predominance of the English language in World Wide Web content and computer-mediated discourse generally. What makes this chapter unique is that it is a product of an ongoing multiuniversity student research project that is entirely computer mediated. Over 150 students and faculty from six universities in Mexico, The Netherlands, the United Kingdom, and the United States are addressing issues of their own status as digital citizens, their perceptions of their own cultural identity as represented on the World Wide Web, and their analysis of the impact of the Internet on international communication.

This chapter discusses how an electronic dialogic space can provide opportunities to question cultural identity and create the grounding for a more comprehensive understanding of international communication. Overall, it analyzes in concrete terms how users of the Internet from nearly 100 different countries perceive the Internet as a device of cyberimperialism and/or as a tool for virtual democracy.

Impact of Internet Access on Ethnicity, Nation, and Citizenship

To adequately explore the impact of new communications technologies on ethnicity, nation, and citizenship, one must first analyze who and what is welcome in the digital world. Internet access and user opportunity have been widely problematized (e.g., Adeya 1996; Carter 1997; Escobar in press; Hacker 1996; Kroker 1996; Lengel 1998a; Loader 1997; Reeve 1995; Riberio 1998; Sardar 1996). As these writers assert, the technology poor, particularly those in developing nations, are left on the margins of the information superhighway, often unable to participate in electronic discourse and disenfranchised by the power and influence of the technology rich.

While computer-mediated communication (CMC) is capable of forming the basis of the much-hyped global village by creating a means for all persons to be equally heard (cf. Grant 1998), the opportunity for global discourse is granted to a select few, a privileged technology elite that excludes those global regions traditionally marginalized politically, socioculturally, and economically. This marginalization occurs despite the fact that new communications technologies, primarily the Internet, were originally designed to be participatory media. For example, Tim Berners-Lee, credited with inventing the World Wide Web while at CERN (the European Laboratory for Particle Physics) and now with the W3 Consortium at MIT, stresses that the Web is in need of *providers* from the public, not just readers (The Web Maestro 1996).

While the Internet can provide a much-needed forum for voices outside the dominant powers that typically control international mass communication (see Owen 1998), the overall result is hardly Habermas's (1989) notion of the "public sphere" where democratic discourse takes shape in the absence of commercial and state interests. First of all, the minimum needs to access this technology require maximum cost, which includes obvious items such as computers, modems, and ISPs, and others such as telephone lines and electricity, requirements often overlooked by and taken for granted in the technology-rich First World. In technology-poor nations, where computers and links exist only at a premium and where the monthly charge by local ISPs costs more than monthly rent, electronic communication is not a viable option (Wresch 1996). Second, it is often not uniquely the fault of those individuals who own and manage the ISPs; in locations such as North Africa government tariffs make affordable Internet service impossible (Fedak 1998). Add to this the irony that such costs run parallel with that of technology generally in developing nations, thus making its acquisition even more expensive than for industrialized countries (Hanson 1990). While new communications technologies like the Internet are surprisingly available in remote areas of Africa, Latin America, and Asia, with few exceptions those who have access to them are members of the economic upper echelon. Most troubling about the convergence of these circumstances is that those who are perhaps most in need of the benefits of new communications technologies (e.g., alternative social and political entities) are too often unable to seize the opportunity to "speak" through them.

Cyberimperialism and the Marginalization of Cultural Difference

Much of this disequilibration of information flow and access could be labeled cyberimperialism. But if we are to evoke a notion like cyberimperialism heading into a new millennium, it must be understood as something more than simply a technological imbalance between rich and poor regions of the globe. That is, not only can cyberimperialism be understood as a set of conditions whereby the technology poor are marginalized by the prohibitive nature of new technologies, it is also a process marked by the marginalization of cultural difference. Recent research (González-Pinto and Roman 1998; Lengel in press) has found that persons in regions such as Africa, Latin America, and Central and Eastern Europe believe their voices are not adequately heard in the dominant global discourses, through either traditional or new media. Hindered both economically and by governments "concerned" about the proliferation of the Internet, persons in the technology-poor regions are unable to use the technology to disseminate what they believe are accurate and sensitive representations of themselves and their cultures. Instead, they are spoken for by government and commercial powers, or misrepresented by the technology rich.

On the World Wide Web, for instance, indigenous content is lost in a sea of Americanisms and corporate discourse. An overabundance of World Wide Web material is increasingly commercial, and the vast majority of Web sites are in the English language (Frost 1996; Stokes and Stokes 1996). These tendencies are only likely to increase as the distinction lessens between traditional telephony and other types of media coverage under the "guidance" of "the market" and a global commercial media system controlled by a handful of conglomerates (Brown 1998; Corporate Culture 1996). Moreover, as processes of conglomeration and convergence clearly show, "The notion that the Internet will permit humanity to leapfrog over capitalism and corporate communication is in sharp contrast to the present rapid commercialization of the Internet" (McChesney 1997, 30).

In fact, the current trend seems to once again confirm hegemonic culture's ability to extract power from even those socioeconomic tools that offer the most potential for counterhegemonic activity. But within the tightly sewn tapestry of power negotiated and resisted, the Internet is still a young-enough communications channel to suggest an unfinished script. And it is within this script that we find ourselves standing at a fork in the information superhighway: Can the Internet be used to foster sociocultural forms of resistance, rebellion, and tradition? Or will the Internet increase the rate through which local and regional forms of resistance, rebellion, and traditional culture are drawn on by marketing firms, and thus increase the likelihood of their absorption into consumer culture as just another commodity?

COMPUTER-MEDIATED RESEARCH ON CYBERIMPERIALISM

The computer-mediated research project, named Frontera (Frontiers of New Technologies Education, Research, and Activism) by the founding faculty, is the first significant computer-mediated, multiuniversity study about the impact of new technologies on intercultural and international communication of which we are aware. The project was conceptualized in 1996 by faculty at the Instituto Technologico Y de Estudios Superiores de Monterrey in Querétaro, Mexico (ITESMCQ), the University of North Dakota, Portland State University, Maastricht University in The Netherlands, Southern Illinois University at Edwardsville, and the American International University in London. At the start of 1997 students at the six universities, who represent nearly 100 national backgrounds, were asked to both interrogate the Internet and encounter it as a discursive tool to explore critical issues in international and intercultural communication. The project afforded students the opportunity to learn across borders and cultural differences. Through computer-mediated communication students work "together" in "cyberclassrooms," across national borders and cultural differences, to explore ethnicity, nation, and citizenship, the potential for democratic dialogue (e.g., "public sphere"), as well as the problems associated with cyberimperialism.

Grouped into twenty CMC teams and using their university e-mail accounts, students were informed that they were part of an experimental group of international students and professors. They were also told that the other student participants were representative of a broad range of nationalities (from Mexican, Norwegian, Nigerian, Brazilian, Indian, Spanish, Turkish, English, and American, to others—because of their dual citizenships and parents from two different countries—who felt as though they have "split" or multilayered national and ethnic identities), and that they were to explore their differences; differences created by the boundaries of nationalism, but also boundaries of race, class, ethnicity, and one's own identity. Our use of cybercommunications was positioned as a mechanism through which to explore this crossing of boundaries because it made possible the students' ability to journey virtually to other places, thus facilitating an "imagined community" of classmates and professors. To help frame their interactions, students were given two specific lines of inquiry to discuss:

1. The Digital Citizen: What does it mean to be a digital citizen? For example, is a digital citizen a person more connected to cyberspace, "interpersonal" relationships, and society via technology than by local or national events or issues? Does new technology allow people to transcend socioeconomic class or does it distance people from the lived (as opposed to virtual) experiences of life and human interaction?

2. International Relations and the Internet: Is the Internet transforming international relations and global conflicts? Are new tensions emerging between the technology-rich and technology-poor nations because of the Internet? Will the Internet homogenize the world into a consumer, American-style culture? What is the potential for democracy to be facilitated by virtual communication networks?

Responses to these questions, along with the introductory messages to their teammates and other correspondence that students were willing to share, were copied to the participating faculty for use in our research. Reflections written by students as well as a sample of the computer-mediated responses were included in a World Wide Web site (Lengel 1998b). Further, students at some of the six institutions wrote final reports and exam essays that afforded opportunities for self-reflexive analysis of discursive experiences with counterparts in their cyberclassroom. Examples of their commentary have been thematized as part of our research and will follow in this chapter.

As implied by our two guiding lines of inquiry, cyberimperialism is one of the most significant topics of investigation in the Frontera project. Students interrogated access and user opportunity to the Internet, primarily from their own socioeconomic privileged position. Many had never taken the opportunity to self-reflexively critique their status as university students, especially at private institutions with high tuition rates. Although a large number of students, such as those attending the American International University in London and ITESMCQ in Mexico, came from developing nations, the fact that their families were able to afford such tuition fees placed them in the elite of their home communities. Many had never contemplated the socioeconomic implications of both their own status as university students and their status as digital citizens, if they considered themselves as such. As university students, they were afforded easy access to computer labs, their own e-mail accounts, and the luxury of the institution-as-ISP to defray the monthly costs of ISPs such as Compuserve or the countless other service providers. Further, in their conversations with students at ITESMCQ, students in Europe and North America were able to learn firsthand about the lived experience of a digital citizen in a less technology-rich nation. Thus, students had ample opportunities to self-reflexively explore the challenges, particularly in developing nations, to accessing the Internet. In addition, they discussed among their teams the assumptions often made by uncritical thinkers that everyone in the so-called global village can communicate via the Internet.

The Digital Citizen

The notion of the digital citizen received much attention after *Wired* magazine published results from a survey about the impact of new technology. The survey, conducted by *Wired* and the Merrill Lynch Forum on a random sample of 1,444 Americans, hailed the digital citizen as the "bellwether of the 21st century" (Sieg and Kurdziel 1997). The digital citizen, *Wired* and the Merrill Lynch Forum press release announced, "is about the most plugged-in, connected optimistic and opinionated person we are likely to find in America today." In *Wired's* December 1997 cover story the survey was positioned as the "first in-depth poll" of technology users in the United States. Contributing editor Jon Katz (1998) reported that digital citizens are "optimistic, tolerant, civic-minded, and radically committed to change."

Those who have critiqued the *Wired*/Merrill Lynch Forum study (cf. Gamberutti 1998; González-Pinto and Roman 1998; Hedani 1998; Moore 1997) are not quite as optimistic about either the survey or its results. In his article "The Digital Citizen: More Nonsense from *Wired*," Richard Moore (1997), for instance, contends, "The poll results reflect the education, political power, economic strength, and faith in the existing order characteristic of a relatively privileged class—namely, those who are 'able' to get connected and are equipped to capitalize on their connections." Katz's (1998) *Wired* article and the digital citizen survey look only at those who either were or could get wired, and the results make no effort to analyze the problems of access that emerge from a lack of socioeconomic privilege.

Like Moore, the Frontera students critiqued the notion of the digital citizen and looked beyond the United States for an indication of who is, who desires to be, and who cannot be a global digital citizen. Writing to her CMC group, student participant Allison, commented, "As for being a digital citizen, it somewhat bothers me, knowing that I am a number on the net. However, I believe that there are some benefits to this issue, because your identity is unknown, and for most people, identity is a difficult thing to accept. Having a censored identity is non-discriminatory, and gives everyone a chance to speak to everyone, rather than just judge them on their first impression appearance" (AK, 31 March 1998).

Commentary on the anonymity of the digital citizen such as Allison's was echoed by other student researchers. For example, reacting to Allison's argument that "identity is a difficult thing to accept," Emily O. speculated that a digital citizen might be "someone who is more conformable in a computerized society than in a society where they can be seen. They are hiding maybe because society wronged them in some way or because they are not socially accepted" (EO, 24 April 1998). Her understanding of a digital citizen, then, is not the wired/empowered individual about whom Jon Katz (1998) writes, but rather a person who has been marginalized by societal norms and who is trying to survive in a more compassionate "virtual" rather than "real" world. And then there is a rather succinct response by Chad, a U.S. student who stated that a digital citizen is someone who

- wakes up in the morning and instead of going to get the newspaper, surfs the net and reads newspapers sites across the world.
- reads his "mail" with a click of a couple buttons instead of an envelope opener.
- wonders if his modem is good enough or fast enough.
- is identified by a password or user name instead of his clothes, face or personality. (CMB, 30 March 1998)

Other Frontera participants had different conceptualizations of the digital citizen that focused less on how the technology defined the user than how the user could speak through the technology. For example, Michelle, a Chinese–South African student, considered how gender and technology converged. "Being a woman and a digital citizen, and myself I am lucky to be part of this technological revolution." Although Michelle critiqued the problems with the "technological revolution," particularly that "the gap between the information rich and information poor is getting bigger" and the possibilities of being distanced from one's " 'real lives' . . . as they get self-absorbed in the 'virtual' world of the Internet, e-mail and chatrooms," she acknowledges advantages to her own life: "The Internet allows the opportunity to let your voice be heard and allows you to be part of this 'virtual' world. In today's technology and information age, being a digital citizen is better than [n]ot being one at all" (MK, 3 March 1998). Another woman, Jane, concurred, adding, "As for being a woman, I also feel that the censored identity [of the Internet] allows everyone to have a voice to be heard. . . . It is important to be heard and not be neglected by society by your race or your gender" (JK, 12 March 1998).

Some of these discussions led to CMC groups addressing gender in terms of the haves and have-nots that transgress the geographical boundaries between developed and developing nations. Jasmina, a Croatian student in London, wrote,

We also tried to tackle a slightly different "haves" and "have-nots," but still relevant in terms of intercultural communications. We looked at how socially "haves" and "have-nots" can transcend this discrimination via the Internet, where these attributes can be hidden, disguised or simply non-apparent. For instance, women, who have been fighting for equality throughout the whole century, and still are, can reach this equality within the domain of the Net. (JK, 23 April 1998)

Meanwhile, other voices, particularly those from developing countries, tended to ground the dialogue in very concrete terms. Brazilian student Camilla concluded that despite potential for empowerment, the notion of the digital citizen was a muted possibility. "Developing nations such as Brazil present a problem where technological access will be limited only to the privileged— wealthy, upper-middle class individuals. Thus, the notion of the 'digital citizen' is an unrealistic one [for] millions of people" (CDS, 27 April 1998).

The Technology Rich Become Aware of the Technology Poor

The argument that the notion of the digital citizen is an "unrealistic one [for] millions of people," particularly those in technology-poor regions, leads to a more broad-based exploration of the imbalance of world communications flow. Before the emergence of the digital citizen from the technology-rich world, a world that dominates cyberimperialist enterprises, was the "informed citizen" from the information-rich world, a world that emerged from a more traditional imperialist power structure. Examining this imbalance and the challenges of information have-nots has been long established in communications scholarship. The debates about cultural and information imperialism in the 1970s reached a peak in 1980 during the first MacBride Roundtable, where communications scholars from both industrialized and developing nations met to interrogate and attempt to reduce the impact of what they termed a "one way flow" of information from the industrialized powers to the developing world (MacBride et al. 1980).

Despite decades of established scholarship, such ideas are often heard for the first time by our students. For students living in the United States, the United Kingdom, and elsewhere in technology-rich regions, it is easy to overlook the one-way flow of information and lack of opportunities to those outside the technology-rich world to have a voice, either through traditional communicative means or through new communications technologies. Teresa, a Spanish student in London, revealed that "before working as a team member in the Frontera, I had never realized the fact that there are people in the world that have no access to computers. As part of a developed country you take for granted having access to computers and you do not realize that you are probably one of the few privileged countries with easy access" (TB, 6 May 1998).

Such confessions stimulated a discussion about access between those participants from industrialized nations and those from developing nations about new technologies and access to them. For example, Ahmed argued that while most of the participants of Frontera "have enough access to technology, and we are all basically from industrialized countries ('The Haves'), we each have different backgrounds to be able to come up with opinions and ideas about computer mediated communication throughout the world concerning 'The Haves' and 'The Have Nots'" (AM, 30 March 1998).

Others, drawing on their lived experience in developing nations, were well aware of the one-way flow of information. Olakunle, a West African student, wrote that the

"Information superhighway" as the name suggests is meant to be a two-way communication affair between the technology haves and the have-nots, but this is not the case in reality. Rather, what is often observed is that information flow from the more developed to the less developed countries is far greater than info flow in the other direction. This of course creates an "information gradient" in which less developed countries now seem more like "dumping grounds" for some information from the developed ones. (OKA, 27 February 1998)

Comments like those of Olakunle and the reaction that they generated stimulated heated and sometimes intimate discussions. Moreover, this interactivity created an ideal atmosphere for teaching and learning about disparities, because the students were teaching and learning from each other. For instance, that the digital citizen was defined in the *Wired* article in terms of economic, professional, and political power, along with more mundane issues like increasing bandwidth and the speed of their computers' operating systems, modems, and browsers, caused student Jasmina to assert that

Despite the libertarian spirit of the Net-users, the drawback is that it [the Net community] does not really tackle issues that don't directly concern it. This I can only report because one of my Frontera partners, Paulina from Mexico, who in one of her letters told us about the situation of the Internet accessibility in her country: it was low on all levels, even on university levels, and apparently only the more acclaimed universities got access to the Net. She was among the lucky universities to have this luxury. (JK, 30 April 1998)

Mexican coresearchers like Paulina critiqued access to technology in both their own country and other developing nations. Jon from Mexico shared with his Frontera group the problems of access to new technologies in developing nations: "I think that the main problems with technology in a country like mine is that a very small group has the access to new technologies . . . [and] the information has always been only for a selected group of people" (JG, 3 March 1998).

As these excerpts attest, as the students encountered each other's ideas and worldviews they became more conscious of the fact that all did not benefit equally from technological advancements. Rohan, for example, explained,

"Through my work on the FRONTERA project I have found that not everyone from all over the world share [*sic*] the concept that there is a widening gap between those that have access to computers, phone lines and the Internet, and those that barely have access to clean drinking water" (RK, 26 April 1998). Another student, Tamara, concurred that "basic living conditions versus installation of computer systems leave a very large gap in living standards and its essentials" (TMG, 15 April 1998).

But as the students found, the divide between the information/technology rich and the information/technology poor is evident not only in the bipolar opposites of First World and Third World, West and East, and North and South, but also within these oppositions. Nicole, a student at the University of North Dakota, asked her group, "In class, we have been discussing the 'information gap.' I was wondering what all of you think about this, and if you think the gap is due to social, economic, or generational problems among individuals. What do you think the implications are in the countries you live in?" Critiquing the situation in her own country, Nicole posited, "Here in the United States, I do see a potential problem in the future because of economic differences. The technology is available in this country, but not everyone has access to it because it is so expensive" (NLK, 3 March 1998). Responding to Nicole's inquiry, Andy added, "I think the 'Information Gap' is a big thing. Who can afford the latest in technology? [Only] the more developed (industrialized) countries. Is this fair?" Yet Andy then countered with, "One thing to leave you thinking about. Should we close this Information Gap so that other countries catch up, or should we keep the gap and keep a competitive edge?" (AW, 9 March 1998). Desire for the competitive edge in technology development and acquisition certainly parallels that of technogiants like Bill Gates, king of cyberimperialism. It also can reinforce problems associated with international relations.

International Relations and Cybercultural Politics

In the last few years Internet listserves provided a global forum for a Yanomani chief in Brazil to defend his land from gold miners, helped the Zapatista movement in southern Mexico circumvent government censorship, and allowed average citizens to challenge the labor practices of a mulitnational athletic-shoemaker. These are inspiring efforts for those concerned with confronting imbalances of power and information and their relationship to human rights. However, as Colombian anthropologist Arturo Escobar (in press) has argued, in order for cybercultural politics to be effective, it must fulfill two conditions: "awareness of dominant worlds that are being created by the same technologies on which the progressive networks rely (including awareness of how power works in the world of transnational networks and flows); and an ongoing tacking back and forth between cyberpolitics (political activism on the Internet) and . . . political activism in the physical locations at which the networker sits and lives" (p. 2).

At the level of international politics, Frontera students demonstrated a degree of sensitivity to Escobar's first condition, though it emerged conflicted and disjointed. For example, Camilla announced, "Being from a third world country I am aware of how most developing nations already struggle to gain hold of technology, thus it is probable that this form of communication will be available to not only developed nations, but to the wealthy upper classes. Perhaps this is going too far, but I have this image of a 'Brave New World', with caste systems, and such" (CDS, 26 February 1998).

Judging from recent transnational trends in communications ownership, development, and acquisition, perhaps Camilla is not going far enough. But as threatening as these trends of information control seem, they are not always easy to get a handle on, as cybersnook code breakers and hardware and software cyberpirates, along with cyberpolitical activities, complicate the purity of cyberimperial divisions of the powerful and powerless. Reflecting on the avenues for prosocial potential, more than a few students seemed hopeful. Olakunle, for instance, suggested,

As far as I am concerned, one positive effect which the web might have on international relations is to lessen global conflicts. Nowadays, a lot of info on the Internet take into account the cultural differences existing among its users with a result that these info try to avoid misrepresentation [sic] of "foreign" values. Also, some political web sites put up mediating views on line in order to lessen clashes between communities where there are clashes. There is therefore a tendency that we might be in for a convergence in cultural values if a trend like this emerges. If democracy is achieved on the net, then nearly everybody gets faily [sic] represented and the chances of understanding our differences more would be high. Consequently, this would result in less chances of global clashes or conflicts. (OKA, 22 April 1998)

Antonia, from Germany, referring to an earlier message from her counterpart, stated, "To learn something about a new culture, different traditions, different societies, or different governments, are implications of electronic networks for the development of personal, professional and political relationships across national boundaries" (AVB, 25 April 1998).

As these excerpts suggest, many of the Frontera students were encouraged about how new modes of knowing, doing, and being based on principles of interactivity and collective engagement could be facilitated via the Internet. However, returning to Escobar's thoughts on cybercultural politics, these e-mail interactions must go beyond electronic observations to truly question power in the international arena. Unfortunately, activism as an extension of these electronic dialogues is not a theme that emerged with any saliency. But what can be said about the Frontera students' use of cyberspace to discuss international relations and power is that through the transborder interactive process the Internet begins to take on a new meaning and dimension, and thus opens up the potential to serve other political and life projects. Much of this kind of recognition was most salient when the students took on questions of cultural identity.

Cultural Identity in Cyberspace

As discussed earlier, part of the research involved the investigation of how cyberimperialism marginalizes cultural differences inherent in technology-poor regions. Students not only discussed their reactions to the representation of cultural identity, ethnicity, and nation by new communications technologies and users of them, but also researched these representations themselves by examining content on the World Wide Web from and about developing nations and traditionally marginalized communities. Olakunle argued that one "indirect consequence of [the technology gap] is that a few attempts by the very minute priviledged [*sic*] who have access to on-line facilities to represent 'their people' on the web often result in mis-representation. After all, these priviledged [*sic*] do not constitute the bulk of the population" (OKA, 17 March 1998).

There is also much discussion about the "loss" of culture and cultural identity through new technologies. Issues of globalization, a term used interchangeably by some students with Westernization, prevail in the computer-mediated communication. Camilla, for instance, wrote, "I feel that globalisation through the Internet is fast becoming a reality. People in Western, developed nations are proof of Marx's theory of 'commodity fetishism,' which states that we want to consume goods, even if they are not needed." She argued that such consumption ultimately spills over to developing nations, resulting in their uptake of Western cultural values. "The only way in which I see the Internet resisting globalisation is to allow more 'cultural voices' to be heard, to encourage those who have access to it in developing nations to represent their own culture" (CDS, 27 April 1998). Accordingly, Paul seemed fearful of the possibility of the Internet "homogenising us into an American style culture. . . . Is web material . . . strong enough to begin eroding peoples's [*sic*] internalised values?" (PL, 27 March 1998).

Further discussions sometimes appeared to be more normative in nature. For example, Tamara, who is also concerned about indigenous cultures buying and buying into cyberimperialism, argued for greater control of Internet growth and adoption. "It would be a shame to ruin the communities they have established for the sole purpose of needless technological advancement. It would probably deplete their community more than benefit it. It is like messing with the rainforests—if it isn't broken, don't try to fix it" (TMG, 15 April 1998).

The computer-mediated collaborators also discussed other areas of concern, such as generational factors. Andy predicted an information gap to widen between young and old, noting, "Younger people are going to be using newer technologies because the younger generations learn new technologies faster" (AW, 9 March 1998). Susan concurred, "In media technology class, that we are doing this project for, we are talking about the division of the use of technology being a generational thing. I know from my own experience that I know a lot more about computers than my older sister, and she knows more than my parents, and I would be surprised if my grandma even knew how to turn a computer on. My younger brother truely [*sic*] is the genius" (SRD, 3 March 1998).

Finally, a particularly interesting discussion about cultural identity emerged in a CMC group, one member of which was Dawn, an African-American woman. She asked her counterparts how the Internet impacts consumer culture and how technology reflects oneself: "Say, do you think that purchasing new technology (like computers) is now a way of defining one's self in a society? The technology we have today has combined all of our global differences and took that information to create a marketing strategy that permeates the globe. Do you guys think that this new technology is just another ploy to get us to buy, buy buy?" She presented her own opinion on how ownership of technology impacts cultural identity: "I do think that the purchase of computers and other telecommunications technology does enable people to claim a status. The tecnologically [*sic*] elite, I guess you could say. But only those who have disposable incomes can really afford to spend money on that kind of technology anyway. . . . So how does this new consumer culture over the web affect those who don't have access?" (DY, 15 April 1998). As a reaction, Olakunle offered the following: "In response to Dawn's question, having a computer in a family in Africa is luxury, having computers in schools reflects affluent schools and having PC's with lots of modems differentiate the so-called first class citizens from the 'still behind' citizens." He continues by analyzing the computer software and hardware marketers, who "might be exploiting us in undefinable ways. Their impact in getting more and more people to be a part of the 'computer community' is profound" (OKA, 18 April 1998).

Reflecting on the CMC Research

The impact of "getting more and more people to be part of the 'computer community'" has certainly been profound in our research. The students in Frontera represented over 100 nations and came from a rich variety of cultural backgrounds. Despite the diversity of this dialogic community, students were linked by a similar theoretical base of cultural studies, the understanding of the possible inequalities of communications access and flow, the an incentive to create access to and opportunity for new communications technologies to build further discursive communities in the future. In fact, a very common daily entry into CMC discussion was that of a student reflecting on his or her experiences, on what he or she had learned, and how they communicated with one another:

The objectives of these projects were for us to learn—either about Dr. Murphy's thought provoking questions and opinions, or about the credibility of Web sites. We also, I believe more importantly, learned about communication and its complexity.

This was a new way of communicating for me. That was very important personal learning. I also learned about people from other cultures, and I successfully communicated with them through e-mail. I learned that you can talk with people with cultural barriers (mainly the English as a second language for some) obstructing the communication process, and you can overcome those hurdles—successfully. I was comforted and delighted by this new knowledge. (ET, 8 May 1998)

Another commented on collaborating with a culturally diverse group: "Working as a member of not just a team but a culturally diverse team, I have learnt that understanding one another is a key tool in effective collaborative work. What I, as an African, think from the wealth of my cultural experiences will definitely be different from what another team member who is Polish thinks. There is a need to sometimes stand at compromise in order to arrive at a convergent conclusion about an issue" (OKA, 8 May 1998). Stuart noted, "Being able to sit down comfortably and type to others in cultures, languages and societies different to our own was truly a remarkable experience" (SM, 25 April 1998).

It is important to note that many of the students participating in the computer-mediated research project were, at first, extremely uncomfortable sitting down and typing to their counterparts. Many had never used e-mail and Internet browsers. Some had never used a computer before. Most were unclear what the difference was between the Internet and the World Wide Web and the relationship of the Internet and e-mail. Many had extremely negative views on new communications technologies which emerged from their fear as beginner users. In one of her early e-mail messages to her group, Allison wrote, "I seem to hold a strong disliking towards the computer and advanced technology, however, I seem to have more postiive [*sic*] outlooks on this advancement. Some people are absolutely afraid of the computer (like me) and also advancements in technology, however, I am beginning to accept it" (AK, 3 March 1998).

Some students were afraid not of the technology but of the means of communication and the possibility for self-misrepresentation. "The thought of using e-mail is scary as we will never see or hear the real you" (MK, 22 February 1998). Others required special assistance in conducting even simple tasks, such as developing an e-mail group, copying and pasting URLs to group members, and saving e-mail messages in a word-processing application for their final reports. However, after a few weeks or months they felt a level of power that comes from mastering a skill set that is touted as necessary for contemporary academic and professional life. Conversely, they realized that knowing how to use the Internet is not the end-all-be-all; because they had developed a solid critical assessment of new technologies, they could distance themselves from the "hype" and instead concern themselves with how the Internet could best be utilized to enact intercultural and international communication, to enact dialogue between those in developed and developing nations, and to use the technologies for some social good.

CONCLUSION

With huge companies like Intel, Worldcom, Lucent, AT&T, Time-Warner, and others combining financial power and market leadership to define the boundaries of the digital interactive world (cf. Brown 1998), what lessons for alternative interactivity does a pedagogical experiment such as Frontera really afford its student participants? Ironically, the answer may lie in the corporate world's motto, "Loyalty is just one mouse-click away" (Friedman 1998, 8). Due to the intense competition between various communications companies, mouse-click loyalty has emerged as a sort of insurance measure to soften, or even profit from, corporate mergers and acquisitions. But mouse-click loyalty is not just a game for elite commercial interests, as it is precisely this kind of activity that can foster dialogue among alternative voices; transform ordinary citizens into publishers, artists, reporters, advocates, and organizers; and ignite cybercultural political efforts.

The Frontera project required that the participants use their mouses, so to speak, for the exploration of such alternative and potentially proactive purposes. Rather than putting the technology into play for reasons of convenience and profit (e.g., electronic malls or cybermerchants), students interrogated the very tool they were communicating with through an international network of voices and experiences. As the previous pages suggest, the result was fruitful on a number of levels, and the emerging dialogue was itself disseminated to a worldwide audience via a Web site (see Lengel 1998b). This process of dialogue and display both worked through and questioned the Net's global role. And it was precisely by drawing on this dual process that students became cognizant of how imbalances of technology and power create a fertile environment for cyberimperialism, and in turn begin to speak to the need to address these imbalances. Teresa, for example, wrote,

The Frontera project has made me see that as a country which "has" access to new technology we have to make a move to help narrow the gap between "the haves" and "the have nots." We have to try make [the have nots] see that they are taken into consideration and that they are not left behind or apart in the development of new media technology. . . . The "have nots" have to see that there are people in "the haves" who want to communicate with them and make them a part of the democratic use of the WWW. They have to feel they are a part of it and not left out. (TB, 8 May 1998)

Other students concluded a semester's work in Frontera with unanswered questions and an ambiguous feel for the potential of cybercultural politics. "Before anything else, can I just say that I'm never clear as to what 'democracy' among on-line users really entails" (OKA, 1 May 1998). After discussing access, equal discourse, and one-way flow of information, he learned enough to know that there are no easy answers. "When 'everybody' has access to the web and its material without restrictions on any grounds and each individual has the right to voice out their opinions about any issue as well as put up information on-line . . . will this be 'democracy'? If it sounds like it then, can we ever get to this stage? Will there be a 100% 'democracy' on the net then?" (OKA, 1 May 1998).

Despite the ambiguity and unanswered questions, the computer-mediated research project raised important issues and shaped a critical appreciation for the present and future of the Internet. Students opened their eyes to the problems dividing the technology rich and the technology poor, but also saw the future possibilities for equal dialogue through new communications technologies. These possibilities, Jasmina pondered, can only happen "the moment when there will be no more 'haves' and 'have nots' in the context of Net users. [Then] we will know that the Net has made a revolutionary impact on society" (JK, 8 May 1998). Despite intentions for developing a truly equal dialogue and creating a "virtual world" that is devoid of cyberimperialism, the reality of such goals are a significant and ongoing challenge.

REFERENCES

Adeya, N. 1996. Beyond Borders: The Internet for Africa. *Convergence: The Journal of Research into New Media Technologies* 2 (2): 23–27.

Brown, E. 1998. New Media 500. *New Media,* July 1998, 32–46.

Carter, D. 1997. "Digital Democracy" or "Information Aristocracy"? Economic Regeneration and the Information Economy. In *The Governance of Cyberspace: Politics, Technology and Global Restructuring*, edited by B. Loader. London: Routledge.

Corporate Culture. 1996. *The Nation* 262 (22): 3–4.

Escobar, A. In press. Gender, Place and Networks: A Political Ecology of Cyberculture. In *Women @Internet: Creating New Cultures in Cyberspace*, edited by W. Harcourt. London: Zeb Books/UNESCO.

Fedak, D. 1998. Africa in the Third Millennium: Organizing New Communication Technologies for the Future. Paper presented at the International Communication Association and National Communication Association conference, "Communication: Organizing for the Future," 17 July, Rome.

Friedman, T. 1998. High-Tech Wizards Can't Win Without Smart Politics. *International Herald Tribune*, 20 April, 8.

Frost, R. 1996. Web's Heavy U.S. Accent Grates on Overseas Ears. *Wall Street Journal*, Eastern Ed., 26 September, B6.

Gamberutti, M. 1998. I Agree! 25 January (cited 8 June 1998). <http://www.enthuz. com/HyperNews/Public/cgi-bin/get.cgi/forums/digit/5/1.html>.

González-Pinto, R., and M. Roman. 1998. Digital Citizens Down the Border: How They See the World Now and in the Future. Paper presented at the National Communication Association Convention, November, New York.

Grant, A. 1998. Communication Technologies and Social Change. Paper presented at the Re-Developing Communication for Social Change conference, June, Austin, Texas.

Habermas, J. 1989. *The Structural Transformation of the Public Sphere*. Cambridge: MIT Press.

Hacker, K. L. 1996. Missing Links in the Evolution of Electronic Democracy. *Media, Culture & Society* 18: 213–232.

Hanson, J. 1990. *New Communication Technologies in Developing Countries.* Hillsdale, N.J.: Lawrence Erlbaum.

Hedani, J. 1998. The Digital Citizen Survey Is Hype. 25 January (cited 8 June 1998). <http://www.enthuz.com/HyperNews/Public/cgi-bin/get.cgi/forums/digit/5.html>.

Katz, J. 1998. The Digital Citizen. 4 February (cited 8 June 1998). <http://www.dealertech-mag.com/features/feat1b.htm>.

Kroker, A. 1996. Virtual Capitalism. In *Techno Science and Cyber Culture*, edited by S. Aronowitz, B. Martinsons, and M. Menser. London: Routledge.

Lengel, L. 1998a. Access to the Internet in East Central and South-Eastern Europe: New Women's Voices, New Media Technologies. *Convergence: Journal of Research into New Media Technologies* 4 (2): 38–55.

———. 1998b. The International Links Project Web Site (see, in particular, Student Research). 30 April (cited 9 June 1998). <http://www.richmond.ac.uk/intllinks/student1.htm>, and Frontera. <http://www.richmond.ac.uk/intllinks/Fronter1.htm>.

———, ed. In press. *Culture and Technology in the New Europe: Communication in Transformation in Post-Communist Nations.* Norwood, N.J.: Ablex.

Loader, B. D. 1997. The Governance of Cyberspace: Politics, Technology and Global Restructuring. In *The Governance of Cyberspace: Politics, Technology and Global Restructuring*, edited by B. D. Loader. London: Routledge.

MacBride, S., E. Abel, H. Beuve-Mery, E. Ma Ekonzo, G. Garcia Marquez, S. Losev, M. Lubis, M. Masmoudi, M. Nagai, F. I. Akporuaro, B. Osolnik, G. El Oteifi, J. P. Pronk, J. Somavia, B. G. Verghese, and B. Zimmerman. 1980. *Many Voices, One World: Towards a New More Just and More Efficient World Information and Communication Order.* London: Kogan Page.

McChesney, R. W. 1997. *Corporate Media and the Threat to Democracy.* New York: Seven Stories Press.

Moore, R. K. 1997. The Digital Citizen: More Nonsense from *Wired*. 17 December (cited 8 June 1998). <http://www.findmail.com/list/cyber-rights/?start=661>.

Owen, C. 1998. Women's Organizations' Utilization of On-Line Communication in the Mexican Women's Movement. Paper presented at the Re-Developing Communication for Social Change conference, June, Austin, Texas.

Reeve, C. 1995. Democracy Through the Information Superhighway. Paper presented at the "Shouts from the Street: Popular Culture, Creativity and Change" Conference, 7 September, Manchester Metropolitan University, Manchester, England.

Ribeiro, G. L. 1998. Cybercultural Politics: Political Activism at a Distance in a Transnational World. In *Cultures of Politics/Politics of Cultures: Re-Visioning Latin America Social Movements*, edited by S. E. Alvarez, E. Dagnino, and A. Escobar. Boulder, Colo.: Westview Press.

Sardar, Z. 1996. Alt.civilizations.faq: Cyberspace as the Darker Side of the West. In *Cyberfutures: Culture and Politics on the Information Superhighway*, edited by Z. Sardar and J. R. Ravetz. London: Pluto.

Sieg, A., and M. Kurdziel. 1997. Move Over "Soccer Moms"—The *Wired*/Merrill Lynch Forum Survey Uncovers "The Digital Citizen" as Bellwether of the 21st Century. 12 November (cited 8 June 1998). <http://www.ml.com/woml/forum/press.htm>.

Stokes, P., and W. Stokes. 1996. Pedagogy, Power, Politics: Literate Practice Online. *Computers & Texts* 13 (December): 5.

The Web Maestro: An Interview with Tim Berners-Lee. 1996. *Technology Review*, July, 32–40.

Wresch, W. 1996. *Disconnected: Haves and Have-Nots in the Information Age.* New Brunswick, N.J.: Rutgers University Press.

14

Between Grassroots and Netizens: Empowering Nongovernmental Organizations

Ellen S. Kole

As with any fast-growing technology, there are a lot of speculations about the impact of the Internet.[1] Two visions—an optimistic one and a pessimistic one—frequently theorize about its empowerment potential for nongovernmental organizations, particularly in the developing countries of the South. "Empowerment" encompasses "the processes of people acquiring the experiences, knowledge, tools and techniques to be able to transform their lives and the society. Within this process transformation of the existing power relations is crucial" (Claessen and Wesemael-Smit 1992, 17).

Optimistic authors see the Internet as an option to strengthen NGO empowerment processes (Frederick 1995; Ruth and Ronkin 1992; Bellman, Tindimubona, and Arias 1993; Ezigbalike and Ochuodho 1991; Polman and Pouw Kraan 1995). NGOs can, for example, combine literacy courses with computer skills. They can increase the "critical mass" of political actions against human-rights violations or environmental destruction by sending electronic alerts to the world. The Internet also supports the quick exchange of vital information between NGOs preparing for an international conference. Pessimistic authors are critical about the empowerment options of the Internet and information and communication technology (ICT) in general (Servaes 1989, 24–25; Hamelink 1994, 1997, 27–28; Frederick 1993, 124–126). They believe that Southern NGOs become increasingly dependent on the North for finances, technology, and knowledge.

In the last few years academics have suggested and elaborated new conceptual frameworks. These incorporate both positive and negative impacts of internetworking for empowerment as two sides of the same coin (Kole 1996; Fortier 1996; Mwangi 1997; Hamelink 1997, 29–30). An important aspect of these critical visions is the coevolution of technology and society.

Whom Are We Talking About?

Looking into the crystal ball of Internet impact on NGO empowerment, one often forgets that NGOs are not a homogeneous group. Authors write about NGOs as if there are no differences between and within them. This is of course not the case. There are small NGOs with only a few volunteers and there are big ones, such as Amnesty International and Greenpeace, comparable to transnational corporations. There are well-equipped organizations and NGOs with only the most necessary devices. Some organizations working in the slums do not even have an office. NGOs may be active on the local level, but also on the national, regional, or even global levels. While one NGO is a religious charity organization, another is an advocacy organization defending women's reproductive rights, and still another NGO is a radical "guerrilla" organization actively opposing the government.

The plurality of NGOs makes it hard to define and delimit exactly what an NGO is. For instance, where does one draw the line between community-based organizations (CBOs) and local NGOs? Or between international NGOs and NGO programs within intergovernmental organizations? Here, the concept of NGO refers to nonprofit, non-(inter)state organizations representing CBOs, people's initiatives, and local issue groups (such as squatters and soup kitchens) in a broader movement for social change.

Variations between NGOs, principally in relations of power, influence Internet impact on empowerment processes. Variations among persons working for an NGO cause a similar effect. This chapter enlists the most important differences between and within NGOs in the South relating to Internet implications in terms of empowerment. Special attention is paid to the NGO function as representative of the grassroots. The grassroots are the more-or-less organized people's initiatives, local issue groups, and CBOs at the local level who have little economic capacity, political power, or other resources. Will these groups profit in the end from the fact that NGOs use the Internet? Or will NGOs alienate their grassroots, becoming more cosmopolitan "netizens" (i.e., capable members of the virtual Internet community)? Will NGOs, with the introduction of the Internet, become more equal partners to the donor organizations in the North who support their work?

To answer these questions, data of various case studies on computer networking and empowerment were analyzed. One set of data is the author's research on electronic networking by NGOs for the 1995 United Nations World Conference on Women (UNWCW) at Beijing.[2] The author takes the experiences of NGO users as a point of departure, and relate these to international relations in the discussion section.

TECHNOLOGY HAVES AND HAVE-NOTS; INFORMATION RICH AND POOR

Part of the pessimistic view of ICT and empowerment is the belief that new social divides will emerge with the introduction of the Internet: technology haves versus technology have-nots and information rich against information poor. The authors call the people with a connection to the Internet or who have access to network applications such as e-mail the technology haves. People devoid of computer network technology are the have-nots. Information rich are those who have access to electronic information, while the ones without access are the information poor.

Can we find these social divides in computer networking in the NGO sector? Who are the haves and have-nots, who is information rich or poor? This section presents some differences between and within NGOs with regard to these categories. The intention is not to arrive at a sophisticated, scientifically sound scheme to categorize NGOs. Rather, it is to make visible variances that have an impact on empowerment through internetworking.

Connectivity

The most obvious difference is of course the one between NGOs linked to the Internet and nonwired organizations. Reading about the marvelous Internet benefits, we may forget what this means to the NGOs without network connection. An experience from the NGO-Forum, accompanying the UNWCW, gives us an idea. Women's libraries and documentation centers from South and North collectively organized a one-day workshop for the NGO-Forum, prepared through electronic networking. One of the largest women's libraries, an NGO of international reputation, was excluded from this event. Even worse, the library had no idea that the workshop was going to take place. It happened out of its sight, on the Net, because the NGO had no link to the Internet. The organization experienced the exclusion as loss of face (Kole 1996, 60). The NGO feared a decline in position unless it connected to the Internet. Today, the library is prominently present in the national activities of women's organizations on the Internet. We should, however, not forget that other NGOs experiencing a comparable exclusion may not have the means (financially or other) to become wired.

The popularity of the Internet obscures the fact that there are more computer network technologies in use. In countries where the Internet is not available, people may still be able to use alternative networks, such as FidoNet or

CompuServe.[3] Such systems usually offer e-mail, newsgroups, electronic conferencing, and file transfer facilities. They are based on store-and-forward technology, which means that every connection in the network needs explicit establishment in order to transport data (Vanheste 1994, 23–25, 36). Users establish a connection ("dial-up") once or a few times a day to send and receive a batch of off-line prepared messages and files.

The disadvantage of this technology is that users cannot use applications requiring on-line (interactive) communications, such as chat boxes, real-time discussions, and video conferencing. Neither can a FidoNet user surf the World Wide Web. This may well be the reason why the Internet is generally regarded as superior to other computer networks. But is it not also the cultural idea that technologies prevailing in the North are better than technologies in the South? Do expressions like "Information Super Highway" (with capitals, indeed) not make us believe that the Internet is the best among digital networks (Kole 1996, 75)? Nevertheless, for NGOs remote from an Internet host, an alternative network may be preferable to not being connected at all. And when a poor organization only needs full Internet access occasionally, why invest in a sophisticated technology? After all, technology such as FidoNet is cheap and easy to use, and an out-of-date computer suffices. One cannot always say the same about the more complex and sophisticated Internet applications.

Location

Considering the speed of Internet expansion, one may ask if Internet availability is a real issue. Even on the African continent there are already forty-four countries with full Internet access (Jensen 1998, 1). Nevertheless, there are great disparities between North and South in availability of phone lines, internet service providers, and bandwidth.

The low-income countries, where 55 percent of the global population lives, possess less than 5 percent of the world's telephone lines (Hamelink 1997, 18). South Africa's deputy president Mbeki reminded us that there are more phone lines in New York's Manhattan than in sub-Saharan Africa altogether (M'Bayo 1997, 346). In the high-income countries, the average teledensity (i.e., the number of telephone lines per 100 inhabitants) is fifty. In developing countries the teledensity is often less than one. In Africa, for example, most countries have a teledensity of less than one; and except for South Africa the number nowhere exceeds five lines per 100 inhabitants (M'Bayo 1997, 346–348; Hamelink 1997, 18). Many are of poor quality and restricted in bandwidth.

At the approach of the millennium, there are a great number of initiatives by public and private organizations to extend and upgrade telecommunications infrastructure in developing countries. There are also many initiatives to provide the South with Internet connections and services. Examples are the Information for Development Program of the World Bank, the WorldTel project by the International Telecommunications Union, AT&T's Africa One, and the Leland Initiative of the United States Agency for Development (M'Bayo 1997, 354–356; Hamelink 1997, 18–19). Yet the majority of these projects focus on urban areas, usually a country's capital. This urban bias is in contradiction to the fact that a large proportion of people in developing countries lives in rural areas. Uganda's capital Kampala, for instance, has 4 percent of the nation's population but 60 percent of the share of national telephone lines. In Vietnam, where 80 percent of the population lives in villages, phone lines are available almost exclusively in five major cities (UNU/INTECH and UNIFEM 1997, 2).

Returning to the question of technology haves and have-nots, it thus makes a great difference whether we are talking about NGOs in the North or in the South, in urban or in rural areas. Particularly the social organizations in rural areas of the South are likely to be excluded from electronic networking, simply because no phone lines are available. There are technological alternatives like satellites to solve this problem. Yet these are either too expensive or they offer restricted (store-and-forward) use. When the satellite passes "the jungle," users of the cheap low earth orbit satellites have about twenty minutes to send and receive data (Hegener 1994a, 11). Consequences are delay in information exchange and deprivation of on-line interactive applications. Still, using this technology in communicative isolated areas generates positive experiences and new options (Hegener 1994b, 6).

Gender, Race, and Class

Internet access is entwined with structural gender aspects, such as variances in income, tasks, and education. Women constitute the majority (60 percent) of the poorest worldwide (UNU/INTECH and UNIFEM 1997, 2). The potential to increase their income is generally very small, because women have a low educational level compared to men. Many women in the South are illiterate. If they get an education it is usually for nontechnical professions. Technology is often considered incompatible with reproductive tasks and the domestic sphere, and therefore considered inappropriate for women. Furthermore, women have limited time for their personal development. They have community, household, and reproductive tasks next to their duties in the productive sphere (UNU/INTECH and UNIFEM 1997, 2; Huyer 1997, 2–3, 7; Kole 1996, 46; APC 1997, 43–44; Carr 1997, 23). Huyer (1997) illustrates how all these aspects influence women's access to ICTs in the African continent:

The economic hardships in our countries make it impossible for women, who have to pay school fees for children and to cater for other basic needs, to save money to buy computer hardware, for example. That is why after attending computer courses, if one does not have a computer in the office to practice, then one will lapse back into illiteracy because she cannot afford a computer for herself. Many men are already computer literate because they have more time to themselves, access to ICTs and a supportive environment for them to acquire whatever new skill comes up. (pp. 7–8)

Women constitute the majority of the inhabitants in rural areas. The urban bias in Southern Internet projects thus seriously hampers women's access. Another bias in ICT processes favors the formal economy. This also puts women in the South at a disadvantage, as many of them work in the informal sector (UNU/INTECH and UNIFEM 1997, 6). At the same time, it renders women's contributions to the economy and to communities invisible and un-recognized. The important knowledge that many women in the South possess on health, nutrition, crops, indigenous technology, and so forth is not made available through the Internet. Therefore people cannot know, use, and value it like other information collections around the world (Huyer 1997, 2, 5; APC 1997, 7).

In view of the relationship between general gender issues and gender dis-parities in Internet access, it is very likely that similar dissimilarities occur between people of different races or classes. For example, the caste system in India influences to a great extent who is rich, who is literate, who has a high position in an organization, and so on. We may presume that people belong-ing to a low caste (or to a minority group or low class) encounter access problems comparable to women.

Organizational Characteristics

The Internet is often promoted as a cheap medium for organizations in the South. Yet this seems to apply solely to e-mail and related applications, such as mailing lists. Not only can one use these applications on older (and there-fore cheaper) computers, they require no more than dial-up phone costs plus a couple of minutes for the data transfer. To search for information on the World Wide Web, however, takes much more time and thus a lot more dol-lars. Moreover, it requires a state-of-the-art computer and full Internet con-nection. If NGOs in the South are able to afford a network connection at all, then it is either non-Internet or the organization becomes financially depen-dent on external funding (Kole 1996, 58, 72).

What we then see in the South is that the rich, well-equipped NGOs are the ones having links to the Internet. The small, poorly endowed organizations are more often than not devoid of connections. The former are generally NGOs work-ing on the international level, frequently located in a country's capital. This is not to say that these organizations have the money and other resources to afford ex-tended Internet use, but they are more likely to have (international) contacts to acquire those resources. It is my experience that they are also the ones that are approached by international Internet implementation initiatives.

Besides resources, the type of work NGOs engage in affects which NGOs have Internet connections. For NGOs active in local, basic issues like popular education, religious charity work, or food security in the slums, the Internet may not be so interesting. Popular media, like street theater and face-to-face sessions, may be more appropriate communication instruments for them. Yet for advocacy NGOs defending a cause on the national, regional, or global level, the Internet is useful for propaganda purposes. Think about how the Zapatistas used computer networks to inform the world about their struggle and to gain support. There are numerous examples of NGOs using electronic networks for political aims (Young 1994; Polman and Pouw Kraan 1995; Frederick 1995; Ruth and Ronkin 1992; Kole 1996, 62).

NGOs with a coordination function benefit substantially from Internet use, too. They are the focal points in a social network, providing services to other NGOs and the grassroots. They can use the Internet for information collection and dissemination, coalition activities, lobbying, and so forth. Many case studies describe how these NGOs distribute information from the Net to grassroots organizations. If necessary, they supplement electronic networking with additional media, such as fax, radio, and newspapers, for further information dissemination (Kole 1996, 63; Huyer 1997, 37–38; Mwangi 1997, 41–43; Fortier 1996, 68–69). So even organizations without computers can receive information originating from the Internet.

Position

After discussing some differences between NGOs, it is appropriate to proceed with examining variations within NGOs. Many NGOs in developing countries can afford one computer at the most. Circumstances like tropical temperatures and lack of air-conditioning equipment to cool all office rooms make it impossible to link all members of the organization to a computer network. On top of that, it is common that only a few employees learn how to operate the system. So, generally, computer access is centralized.

With the introduction of the Internet, computer users grow from "data typists" to information specialists. It is no longer a matter of knowing how computer programs work; using Internet applications requires information management as well. Users need to be capable of presenting information on the World Wide Web in a useful and meaningful way to clients. They need to know such things as where to find relevant electronic information and how to apply search strategies.

Next, the users' range of vision changes. Generally speaking, the local or national environment used to delimit their range. Users could maintain international contacts, but these were probably rather scarce due to the costs, slowness, and limitations in available communication media—especially in the South. Yet once connected to the Internet it is very easy to establish and maintain contacts in distant parts of the world. The person operating the computer may in due time obtain a more cosmopolitan scope. He or she is at the heart of exchange with persons from foreign countries and other cultures. The user also acquires computer jargon and "netiquette"—language, norms, and values that apply to the Internet. An experienced user so becomes a netizen.

This may be in striking contrast with other members of the organization. In many NGOs there are no procedures to circulate electronic information. Non-users have difficulties in obtaining Internet information because its access is often as centralized as the access to the technology (Kole 1996, 45–46; Huyer 1997, 8–9). The result is a lack of awareness of the availability of information. Even worse, it leads to a gap in information access between the computer operators and the other employees.

In summary, technical aspects (availability of phone lines), organizational aspects (NGO characteristics, tasks), context (location), and social relations (gender, class, race) all effect the question of who is able to use the Internet. The outcome is, however, not a strict dichotomy of technology haves versus have-nots, or information rich against information poor. Rather, individual NGOs and NGO members are somewhere on a continuum. This continuum has full Internet access on one pole and complete exclusion from computer networks and electronic information on the other (see Figure 14.1). NGOs may have Internet connections, but only use applications that require a less sophisticated computer. Others have a store-and-forward connection. Still others receive information originating from the Internet by radio, newspaper, fax, or any other medium, without actually being linked to the Net.

We need to answer the empowerment question of this chapter differently for persons and NGOs who are more on one side of the continuum than individuals and organizations on the other side. Organizations and employees completely excluded from electronic network processes will of course not gain from Internet information, new skills, new employment opportunities, and other benefits. Users with restricted access have an advantage, but not in comparison to NGOs and employees with full Internet access.

EMPOWERMENT REQUIRES MORE

But does this mean that the NGOs and NGO employees with full Internet access automatically experience more benefits? Are they and their grassroots more empowered simply because they have access to the Internet? This section answers these questions by taking a closer look at the actual practices of NGO computer networking, and illustrates the process with data from research on the UNWCW, a process often referred to in the context of empowerment. It is important, first, to return to gender issues, based on multiple studies.

Figure 14.1
Electronic Network Connectivity Continuum

no access to e-networks or to e-information	no access to e-networks but access to e-information	access to store-and-forward e-networks	restricted access to the Internet	full Internet access

Gender

Women in the South who do have access to electronic networks struggle with many more problems than male users. In a high number of cases they are unable to maintain access. As soon as management—often men—realizes the value of the technology in terms of status, they deny women access to computer equipment (Kole 1996, 46; Huyer 1997, 8).

Projects implementing new technologies in the South, either by commercial firms or public institutions, generally lack gender sensitivity: They yield fewer benefits for women than for men (Carr 1997, 24). Technology assessments to define user needs frequently consult men only (p. 22). The risk is introducing a technology that is inappropriate to the needs, priorities, and circumstances of women (Huyer 1997, 7, 13–17; APC 1997, 28). For instance, surfing the Net is a very time-consuming activity. Female users do not always have the time for this because of their multiple tasks (Kole 1996, 66). Another concern is that technical-assistance projects treat women as passive recipients of technologies rather than offering them an active role in the development. This cuts off the options for women to participate in technology practice and policy (Carr 1997, 20, 22).

There are also psychological barriers for women to use the Internet easily. The tendency to direct women into nontechnological professions causes discomfort, insecurity, fear, and embarrassment among women when confronted with the new technology (Huyer 1997, 8); so does the social association of technology with masculinity. Male users generally take an active approach, exploring and mastering the Internet. Women show a waiting attitude and feel lack of control. Many women who have already used computer networks for two to five years still feel insecure and are afraid to use more complex functions (Kole 1996, 66, 85; APC 1997, 7–8, 27–28, 43–45).

Information on the Internet is sometimes pornographic, sexist, harassing, or hostile to women.[4] This causes stress and reluctance among women who use the networks; for instance, for feminist activities (APC 1997, 41, 43; Kole 1996, 68). Process aspects of electronic networking may intimidate women as well. An example of a woman lawyer from Uganda illustrates this: "She has to wait two days to pick up replies, but most e-mails she sends never arrive at their destinations, because the addresses are keyed in by the library personnel, who, she reports, 'tend to make mistakes' in keying in the addresses" (Huyer 1997, 8).

Policy and Conceptual View

The research on the UNWCW was striking because none of the NGOs employed a political vision toward electronic networking. Hardly any NGO issued policy on information and communications in relation to the organization's objectives: the empowerment of women and of their grassroots. The same applies to Northern nongovernmental donor organizations (Kole 1996, 46–47).[5] While the NGOs expected much political impact from electronic networking, they used it merely as an instrument to improve efficiency. An example is the lobby process, supported successfully through e-mail use (p. 61). Still, there was no lobbying in the sense of individual NGOs or NGO members e-mailing personally to U.N. representatives. Computer networks solely provided lobbyists with up-to-date information for later use in face-to-face sessions with government delegates (p. 52). The democratic ideal of decentralized political participation through network use (Rodriguez 1987; Schuler 1994) in no way came through.

One can also raise questions about the influence of electronic alerts. While the interviewees all valued the impact of alert actions positively or even very positively, no one could tell me about the actual impact. For instance, e-mail messages reported human-rights violations by China, the country hosting the UNWCW. The intention was to counter the image that China presented in the mass media (Kole 1996, 61–62). Clearly, e-mail offered the NGOs an instrument of independent news provision, a valuable empowerment instrument (pp. 63–64). Yet did the alerts really change the view of the mass audience following the conference news on CNN? Did it stop the human-rights violations against Tibetan conference attendants and other organizations opposing the Chinese government?

Self-Reliance

In the UNWCW study, women from the South repeatedly reported lack of insight into organizational aspects (Kole 1996, 56–57; see also Huyer 1997, 30). A striking example is the design of a World Wide Web site by a Northern expatriate to enable a UNWCW focal point in Latin America to distribute conference information. After the expatriate had left the NGO realized that the Web site needed continuous management—and thus time, money, skills, and knowledge of the English language (Kole 1996, 46, 56–57). For these needs the NGO was again dependent on the North.

Lack of "capacity building" (creating conditions for self-reliance and technological institutionalization) is indeed a recurring phenomenon in computer network implementation in the South. For instance, computer training habitually addresses users and systems operators only, without educating trainers to anticipate future needs. Too often the emphasis of an Internet project is on "instant" manifest results, such as graphical Web pages. Project managers hardly consider the fact that maintaining such a system demands sophisticated hardware and software, plus substantial skills (Kole 1996, 45; Huyer 1997, 31).

Participation in electronic discussions presents a similar problem. Too often the technical establishment of a virtual discussion space clouds issues such as active involvement, discussion styles, and language. For instance, many social groups can not voice their opinions on affairs that affect them for the simple reason that they do not speak English. Discussion groups in Central Asia and Africa completely failed for such nontechnical reasons (Kole 1996, 46, 52; Huyer 1997, 31).

Culture

Research by Ishii (1993) illustrates that cultural context also influences the ability to make use of electronic discussions. Ishii analyzed electronic decision-making processes by North American and Japanese users. The former extensively used the features of discussion software to express their personal opinions. The active contribution by individual participants and the final decision based on the contents reflect the individualistic character of American debating (pp. 148–150).

In Japan, decision making and discussions are more collective processes. Japanese take formal decisions on the basis of consensus acquired through multiple personal, informal contacts, mainly behind the scenes. The sole purpose of Japanese discussion sessions is to share and confirm each other's point of view. Therefore, group communication depends strongly on contextual aspects like facial expressions and body language; for instance, nodding assent. This discussion style concurs with Ishii's (1993) findings that Japanese computer users preferred the use of videoconferencing preceded by personal e-mail, rather than discussion programs (pp. 148–150).

The study demonstrates that people actively give technology meaning and use it in a way that conforms to their cultural frames of reference. However, the findings also make it questionable whether Internet applications are suitable for all cultures under all conditions (see, for instance, Kole 1996, 75–76). This is even more significant in view of empowerment processes: How can people with an oral tradition, like in Africa, disseminate their knowledge and express their opinions through an electronic medium and still maintain their cultural identity?

Information and Communication Flows

The United States distributed the majority of the UNWCW information, particularly in the period preceding the conference. There was scarcely intercontinental South–South communication. The Southern users participating in my research hardly ever addressed Southern continents other than their own. Reasons for this are technical (low connectivity), economic, and political. It is, for instance, easier and cheaper for a Francophone African country to establish a telephone contact with an Anglo-Saxon neighboring country via Paris than through a direct connection. This phenomenon is a result of former colonial relations, which shaped the national telecommunications structures in developing countries (Kole 1996, 70).

While colonial relations and other political aspects influence computer networking, the technology in its turn affects issues of boundaries. At a UNWCW project in Amman, Jordan, Arab NGOs did not obtain permission to use the nearby network node at Jerusalem because of the Arab–Israeli conflict. Still, they overcame this barrier by linking to a remote computer in London. This relieved the Arab women, previously cut off from other women's organizations, from their isolation (Kole 1996, 67).

DISCUSSION

The previous section demonstrates some options of the Internet to contribute to empowerment processes like influencing policy and breaking through communicative isolation (see also APC 1997, 22–23; Fortier 1996, 63–64; Huyer 1997, 10–13). It is, however, clear that networking NGOs and users in the South suffer a lot of problems, limitations, and increased dependencies (see APC 1997, 23–24, 43–47; Fortier 1996, 74–76; Huyer 1997, 7). Main barriers and constraints are rooted in existing social relations, nonadapted management styles, and context aspects. The gains of digital networking are not equally distributed. Furthermore, NGOs do not employ the potentials for empowerment purposes extensively. Clearly, empowerment does not occur "of itself" simply by linking up to the Internet.

Mutual Shaping of Technology and Society

A position on the electronic network connectivity continuum does not determine Internet empowerment options. On its own, Internet connectivity does not generate technology haves and have-nots or information rich and poor, as would be expected from a deterministic, pessimistic vision. Even when a Southern NGO has full Internet access, the problems encountered may be huge and manifold. In the end, the organization becomes more dependent on the North than before the introduction of the Net. In another scenario, new skills, access to electronic information, and extension of social networks empower computer users. Still, as long as they do not share these assets with other NGO employees or with the organization's grassroots, there is no question of empowerment of all, and certainly not of the poor and underprivileged.

NGOs need to effectuate the potentials that connectivity offers. Adaptation of management style, Internet policy, considering the relationship with CBOs, incorporating sociocultural aspects, and so forth are all means to achieve this. Nonetheless, there are always unpredictable influences and processes beyond the control of a single organization. Think about government regulations and neocolonial relationships. As we have seen, such aspects may obstruct the contribution of internetworking to empowerment processes.

Technology does not stand on its own. It shapes and is shaped by its environment (Callon 1987; Grint and Woolgar 1997; Mackenzie and Wajcman 1992; Bijker, Hughes, and Pinch 1987). This environment includes the organization, the local situation, and national, regional, and even global structures and relationships. Technology and society coevolve, and so do empowerment and computer network processes. The UNWCW and other case studies illustrate that the Internet influences empowerment processes of Southern NGOs in both positive and negative ways. The complex interplay of technological and social features provides options to reconsider social relations (in the UNWCW case by influencing U.N. gender policy) at the same time it reinforces them (such as men depriving women of computer access).

Nontechnological aspects play a considerable part in shaping the possibilities and constraints of internetworking for empowerment. For example, rural organizations are not devoid of the Internet because of technical impossibilities but due to the choices made in ICT projects. Transnational conglomerates like AT&T or Teledisc introduce ICTs in modernized urban areas because there lie their chances for market expansion.

Power relations are an important factor in the shaping of technology. Actors with more resources, such as money, knowledge, high positions, contacts, and access to tools, are dominant in the social shaping of network processes. NGOs with full Internet access can, for example, determine which electronic information they will or will not forward to CBOs. At the same time, technological processes reconfirm dominant positions and identities (Law 1991; Cockburn 1985; Wajcman 1991; Noble 1978; Winner 1980). Unequal relations between North and South, between men and women, and between NGOs and the grassroots in internetworking reinforce existing disparities. Many inequalities have less to do with technology because of existing technical alternatives. They have to do with the awareness, interests, and will to make these alternatives available and appropriate. But available to and appropriate to whom?

Internet and Empowerment

To strengthen their empowerment processes, NGOs need to change their attitudes toward the Internet: from technical device into political instrument. Instead of emphasizing improved efficiency, NGOs need to deal with questions such as equal distribution of electronic information, needs of the grassroots, and gender aspects in computer networking. If not, they may end up serving the interests of bodies like the United Nations or governments; for instance, as spokesmen of civil society to facilitate global processes. An evolution comparable to the one of unions—from labor representatives opposing employers into mediators between states, employers, and laborers—is well conceivable.

The relation between Southern NGOs and their funding agencies in the North is delicate as well. Too much stress on efficiency on the donor's side turns the Internet into an instrument of control. It forces NGOs to become more accountable through electronic communication and so reduce their autonomy. It is thus imperative that donors change their attitude to the Internet, too. They can use it, for instance, to increase mutuality in policy making. Donors also need to accentuate capacity building in ICT projects.

The most important danger, however, does not apply to the international level, but to national relations within civil society. As cosmopolitan netizens, international NGOs may handle electronic communication, netiquette, and electronic information management very well. Yet unless NGOs adapt their stand and vision toward computer networking, they will alienate themselves from the poor and underprivileged. Using the Internet at the international level to become more successful in fostering social change soon results in a friction with the NGO task of representating the grassroots. International intermediate NGOs and their highly educated employees who have access to the Internet claim to represent grassroots organizations. Nevertheless, there is a huge gap in understanding (Mwangi 1997, 45–46) and, consequently, in empowerment benefits.

Mwangi (1997) puts forward the central issues in the alienation process between NGO computer networks and local communities (pp. 36–38). First is the inability to bridge the gap between the goals and expectations of different social groups. Second is that there is not enough attention paid to the role that ICTs play in altering the power balance among groups within civil society. Third, networking tends to focus primarily on passing on information, relevant or not, without sufficient efforts to make such information meaningful to people at the grassroots level. Finally, the networking NGOs are usually not selected and supported from below, and may not feel accountable to the CBOs.

The core issue, Mwangi (1997) writes, is the "interconnectedness of information flow and communication with deeper structural issues—of democracy and equity in NGO and CBO relations" (p. 38). As long as these structural issues are not addressed, the use of computer networks such as the Internet will only reinforce existing inequities (p. 39; Kole 1996, 96–97). Under those circumstances, empowerment through internetworking certainly does not apply to the world's poorest and most marginalized groups.

CONCLUSION

When we study the implications of the Internet on social relations, a technological approach anticipating positive or negative consequences only, it is not very fruitful. Neither is an approach that merely addresses social dependencies in terms of haves versus have-nots. It is equally important to develop a conceptual framework that recognizes the mutual relationship between technology and society. Only such a framework enables us to better understand the many-sided implications of the Internet for different actors. It would provide the means to analyze empowerment and disempowerment processes simultaneously, for distinct types of NGOs and for diverse persons within or represented by these organizations.

Several theoretical approaches are applicable. One may consider a communications theory that incorporates both positive and negative implications

(Servaes 1989). Another option is a sociological theory linking local and global processes comparable to Giddens's structuration theory (Orlikowski 1992). Political economy theories (Fortier 1996) and constructivist technology studies offer fruitful frameworks, too.

In Internet practice, many conditions need to be met at all levels of society. The NGOs themselves can actively contribute to creating these conditions. They can involve people who are likely to be excluded from networking processes; for instance, by sharing electronic information throughout the organization or by integrating a gender approach in electronic networking. NGOs can also pay attention to socioorganizational aspects of internetworking such as maintenance, dependencies, and technological appropriateness with regard to culture.

Most important, international network processes need to be supplemented with linkages to and from local initiatives. This enables NGOs to share information and speak on behalf of the grassroots more adequately. The grassroots themselves should play an active role in the linkages, which requires complementary media. Finally, it seems wise that donors and NGOs develop collective political strategies to use the Internet as an instrument for empowerment. This may call for a redefinition of empowerment in Internet processes: Empowerment for whom?

NOTES

1. Part of this chapter is based on the author's research for her Master's thesis (Kole 1996). I would like to thank Grietje and Willem Kummer for their editorial revisions.

2. An in-depth elaboration of this study can be found in Kole (1996). Despite the low response, the data are illustrative of the issues in NGO computer networking.

3. These differ from the Internet in the technical specifications (protocol) of the data transport mechanism. The Internet uses the TCP/IP protocol, other systems use different protocols like UUCP (Vanheste 1994, 31, 43, 174). The distinct systems are linked through dedicated computers (gateways) that convert data for exchange.

4. I experienced this myself when working at the Internet support group of the Amsterdam Women Center. There was a need to moderate the electronic discussions because of the frequently posted contributions of the tenor, "Why argue about this, women are dumb anyway."

5. This observation is based on personal experiences from my traineeship at a Dutch development donor organization.

REFERENCES

APC. 1997. *Global Networking for Change: Experiences from the APC Women's Programme*. Report of the Gender and Information Technology Project. London: APC Women's Networking Support Programme.

Bellman, B., A. Tindimubona, and A. Arias, Jr. 1993. Technology Transfer in Global Networking. In *Global Networks: Computers and International Communication*, edited by L. M. Harasim. Cambridge: MIT Press.

Bijker, W. E., T. P. Hughes, and T. J. Pinch, eds. 1987. *The Social Construction of Technological Systems: New Directions in the Sociology and History of Technology*. Cambridge: MIT Press.

Callon, M. 1987. The Sociology of an Actor Network: The Case of the Electric Vehicle. In *Mapping the Dynamics of Science and Technology: Sociology of Science in the Real World*, edited by M. Callon, J. Law, and A. Rip. Basingstoke: MacMillan.

Carr, M. 1997. Gender and Technology: Is There a Problem? In *Technology and Development: Strategies for the Integration of Gender*, edited by S. Everts. Presentations from the Technologie Overdracht Ontwikkelings Landen (TOOL) conference, Amsterdam, 6 June.

Claessen, J., and L. van Wesemael-Smit. 1992. *Reading the Word and the World: Literacy and Education from a Gender Perspective*. Oegstgeest: Vrouwenberaad Ontwikkelingssamenwerking.

Cockburn, C. 1985. Technology, Production and Power. In *Machinery of Dominance: Women, Men and Technical Know-How*, edited by C. Cockburn. London: Pluto Press.

Ezigbalike, C., and S. Ochuodho. 1991. E-mail for Developing Countries: What They Never Tell You About It. Paper presented at AITEC South Conference, 13–16 November, Harare.

Frederick, H. H. 1993. *Global Communication and International Relations*. Belmont, Calif.: Wadsworth.

———. 1995. North American NGO Computer Networking: Computer Communications in Cross-Boarder Coalition-Building—The Case of Mexico. Research report for the RAND Corporation and Ford Foundation, Program for Research on Immigration Policy, DRU-234-FF 1994.

Fortier, F. 1996. Civil Society Computer Networks: The Perilous Road of Cyber-Politics. Ph.D. diss. York University, Toronto.

Grint, K., and S. Woolgar. 1997. *The Machine at Work: Technology, Work and Organization*. Cambridge/Oxford/Malden: Polity Press.

Hamelink, C. J. 1994. *Trends in World Communication: On Disempowerment and Self-Empowerment*. Penang: Southbound.

———. 1997. *New Information and Communication Technologies, Social Development and Cultural Change*. Discussion paper 86. Geneva: UNRISD.

Hegener, M. 1994a. Email from the Bush: On-Line in the Third World. *World Press Review*, April, 11.

———. 1994b. Verbinding met Boven: Satellieten bieden de Derde Wereld aansluiting op de electronische snelweg. *NRC Handelsblad*, 27 August, 6.

Huyer, S. 1997. *Supporting Women's Use of Information Technology for Sustainable Development*. Report for the Gender and Sustainable Development Unit of the IDRC. Ottawa: IDRC; Ontario: WIGSAT.

Ishii, H. 1993. Cross-Cultural Communication and CSCW. In *Global Networks: Computers and International Communication*, edited by L. M. Harasim. Cambridge: MIT Press.

Jensen, M. 1998. *African Internet Connectivity*. <http://demiurge.wn.apc.org:80/africa/>.

Kole, E. 1996. The Benefits of Electronic Networking for Women: The Case of the Fourth UN–World Conference on Women, Beijing 1995. Master's thesis. University of Amsterdam.

Law, J., ed. 1991. *A Sociology of Monsters: Essays on Power, Technology and Domination*. London: Routledge.

Mackenzie, D., and J. Wajcman, eds. 1992. *The Social Shaping of Technology: How the Refrigerator Got Its Hum*. London: Open University Press.

M'Bayo, R. 1997. Africa and the Global Information Infrastructure: Prospects, Obstacles, Preferences and Policies for the 21st Century. *Gazette: The International Journal for Communication Studies* 59: 345–364.

Mwangi, W. 1997. *Rethinking the Role of International Communication Networks in Local Empowerment*. Master's thesis. The Hague, Institute of Social Studies.

Noble, D. 1978. Social Choice in Machine Design: The Case of the Automatically Controlled Machine Tools, and a Challenge for Labor. *Politics & Society* 8: 313–347.

Orlikowski, W. J. 1992. The Duality of Technology: Rethinking the Concept of Technology in Organizations. *Organization Science* 3: 398–427.

Polman, M., and P. van der Pouw Kraan. 1995. *Van bolwerken tot netwerken. Datacommunicatie door maatschappelijke organisaties*. Amsterdam: Ravijn.

Rodriguez, G. 1987. Electronic Networking: A New Tool for Development Action. *Media Development* 4: 2–3.

Ruth, S. R., and R. R. Ronkin. 1992. Aiming for the Elusive Payoff of User Networks: An NGO Perspective. Paper presented at the Annual Meeting of the International Society for Systems Science (ISSS), Denver, July 12–17.

Schuler, D. 1994. Community Networks: Building a New Participatory Medium. *Communications of the ACM* 37: 39–51.

Servaes, J. 1989. *One World, Multiple Cultures: A New Paradigm on Communication for Development*. Leuven/Amersfoort: Acco.

UNU/INTECH and UNIFEM. 1997. *Gender and Telecommunications: An Agenda for Policy*. Maastricht/New York: UNU/INTECH and UNIFEM.

Vanheste, J. 1994. *Internet: Gids voor wereldwijd netwerken*. Compact computer course. Utrecht: Het Spectrum.

Wajcman, J. 1991. *Feminism Confronts Technology*. Cambridge: Polity Press.

Winner, L. 1980. Do Artifacts Have Politics? *Daedalus* 109: 121–136.

Young, J. E. 1994. Spreading the Net. *World Watch*, January–February, 20–27.

15

Implications of the Information Revolution for Africa: Cyberimperialism, Cyberhype, or Cyberhope?

Robert G. White

Even though the dust has not yet settled from the information revolution of the twentieth century, it is not too soon to examine the impact that it will have in Africa in the next millennium. Discussions in the advanced industrialized countries of the North suggest a vast and far-reaching revolution in information technology, one that is transforming business, finance, politics, entertainment, education, and many other facets of our lives in a way that leaves them barely recognizable (Stoll 1995). Will this revolution have the same effect in Africa? In other words, what turn does the discussion take when we try to expand it to include Africa? If even part of the constant cyberhype we are bombarded with here in the North is true, what does it mean for Africa? Are the breezes of the current African Renaissance strong enough to allow us to separate the cyberwheat from the cyberchaff? To answer these questions requires an examination of the current state of Internet connectivity in Africa and some of the initiatives contemplated and underway to enhance it.

CYBERHYPE OR CYBERHOPE?

The irrelevancy of much of the Northern cyberhype, at least in the context of Africa, can be illustrated by a statement like this: "Territorial boundaries are rendered meaningless as bits and bytes and electrons and data and faxes and images speed along fiber optic cable, up and down satellite links, and through the matrix of cyberspace, the infobahn, the Internet, the Information Superhighway, the Global Information Infrastructure at the speed of light" (Mills 1998, 1). The image that this statement conjures up in our minds is one of a highly wired society, where everyone has a telephone, a fax, a computer, and a T-1 line. This is not the reality in Africa. And in spite of the rapid expansion of connectivity and improvements in infrastructure, it is not likely to be the reality for a very long time. Let us look more closely at some of the issues involved here.

First, it is true that connectivity is rapidly expanding in Africa. Today nearly 75 percent of the capital cities are connected to the Internet, up from barely 25 percent just two years ago. South Africa is among the top twenty countries in the world in terms of connectivity (Jensen 1998). Kenya, however, is a more typical example. Nairobi, the capital, is the major commercial center for East Africa, a key diplomatic post, and home to important international agencies, including the U.N. Environment Program. It is among the top dozen countries in Africa in terms of connectivity, with a half dozen Internet service providers. Still, fewer than 1 percent of the population have telephones, and there are more than 70,000 people waiting for lines. Many other countries are doing less well. So while it is true that connectivity is increasing, there is a very long way to go (USAID February 1995; Jensen 1999).

Second, a number of important initiatives are underway to increase connectivity in Africa. Among these are the U.S. Agency for International Development's (USAID) Leland Initiative, the African Virtual University with "seed" money provided by the World Bank, the Tyco Corporation's plan to lay a fiber-optic cable around Africa, the WorldSpace Corporation's plan for its AfriStar satellite communications system, and the African Information Society Initiative sponsored by the Economic Commission for Africa. Let us take a closer look at these initiatives.

The USAID's Leland Initiative is described as "a five-year $15 million US government effort to extend full Internet connectivity to approximately twenty African countries in order to promote sustainable development" (USAID February 1995). It "seeks to bring the benefits of the global information revolution to people of Africa, through connection to the Internet and other Global Information Infrastructure (GII) technologies." There are three primary objectives. The first is to create an "enabling policy environment" that will provide low-cost and widely available Internet services free from government interference. Second, it hopes through technical and entrepreneurial training to create a sustainable supply of Internet services, including Internet service providers, with special attention to countrywide access, including rural areas. Third, the Leland Initiative seeks to build capacity in the countries where it is implemented to use the Internet for "sustainable development in manufacturing, business, the environment, health, democracy, education and other sectors."

The first step for countries that wish to participate is the signing of a memorandum of understanding with the U.S. government, in which they agree to promote "Internet friendly policies." A number of countries have taken this first step, including Mali, Madagascar, Rwanda, Mozambique, Ghana, Cote d'Ivoire, Guinea, Benin, Guinea-Bissau, and Zambia. Kenya, Uganda, and Ethiopia, however, have not, and the prospects look dim that they will anytime soon. Indeed, one U.S. government official familiar with the project told me, "In Ethiopia the Leland Initiative is dead" (USIS Official 1998). In Kenya it was described to me as having "never got off the ground" (Ogutu 1998). And in Uganda, no signs of life could be observed (Mutazindwa 1998; Stryker 1998). Clearly, the implementation thus far is uneven, and it is no doubt too early to evaluate the overall project and its impact. Moreover, a number of conferences, training workshops, and so forth have taken place whose value in terms of Internet education and application as well as generally increased awareness is substantial but hard to measure.

The African Virtual University (AVU), on the other hand, differs from the Leland Initiative in that it has a quite specific focus on distance education at the university level (AVU 1999). Distance education is a particularly attractive concept to many African governments. The cost compared to sending students overseas is low, especially in terms of living expenses, travel, and tuition. Moreover, courses can be specifically tailored to meet local needs, whether that be calculus in the mathematics department, hydrology of arid areas in the engineering department, or desktop publishing in the communications department. Finally, and often quite important in many cases, the government does not have to worry about students not returning home from their overseas education. While the AVU was initially funded by the World Bank, it plans to become financially self-sustaining in the next few years. Started in 1995, the AVU finished its first-year pilot phase, successfully delivering several first-year science and engineering courses to a dozen African universities.

The format in the pilot phase is that courses originating in the United States and Ireland are sent by satellite to participating universities previously equipped with satellite dish receivers. Students sit in a classroom at their university in front of a television monitor, taking notes. Although the courses incorporate some of the latest educational technology in their design and delivery, there is little interaction. In addition to the first-year science and engineering courses, there is a remedial instruction program and a professional development program.

One of the most successful of the AVU sites is Kenyatta University in Kenya. Here, under the direction of Dr. Magdallen N. Juma, director of the Institute of Distance Education and the AVU, a separate section of the campus has been dedicated to the AVU. With the full support of the university administration it has been completely retrofitted with multimonitor lecture halls and fully equipped computer laboratories. Electricity supply is assured by a separate back-up generator. With full Internet access and the development of a digital library, students and faculty have access to almost the full wealth of information available to their peers anywhere else on the planet (Juma 1998).

But can such a program actually become financially sustainable, or is this just cyberhype? In spring 1998, at the end of the academic term of the first-year pilot phase, Kenyatta University's AVU decided to test the market in the

Nairobi area for fee-based (i.e., for profit) courses on computer use, including how to use the Internet and various application programs common in the business world (word processing, Windows 95, etc.). Such an effort made sense in that it would allow fuller utilization of the expensive facilities as well as generate revenue for the AVU program, pushing it along the road to being financially self-sustaining. The response to their brief advertisement in local newspapers was stunning, indeed. They were overwhelmed with applications. All the courses and workshops were immediately fully subscribed, indicating not only substantial interest but an important and previously untapped market (Juma 1998).

The AVU plans to offer complete undergraduate degree programs soon, and to incorporate African-originated content in its next phase. The African-originated content will include complete courses produced at one African university and sent via satellite and Internet to other African universities. This next phase will allow for the development and training of African faculty in distance-learning techniques, as well as the exploitation of existing strengths at various institutions. Indeed, the AVU says that one measure of its success "will be the extent to which our program offerings are truly africanized" (AVU 1999).

In addition to expanding access to university education in Africa, the AVU will influence the way faculty, staff, and students interact with themselves, with those at other institutions of higher learning in Africa, and with their peers elsewhere in the world. The advent of e-mail and the Internet, especially H-AFRICA (<http:///www.h-net.msu.edu/~africa>), has already changed the way research is conducted and disseminated and this is likely to continue at an accelerated rate as scholars and students in Africa become connected to the Internet (Polman 1998). In this context it is worth noting the amazing success of what is now the largest private fully accredited university in the United States, the University of Phoenix, which has specialized in Internet-based distance-learning programs in business, management, and technology directed to working adults (<http://www.uophx.edu/online>). To be fair, there has been substantial criticism of cyberbased distance education in the United States, and of the University of Phoenix, in particular. But with prestigious major universities now offering degree courses over the Internet, the criticism seems to be subsiding. Oxford University, for example, is one of the latest to join the trend (Targett 1998).

Two other initiatives underway in the private sector are worth noting here. The first, often known as Africa ONE, is a plan to lay a fiber-optic cable around the continent with secondary links to inland countries. Originally started by AT&T, it was subsequently sold to Tyco Submarine Systems (<http://www.submarinesystems.com>). The current status of the project is not clear. South Africa has not expressed strong interest in it, as it is already linked to Europe and North America by the mid-Atlantic hub in the Canary Islands, and soon will be linked by the South Africa Far East (SAFE) cable from

South Africa to Malaysia (Ogutu 1998). Because of its circular design, redundancy is one of its strengths, since if there is a break anywhere along the line traffic can be rerouted in the other direction until repairs are made. Although when it was first proposed by AT&T the project received a great deal of publicity, recently it seems to have faded from the news. It certainly is not a high-priority project at Tyco Submarine Systems.

The second initiative, also a private, for-profit venture, is WorldSpace (<http://www.worldspace.com>). Noah Samara, the chair and CEO of WorldSpace, himself of African origin, plans to broadcast digital audio and multimedia by satellite to Africa. With over 100 channels available, the potential for an amazing diversity of programming is possible. Many, perhaps most, will be commercial, since this is a private, for-profit company. But Samara (1997) has made it clear that offerings will include "programs in specific areas of information, such as health, women's issues, civic education and conflict resolution." In addition, he is "exploring the establishment of a Peace Channel for all of Africa. This broadcast service would promote dialog and reconciliation, and it would work to resolve conflicts by broadcasting information intended to create an environment of peace" (pp. 9–10).

Finally, there is the African Information Society Initiative (1999), sponsored by the Economic Commission for Africa. Broadly speaking, it is a framework to guide the development of information infrastructure, training, and policy at the national level. The premise of the initiative is that building an information society in Africa will promote a nation's "development plans, stimulate growth and provide new opportunities in education, trade, healthcare, job creation and food secuirity, helping African countries to leapfrog stages of development and raise their standards of living" (20 January 1997, p. 1). Its activities have largely consisted of sponsoring symposia and coordinating meetings of various groups and organizations with an interest in the topic such as the International Telecommunication Union, the U.N. Educational, Scientific, and Cultural Organization (UNESCO), and the International Development Research Center (IDRC).

What are we to make of these initiatives, their potential for success, and their impact? Is this cyberimperialism, cyberhype, or cyberhope? Even if these initiatives, or some of them, succeed, there are still a number of major "potholes" on the information superhighway in Africa, including infrastructure, poverty, and authoritarian rule. Teledensity in Africa is the smallest in the world. It is concentrated in urban areas, although most people live in the rural areas. And it is concentrated in one particular country, South Africa. "Only 1.4 percent of the continent's 700 million population uses the Internet" (Jensen 1998), and about 70 percent of those live in South Africa (Jensen 1998; Hegener 1996; Geerdts 1996). Moreover, the telephone lines are old, the equipment is in poor condition, and the service is frequently unreliable. Indeed, service is sometimes characterized by its absence. New lines are hard to get and there is often a long waiting list. Almost everyone I have talked to in

Africa about this subject has mentioned the infrastructure problem. Unfortunately, there is no quick solution; repairing and building out the telecommunications infrastructure is going to be expensive and will take time.

Privatization of state telecommunications monopolies resulting in increased competition may lay the groundwork for improvements and provide incentives for undertaking them. And there is some cause for optimism in this regard. For example, Uganda has already invited the South African telecommunications company MTN to come in and begin offering service, and they will do so soon. Kenya is also planning a major restructuring of its state telecommunications monopoly, although it is too soon to tell precisely what shape it will take or what impact it will have on the improvement of services. In other countries—Ethiopia, for example—there is really little cause for optimism. The government has made it clear that it has no intention of giving up its monopoly on telecommunications to private companies or allowing other private Internet service providers to enter the market. And the current state of military hostilities with Eritrea over their disputed border may well strengthen Ethiopia's resolve in this respect.

It seems appropriate to ask what contribution the Cyber Age can make to the resolution of the seemingly intractable conflicts in Africa, whether based on borders, ethnicity, nationalism, natural resources, or just the raw lust for power. In most cases the contribution will be minimal, but it has potential. Consider the case of the Ogoni people in Rivers State in the Niger delta of southern Nigeria. After the discovery of oil there in the late 1950s by Shell, the giant multinational petroleum company, the Ogoni began a long, fitful, and frequently unsuccessful struggle to protect their land from environmental degradation caused by oil spills, air pollution caused by the flaring of natural gas, and so forth. Over a fifteen-year period nearly 3,000 spills totaling over 2 million barrels were recorded. But the Ogoni, less than a half percent of the Nigerian population, found themselves facing the ruthless force of the military government, which put itself shamelessly in the service of Shell. The conflict moved into cyberspace with the establishment of an Ogoni Web page dominated by the bright yellow Shell logo dripping with equally bright red blood (see <http://www.oneworld.org/mosop/>; <http://www.sierraclub.org/human-rights/ogoni19.html>; and <http://xs2.greenpeace.org/~comms/ken/hell.html#cont>). While this did not come soon enough to save the lives of Ogoni activists, including noted author Ken Sero-Wiwa and others who were hanged by the military government, it does indicate the potential for a tiny group to use the power of cyberspace to build a worldwide constituency for environmental justice. This is a lesson not likely to be lost on others engaged in similar struggles.

But what about wider conflicts, like the crisis in the Great Lakes region of Africa involving the Democratic Republic of the Congo (formerly Zaire), Rwanda, Uganda, and, more recently, Angola, Namibia, and Zimbabwe. This is a complex and complicated conflict, whose human suffering makes one long for help from cyberspace. It is complex because there are many actors involved, ranging from nation-states to ethnic groups to private business interests. Briefly, following the 1994 genocide of the Tutsi by the Hutu in Rwanda, the Tutsi-led Rwanda Patriotic Front invaded and overthrew the Hutu-led government, in the process creating over a million Hutu refugees who fled across the border into neighboring Zaire. There, with the toleration of the long-time dictator of Zaire, Mobutu Sese Seko, and the United Nations, the Hutu reorganized and rearmed themselves to finish their genocidal task. When cross-border raids from these camps into Rwanda became intolerable, Rwanda, with the assistance of Uganda and dissent elements in Zaire, launched a successful military operation to disperse the refugee camps and to overthrow the Mubutu regime, which had long been supported by the United States, France, and Belgium. Laurent Kabila, who replaced Mobutu and changed the name of the country from Zaire to the Democratic Republic of the Congo, proved little better than Mobutu. So a second rebellion began, again backed by Rwanda and Uganda, but this time Kabila got support from Angola, Zimbabwe, and Namibia, all of whom sent troops and supplies, which proved decisive in the battles near the Atlantic coast. The struggle continues in eastern regions near the Great Lakes.

Several peace conferences have been held, but no agreement has been reached to stop the fighting. What contribution can the Cyber Age make here? Can connectivity contribute to conflict resolution in this case? Not, I think, in any major way. Increased communication between Kabila and the rebels seems like an obvious starting point, but the problem is not one of technology, e-mail, videoconferencing, and so forth, but one of political will. If Kabila will not talk to the rebels when they are in the same hotel, would he answer their e-mail? Connectivity in the region is so low and unreliable that there is little chance of involving large numbers of citizens in cyberdiscussions. On the other hand, dissemination of information about the conflict on the Web is helpful in contributing to a better understanding of this complex conflict in the wider international community, and the knowledge of rapid dissemination of reports on human-rights violations may have some deterrent effect on the combatants (Contemporary Conflicts in Africa 1999).

What about early warnings of international conflict? "Early warning," Bruce W. Jentleson (1999), points out, "actually has been less of a problem than often asserted and assumed." There is, however, some reason for hope. Conflict resolution, especially training, is making an increasing appearance on the Internet. Not much of it is directed toward international relations, especially toward conflicts like the one just described in the Great Lakes region of Africa. But it could be, and I think in the future it might be, so there is some, albeit it small, glimmer of hope (Hauss 1998).

So is the information revolution in Africa a case of cyberimperialism, cyberhype, or cyberhope? The answer is a little bit of all three. To the extent that the hardware and software, basic building blocks of the Information Age, continue to be dominated by the Northern industrialized countries, it may be cyberimperialism. But these are mere vessels, empty of substantial content.

Moreover, there are already signs of erosion of this domination, with the production of hardware components in the Third World and the large and growing Third World software industry. Although this may be at the moment more true for Asia than Africa, the handwriting is on the wall. But what about content? Is there any African content out there?

The answer is yes, there is a lot of African content and it is growing (see, e.g., ANC 1999). Much of the growth in African content is in expected directions: business, education, entertainment, and so on. But sometimes it is in unexpected directions. Consider, for example, that while Ethiopia is still struggling to come to grips with the implications of the information revolution, the struggle of the Oromia, in the southern part of the country, already has its own Web site (<http://www.ourworld.compuserve.com/homepages/osgweb>). In a classic military maneuver, not from the last century but from the next, the Ethiopian government is being outflanked, not on the ground, but in cyberspace.

Moreover, the African content in terms of page design is different in subtle and interesting ways that one cannot help but notice. The graphics, for example, are distinctly African, and there are more of them. It may be, as Professor Jessica N. Aguti (1998), coordinator of the AVU at Makerere University in Kampala, Uganda, told me during a visit there recently, "Africans see the world in a different way, and that is going to be reflected in the way we construct and use the World Wide Web."

I believe the information revolution will have a positive impact in Africa over the next millennium, but in different, perhaps softer and more subtle ways than in the North. And Africa may well influence the direction of the Information Age in the North and elsewhere in the Third World in a way perhaps parallel to the interplay of influences in music, like jazz and reggae. It comes to the West and is transformed in the process. Then it returns to Africa, being transformed again, before returning once more to the West. When an African musician picks up an American banjo, we should not expect to hear American folk music. The same may be true of computers and the Internet.

Let me return for a moment to the discussion of the AVU and distance education. The same technology that permits knowledge to flow from Ireland and the United States to Kenya and Uganda, or from Tanzania to Nigeria, also permits knowledge to flow from Africa to the North. The Internet and distance education via the Internet is not a one-way street. Indeed, it is not a street at all. Students in Ireland and the United States could be receiving courses originating in Africa, based on knowledge generated in Africa, and taught from an African perspective. Consider the subject of agroforestry, for example. Much of the knowledge about this subject is generated and resides in the International Center for Research in Agroforestry in Nairobi, Kenya (ICRAF) (<http://www.cgiar.org/icraf/home.html>). A course originating there might find its way into forestry school curriculums in the United States, many of which might not otherwise be able to offer such a course. This holds for courses in many fields, from art and archeology to marine biology and soil science. In many cases such courses are particularly well suited to asynchronous distance education because the enrollment is spread so thinly across a vast geographical area. For example, there may not be enough students at any one university in the United States to support a course on the history of the Great Zimbabwe ruins or the role of women in the Eritrean liberation struggle, but if there are two in Connecticut, three in Florida, one in Nebraska, and so on it is enough to make a class (O'Donnell, discontinued Web site).

Moreover, the fees generated from such Africa-originated courses would represent a major supplement for the earnings of almost all African professors and, indeed, probably provide full employment for many. Important, too, is the effect on slowing or reversing the brain drain of African intellectuals leaving to pursue careers in the North. Reversing the flow of knowledge in this way could represent an important mode of resistance in an age of cyberimperialism.

CONCLUSION

Is there cyberhope among the cyberhype? Yes, there is hope. Territorial boundaries are not dissolving for the vast majority of people, and they will not for a very long time, if ever. On the other hand, there is the small-scale coffee farmer, who gets up one morning, balances a sixty-kilogram bag of coffee beans on his head, and walks two miles down the path from his little farm to the road, where he catches a bus to the nearest town so he can sell his crop. The buyer there knows about the frost in Brazil yesterday, and the spike it is causing in the coffee futures market; he got the information off the Internet last night. He thinks he will make a killing this week buying low and selling high. What he does not know is that the farmer's daughter recently took a course on commodity trading by distance education from the African Virtual University. The course was taught by an economist in Ghana, and she got it off the Web at her school in Moshi, Tanzania. Naturally, she told her father to listen carefully to the commodity reports before taking his coffee beans to market. So the farmer heard the same information about coffee prices that morning as the coffee buyer, and he heard it on a broadcast from Noah Samara's WorldSpace AfriStar satellite. And he does not plan to sell low, because he needs the money to upgrade his daughter's computer.

So how is the information revolution going to work itself out in Africa? I do not know. I do not think anybody knows. The future is still open, waiting to be created. But one thing is certain: Because of the information revolution, life in Africa in the next millennium, at least for some, is going to be quite different from life in the twentieth century.

NOTE

This chapter is based on research in East Africa during May and June 1998.

REFERENCES

African Information Society Initiative. 1999. <http://www.bellanet.org/partners/aisi/ PROJ/index.htm>.

African National Congress (ANC). 1999. <http://www.anc.org.za/>.

African Virtual University (AVU). 1999. <http://www.avu.org/>.

Aguti, Jessica N., Coordinator AVU Project. 1998. Interview by author. Makerere University, Kampala, Uganda, 26 June.

Contemporary Conflicts in Africa. 1999. <http://www.synapse.net/~acdi20/ welcome.htm>.

Geerdts, Christopher. 1996. Connectivity, Southern Africa. <http://www.idrc.org.za/ connectsa/>.

Hauss, Chip. 1998. Private e-mail to author. 20 September.

Hegener, Michiel. 1996. Telecommunications in Africa—via Internet in Particular. 24 March. <mh@nrc.nl>.

Jensen, Michael. 1996. Bridging the Gaps in Internet Development in Africa. 31 August. <mikej@wn.apc.org>.

———. 1998. The Expansion of African Webspace. *The Electronic Mail & Guardian*, 6 May, 1.

———. 1996. Kenya telecommunications page. <http://www3.wn.apc.org/africa/ kenya.htm>.

Jentleson, Bruce W. 1999. *Preventative Diplomacy and Ethnic Conflict*. <http:// www.synapse.net/~acdi20/links/warning.htm>.

Juma, Magdallen N., Director, Institute of Distance Education and AVU. 1998. Interview by author. Kenyatta University, Nairobi, Kenya, 10 June.

Mills, Kurt. 1998. The Virtualization of Identity: Cyberspace, the Relocation of Authority, and Self-Determination. Paper delivered at the Annual Meeting of the American Political Science Association, September, Boston.

Mutazindwa, David, USIS. 1998. Interview by author. Kampala, Uganda, 25–27 May.

O'Donnell, James J. *New Tools for Teaching*. (Discontinued Web site). <http:// ccat.sas.penn.edu/jod/teachdemo/teachdemo.html>.

Ogutu, Assistant General Manager for Strategic Planning, Kenya Post and Telecommunications Corporation. 1998. Interview by author. Nairobi, Kenya, 12 June.

Polman, Katrien. 1998. Evaluation of Africa-Related Internet Resources. *African Affairs* 97: 401–408.

Samara, Noah A. 1997. To Make As One: A Vision for the Future of African Communications. Paper presented before the Royal African Society, 30 September, Queens' College, Cambridge.

Stoll, Clifford. 1995. *Silicon Snake Oil: Second Thoughts on the Information Highway*. New York: Doubleday.

Stryker, Sara, USIS. 1998. Interview by author. Kampala, Uganda, 25–27 May.

Targett, Simon. 1998. Oxford University to Launch Degree Courses Over Internet. *Financial Times*, 30 July, 1.

U.S. Agency for International Development (USAID) Leland Initiative. <http:// www.info.usaid.gov/regions/afr/leland/kenindex.htm>.

USIS official. 1998. Addis Ababa, Ethiopia, 21 May.

16

Negotiating National Identity and Social Movement in Cyberspace: Natives and Invaders on the Panama-L Listserv

Leda Cooks

> I have lived that moment of the scattering of the people that in other times and other places, in the nations of others, becomes a time of gathering. Gatherings of exiles and émigrés and refugees, gathering on the edge of the frontiers; gatherings in the ghettoes or cafes of city centres; gathering in the half-life, half-light of foreign tongues, or in the uncanny fluency of another's language; gathering at the signs of approval and acceptance, degrees, discourses, disciplines; gathering at the memories of underdevelopment, of other worlds lived retroactively; gathering the past in a ritual of revival; gathering the present.
>
> H. Bhabha (1993, 291)

It is Bhabha's postmodern, postcolonial gathering of peoples—(un)named, (in)authentic, (un)marked, and (in)coherent identities—that is the setting for this chapter. I discuss the existence of both inhabitants and aliens in the virtual cyberspaces of identities, nation, and nationalism, of patriotism to a space that no longer holds the (ideological) claim to physical space and geographic boundary (as in the age of colonialism). Rather, these spaces/communities are imagined in the conversations in which one can be nostalgic for places never visited or people never seen. This movement from the physical space of the nation to the virtual space of the computer has been theorized alternatively as the rebirth of democracy, the crisis of Western modernity, the end of the notion of nation as "territory," the new centralization of power and the reorganization of economic space (Sassen 1996), and the beginning of travel to and residency in virtual spaces/territories by Third World elites, governed increasingly by megafirms and global alliances. Sundaram (1993) notes, "Third Worldist/classical Marxist critiques of 'cyberspace' seem limited. Such critiques have focused on the museumization of Third World cultures in the space of the Web, or the domination of a multinational capital in the political economy of the information superhighway. There is a strong element of truth in both positions but neither can explain the complex implication of virtual spaces in local/regional strategies for re-mapping national identity" (p. 2).

I return to the need for current modern, postmodern, and postcolonial theories to account for ideas of nation, identity, and authenticity later in the chapter. My aim here is to move back and forth from the social constructionist view on the performance of identity, nation, and nationalism to the ways these issues have been theorized in modern, postmodern, postcolonial scholarship. To do this I study the text-based, imagined community created on the Panama-L listserv, a community like many others in which stories of identity, culture, and nation are contradictory and incomplete, and in which rules are constantly negotiated for membership.[1] In this movement from one set of stories about identity and nation within the frame of social action to another, I hope to find the connections and disjunctures between the "account" of identity as it occurs in discourse and the "accounting for" as a product of theorizing about identity in the larger frame of (the end of) nationalism and social movement and change.

Location, space, migration, displacement, boundaries, and nation are terms important to postmodern and postcolonial theory that originated in modernity. As such, the distinctions and differences recognized in modern theories of social/political identities and movements served an agenda that has not disappeared with the advent of postmodernity. Communities of immigrants, once tied to specific physical locations through common bonds of language and ethnicity are increasingly rare; yet, as the experience of migration and displacement has not disappeared, diaspora communities take on new forms, with new rules for membership. These new communities both resemble and mutate the older symbols of nation and the state, but their place in the postmodern, postcolonial space of the Internet does not erase the hierarchies or annihilate the old markers of membership. Indeed, in her study of the creation of imagined Indian communities on the Internet, Mitra (1996) observed that no new stories or alternative ways of discussing what it means to be Indian emerged in the group, even as she argued that this (postmodern) space allowed for such acts to occur.

Kaplan (1996) claims that "the circulation of powerful modernist tropes within postmodern discourses of displacement suggests that postmodernity operates through a contradictory, discontinuous and uneven process of connection with modernity" (p. 23). In this chapter I hope to substantiate Kaplan's argument, through the articulation of contradictions tied to the notion of a postmodern politics of location. Specifically, I focus on the ways in which location emerges through attachment to specific identity claims of nationality and ethnicity, among others, on the national listserv for Panama, Panama-L. I use performance (also known as boundary or critical) ethnography as a methodology that brings together the theoretical commitment of social constructionist, postcolonial and critical scholarship. While much of postmodern scholarship has valorized the local, there is little scholarship to point to as exemplars of "local" research. As Kaplan notes, "To historicize the use of these terms [community, nation, location, displacement] in critical instances rather than simply assuming their value and currency can politicize our critical practices and make them sharper, more meaningful" (p. 26). In this vein, my purpose is to contextualize the social practice of naming identities, particularly as it occurs in cyberspace and with particular ties to nationhood. To do this, however, I must first detail the methodological means and context in which this analysis occurs.

PERFORMANCE OR BORDER ETHNOGRAPHY

Performance or border ethnography can be best characterized as a methodology that situates meaning and interpretation as local knowledge, indeterminate and fragmented even to the "natives" themselves. Within a specific speaking community, the ways in which ideas about identity and difference are communicated construct ideas about culture, community, and nation. This type of ethnography often contradicts and contrasts the modernist notions of the self that have traditionally characterized ethnographic texts. Clifford's (1988, 1992) work on the politics of location or the more recent work in autoethnography (Corey 1998; Crawford 1996; Kaplan 1996) are examples of the displacement of narrative, of the traveler, and of the place that is important to the study of national community in cyberspace.

In addition, border ethnography emphasizes the displacement of the self from the social and cultural place of reflection. Conquergood (1991) observes, "Borders bleed as much as they contain. Instead of dividing lines to be patrolled or transgressed, boundaries are now understood as criss-crossing sites inside the postmodern subject. Difference is resituated within, instead of beyond, the self" (p. 184). This means that reasoning about or the logic of culture is not ontologically given or prior to understanding, but is rather relational and socially constructed. Given such an understanding of culture, identities cannot be stable or fixed, but are constructed in a "polysemic site of articulation for multiple identities and voices" (p. 185). Performance ethnography, then, looks at the social and material context in which both the subject and the object of ethnography occur. The experience of writing about and being "native" to a culture are read as performances (rather than the traditional emphasis on text) of multiple and often conflicting voices.

In an attempt to address the discursive structures of power both within the discourse about imagined communities and postcolonial theory and in the listserv discussion itself, I utilize performance ethnography to examine several general themes (rituals and performances) that have emerged over the years I have been a member of the Panama-L listserv group. I look particularly at one episode or "string," as it simultaneously informs and transcends these ritual constructions. Before turning to the analysis, however, it is important to give some brief description of the listserv to understand better the context in which these discussions occur and my position as researcher/participant/other in this community.

PANAMA-L

The Panama-L listserv, as with most other listserv groups, serves as a kind of community center or gathering place for people sharing a common national bond. To join the list all that is needed is a short message to the list Web site. Numbers of members are difficult to determine, due to the transient nature of the medium and reasons for locating the list. However, a common core exists of approximately thirty members who post anywhere from daily to once a week. List members are (ostensibly) people who are living in, have lived in, or are interested in the country, but also include people seeking information about the country or people conducting surveys or research for reasons which may or may not be related to the group. Message flow ranges from twenty-five to fifty messages per day, with several members posting three to five times per day.

The list was moderated for a short time but has been open for most of the four years I have been a member. Member posts primarily consist of news and information postings from U.S. and Panamanian papers, responses to the news posts, reviews of books and movies related to Panama or Latin America (a recent review of *Titanic* excepted), information about local events, jokes, and political and social commentary. Other types of posts are discouraged unless the person posting the message is well known to other group members. Postings are in both Spanish and English, although the primary (and obviously more acceptable) language is Spanish. The general pattern is that a formal post (e.g., excerpts from the national newspapers) is followed by commentary by group members. Thus, a thread of discussion emerges around a particular topic. A recent example (July 1998) is from a post that discussed an upcoming march in Panama City opposing the tactics of the primary political party. This post was followed by commentary from members on the potential impact of the march, which sparked the frequent debate about which members were in the best position to comment on the state of political affairs in Panama—those living inside or outside of the country. This debate, over boundaries, membership, authenticity, and information, is at its core the modern–postmodern tension over nation/globalization, community/diaspora, and identity alluded to earlier and is the impetus for further examination of these terms as well as the contexts under which they are produced or performed.

My membership in this listserv group reflects this tension or ambiguity. I joined the list after a visit to Panama in 1994 prompted me to seek information and contacts in the country. My participation at that time was limited to asking questions and obtaining addresses of people in the United States and Panama. I returned to Panama on a Fulbright grant in 1997 for a year to research national identity and work in the community on several social-action programs. My continuing interest in the national identity "campaign" (called Panama 2000) and other issues in the country drew me back to this cybercommunity site as a source of information about current events and a place to connect with people from Panama. However, in the past year I have chosen to be an observer on the site, reading the messages posted but rarely responding or attempting to negotiate my membership in this community.

As a critical ethnographer I am both a participant and an outsider to several cultures important to this analysis: As an academic participating in critical and cultural theories and discourses I have a framework through which I view events and performances of identities and culture. As a participant and researcher in social justice projects in Panama I have an investment in some notions of development and community that are native to and alien from those people I have worked with. As a U.S. citizen with no relatives in Panama and whose first language is English I am an outsider to those born and raised in Panama, and to others with various kin and personal ties to the country. Furthermore, I am Caucasian, which positions me as a *fula* (Panamanian label for white woman) by virtue of my skin color.[2] Each of these affiliations marks me as both a participant in the cybercommunity and a researcher of that community. I have been a sojourner in Central America and Panama for quite some time, but I am not from the country. As an academic, I have a view of the world and of the nation that is different from the majority of the population of the country, but that is similar to many of the members of Panama-L.[3]

TEXT, CONTEXT, AND THE INTERNET

Although the text of the Internet has been the subject of much analysis (e.g., emoticons, flaming, spamming, etc.), little of this research has attempted to connect the discourse to the larger (social, cultural, political) context in which it occurs. Some scholars have discounted the possibilities of true "communities" existing on the Internet (e.g., Beniger 1987; Peck 1987), while others have praised the possibilities for new nationalisms, empowerment, and social change. The former set of critics presupposes the physical constraints of space and place as necessities for the true formation of community, while the latter assumes the collapse of these constraints, and thus the pure possibilities for equality in the formation of community. Both approaches are limited in their assumptions about technologies and human systems, yet it is important to look at what makes this medium unique.

Mitra (1996) notes that the Internet, while primarily text based and thus dependent on secondary symbolic forms, is still more immediate and interactive than videotext. As many scholars interested in politeness and norms for disclosure having pointed out, the Internet also allows a degree of anonymity, thus encouraging forms of dialogue that might be face threatening in other (i.e., face-to-face) situations. The images produced on listservs in particular are unstable (changing almost daily) and predicated upon prior knowledge. In order for a participant to enter into the grammar of a particular exchange, he or she must have some knowledge of what came before as well as what the possibilities for responding might be. Mitra also argues that the Internet offers a great degree of empowerment to its users, where rewriting any text is a possibility and new images can replace old ones. While I believe that the anonymity and interactive nature of the forum might provide for more agency than face-to-face communication, I argue that in the case of listserv and other groups, membership rules that structure these communities also limit and regulate what can and cannot be said. Scholars looking at the structuring of gendered discourse on the Internet have advocated both sides of this issue. Herring (1994), for example, looks at how gendered codes are recreated in Internet space, often disempowering and alienating female users, while other scholars (e.g., Ito 1997; Lebesco 1998) note that reading the performance of gender in a particular way does not necessarily reveal some truth about the genitalia of the sender. It is this area of performance, with special attention to nationality (although all other "categories" of being can be implicated here), that I wish to focus on for the remainder of the analysis.

THE INTERNET AS PERFORMANCE SPACE

The Internet differs from other mediums (e.g., television, face-to-face encounters) as a space for performance primarily through its reliance on textual forms (although certainly pictures are disseminated over the Panama listserv with increasing regularity), and the possibilities for immediate creation of and response to messages. From an ethnographic standpoint the social conventions for enacting national identity give insight into the ways national identities are created, maintained, and called into question—where boundaries are constructed and where they collapse. From a critical standpoint such information provides a way of recognizing the role of membership, location, and displacement in the cyberspace of potential social movement and change. In the following section I discuss four recurring episodes or "events" in the Panama-L community where national identity and boundaries have been called into question over the four years I have been a member of this group. Over the years I have downloaded messages on a regular (twice a week) basis and have thematized these messages for the purpose of this analysis. Messages used here as examples of a particular kind of event have been chosen more for their typicality (that is, the frequency of the occurrence of similar messages) than for their uniqueness. For the purposes of this chapter I have organized them into four recurring events: (1) introductions, (2) jokes/humor, (3) commentary on and framing of political/social issues, and (4) rules for participation in the community (who is or is not allowed to respond).

Introductions

Several bits of information are included with every message posted to alert members as to the identity of the participant. Each message contains the name (or pseudoname) of the author and a subject line that summarizes the theme of the message. Members can often also tell something of the background of the participant by the particular codes used in the e-mail address (e.g., .edu signifies that the person is writing from a university). Other information includes where the message has been and to whom else it may be addressed. This allows other users to identify the intended audience for the message, thus allowing for some control over the intended effect of the commentary.

Beyond the general information included in all messages, introductions serve the purposes of informing the group of the new member's background and interests and reasons for joining the group. Often a new member builds credibility first by noting connections that he or she has to people in Panama or other members of the group, or that he or she is from the country, lives or lived there, speaks Spanish, and so on. This information is usually followed by a networking or information request. That is, the new member is looking to meet someone in Panama or from Panama but living elsewhere, or the member is looking for specific information about Panama. This ritual often serves to connect the new member with the community through affiliations previously established in a common space and through identifiers that might mark him or her as otherwise Panamanian. It should be noted here that not all members follow this procedure, but that those who actively stay with the group often cite affiliations that they read as having some credibility with the group. As well, Mitra (1996) observes, "These postings indicate that there is a strong tendency among the . . . users to try and find similar people who share the histories and practices that produce communal identity of the users as they exist outside the network" (p. 54). This practice runs counter to the argument often posed that computer-mediated communication isolates and disconnects people from their communities. The complexities of the locations and displacements of participants need to be acknowledged for such analyses to give insight into how and why such Internet communities occur.

Jokes/Humor

Jokes or humorous stories are often used on this network to identify a particular Latino or Panamanian type of humor and to exclude or differentiate it from other forms (e.g., Irish jokes). Often stereotypes of Latinos are invoked to incite responses from other group members. Due to the tension caused by these jokes, recent humor has been gender related, due in part to the perception that members would find this least offensive. It seems that within the genre of humor members of the group tend to exercise more caution than do Panamanian friends in face-to-face interactions over stereotypes that may offend. An example, sent July 5, 1998, said, "Two kids were having the standard argument about whose father could beat up whose father. One boy said, 'My father is better than your father.' The other kid said, 'Well, my mother is better than your mother.' The first boy paused, 'I guess you're right. My father says the same thing.'"

While not pointing immediately to national identity, such humor is often used to typify the amount of adultery that exists in Panama and the state of relationships between men and women. Often songs are quoted as typifying the state of relationships or of the family as in an example, borrowed from a Calypso tune, sent by Bill on July 3, 1998. It tells of a Grand Cayman family in which the son finds a girl he wants to marry. His father tells him he cannot give permission for the wedding because the girl is actually his sister, although the boy's mother doesn't know this. Then the boy finds another girl who is a wonderful cook. Again the father tells him he can't marry her—this time because the girl is the boy's aunt, although the boy's granny doesn't know this. In shame and confusion, the boy tells his mother about this dilemma. She tells him to go ahead and marry the girl, since his father isn't really his father anyway, although the father doesn't know this. The repeated refrain is "Woe is me. Shame and scandal in the family."

Framing of Political/Social Commentary

The most standard practice for "calling out" or naming someone as Panamanian or non-Panamanian occurs in the context of political and social debate. Typically, this interaction will start with the posting of a news item or the announcement of a debate or march, followed by commentary about the event. Since the most active Panamanian members' politics are often well known to other group members, they are given more leeway and their opinions more credence than members who respond only occasionally or those who are active but are participating from other countries. I discuss this ritual in more depth in a story explicated later.

Rules for Participation

Debates occur frequently over what constitutes information, and whether that information should be addressed (i.e., is it relevant to Panamanians living in the country? To those not living in the country? To those who aren't Panamanian but who are nonetheless members of the group?) Also debated is whether the list should be moderated or censored. A recent example illustrates this debate. After a controversy emerged over the relevance of a posting about a march in Panama City, Meredith (July 3, 1998) wrote, "Creo que en parte es la ansiedad de tener noticias sobre lo que ocurre en Panama. Los que se preocupan por lo que sucede en Panama son solo una parte y entre ellos hay quienes viven en Panama y quienes no" (Those who worry about what occurs in Panama are only a part of the group and the debate is between those who live in Panama and those who don't).

These debates become significant in the context of a national identity to the extent that diaspora experience is what connects and maintains this virtual national space, even as tensions over "authentic" nationalism reemerge frequently. These pressures are part of a new nationalism to the extent that they must be accounted for politically, economically, and culturally, and acknowledged in any attempt to build communities toward social movement and social change. The following story exemplifies and illustrates the events discussed as they overlap and inform each other, creating affordances and constraints as members coconstruct a national identity.

NEGOTIATING NATIONAL IDENTITY AND SOCIAL ACTION ON THE INTERNET

The story is about the construction of a highway through the heart of a tropical forest in Panama. The story can be located temporally in the summer of 1995 and spatially (physically) at my computer terminal in Amherst, Massachusetts. While neither of these facts seem especially important, time and space in this story are both irrelevant and extremely relevant; irrelevant because of the virtual space in which the controversy occurs and relevant because they are still discursively constructed as validation of authenticity for participation in the site.

In the summer of 1995 I received the following message on the listserv:

We need your Support!! STOP ECOLOGICAL DISASTER IN PANAMA'S TROPICAL FOREST. We are writing to you because we are in urgent need of your help in order to avoid the destruction of one of Panama's most precious natural resources.

The letter went on to protest the construction of a highway through the Parque Metropolitan in Panama City. The highway would run deep into the only tropical forest within the city of Panama and part of the biological corridor that connected the Panama Canal Watershed with Panama City. Civic and community groups were protesting the building of this highway because an alternative route, called the ESTAMPA route, would not damage the park system. The campaign called for letters and e-mail to be sent to Panama's president Ernesto Perez Balladares, because a request for World Bank and IMF funding had already been made that would speed up the financing (and thus the construction) of the highway.

The campaign and the implication of a very well-known Panamanian environmental group in the scheme to secure IMF funding produced a flurry of responses among the members of the list. The volume was upward of twenty-five messages a day. While some of the mail was sympathetic, some was critical of the attack on the environmental organization. The criticism, in particular, sparked the beginning of a very interesting debate about who was Panamanian, and thus who could speak authoritatively on the topic of the highway. Although the list was moderated from a university site, the respondents appeared to be quite diverse: there were soldiers (U.S. citizens) who had been stationed in Panama; expatriots living in Slovakia, Germany, and (the majority) in the United States; Zonians (people who were born and raised in the canal zone); and other Panamanian citizens.

The controversy centered on several critical responses, the first sent by a man who claimed to be U.S. military, and who had lived in Panama for several years. He was critical of the attempt to "slow the construction of a much needed highway in Panama City" and suspicious of the origins of the letter. Further, he was critical of the lack of acceptance of controversial opinions on the list. As an endnote to the critique (and perhaps because he knew he was creating a controversy in his declaration of a lack thereof) he wrote, "I love Panama as much as any of you do and it is because of this love that I continue to be interested in the development and preservation of this beloved country. The fact that I am not from Panama does not deny me the right to love the country and to participate on this list" (June 22, 1995).

Subsequent to this message, Charlie was identified as a "flamer" and warned to stop his critiques. Nonetheless, expatriots and others living outside of the country would preface or end their responses with similar declarations of love for their home country, while criticizing the government, criminals, and citizens, or circumstances such as poverty for its demise. As one expatriate, Carlos (from Slovakia), wrote, "It is a shame that in a country so beautiful, with so many resources and a relatively small population, there is so much crime and corruption." Such utterances were frequently met with comments such as this one by Miriam (June 1995): "You put down those of us in Panama for doing nothing to stop a corrupt government, yet you live in the United States—a place far more corrupt and responsible for the problems we experience in Panama today. *Who are you to tell us what we should be doing?*" (emphasis added).

The debate over who could or should participate both in the action to stop the construction of the highway and in the critique of that action reached an interesting point with the distribution of a letter that addressed neither of these issues, but, rather, the construction of Panamanian identity in both the United States and in Panama:

My name is Gregorio. I was born at Gorgas hospital in Balboa and raised between Pedro Miguel (in the canal zone) and Las Savanas (directly next to the Panamerican Institute). . . . I have been living in Seattle for 12 years this August 6. I keep in touch with most of the Panamanian population here in Seattle and we try to do things together whenever possible.

Without meeting any of you, I have already begun some controversy within the group which was not my intention [referring to his earlier comments about living in the United States versus living in Panama]. To those of you that might be slightly irritated with me for entering the question or others for their comments, I give you my sincerest apologies and ask to restore the peace like it once was. As people of color we face too much conflict from some African Americans that have a problem with someone who is a darker shade of brown and has such ties with the Hispanic community; and at the same time with some in the Hispanic American community for being born in Latin America and being a darker shade of brown. Please do not misinterpret what I am saying. Let's just not fight with each other.

Talk, Dark and Panamanian

Gregorio (Springer, June 22, 1995)

All the messages that have been identified were part of the thread that followed the initial call to action to stop the construction of the highway. However, it is Gregorio's letter in particular that I wish to use as the jumping-off point for the analysis of the construction of identity, community, and nation within the context of social action and social movement on the Internet. Although this letter did not register direct criticism of the highway construction, it addressed the conflict that had been going on among the members of the site, while simultaneously pointing to the conflictual representations of Panamanian identity in the United States.

The Space Between: National Identity and Radical Subjectivity

While the earlier messages had each constructed national space geographically (constructing legitimate participation in the debate on the basis of the experience of either being Panamanian or living in Panama), Gregorio reconfigured this space and his place in the controversy with an interesting move. He first replicated the earlier criteria for validating authenticity: He noted the exact locations of his birth and early years within the national space of Panama. Then he discussed his frequent contact with and ties to a "displaced" Panamanian community in the United States, a community that is continually marginalized even by those at the margins of mainstream U.S. society (namely, Latin Americans and African Americans). Thus the primary story for Gregorio was the living out of Panamanian identity in spaces where he did not feel marginalized but rather a part of a community. This virtual space for him was not a space for debating *being* Panamanian, but rather a space where his Panamanian identity could be confirmed and supported. He thus constructed this virtual space as a place for a different kind of national identity and constructed a community of individuals united in their differences from others.

Although the borders constructed in these conversations rely on temporality and spatiality (that is, time spent in a national space) for the validation of one's identity as Panamanian, the location of peoples and the debate itself collapses these same spaces. This raises deeper complexities than those suggested in postmodern arguments about the reconfiguration of the time and space of identity and nation. Temporality (here, the time and date of the messages sent, but also time spent in Panama) and spatiality (from where the messages originated, but also the nostalgic associations with a national space) says more about what Bhabha (1993) calls the "metaphoricity" of the peoples of imagined communities than about the historicity of a national identity or national culture. Bhabha argues that people are a "complex rhetorical strategy of social reference where the claim to be representative provokes a crisis within the process of signification and discursive address" (p. 297).

Gregorio's message illustrates this point. He cites his marginalization within the Seattle community as a basis for his wanting to end the conflict in this cybercommunity. "Peace" thus points to the crisis invoked by the signification of "naming" his identity in other spaces. That he chooses to cite skin color as a marker of his disenfranchisement with both the Latin American community (not light enough to be Hispanic) and the African American community (too dark to be Hispanic) is important here. It is a strategic move toward community, an uncovering of differential hierarchies of skin color that signify the difference of being Panamanian. Where many cite virtual space and communities as a place where identities are irrelevant, it is crucial to note the strategic use of essentialism/authenticity and markers of difference in the name of political action (and social support).

Sundaram's (1993) observation seems relevant here; what is needed in theorizing cyberpractices in the Third World (and among those dispersed and diasporic throughout the world), is a move beyond the oppositional and Marxist arguments that simplify the complex relationships among cyberconnected peoples. Sundaram, borrowing from Laclau, calls for the "radical contextualization" of the discourse of cyberspace, "where the violent abstractions of 'West', 'capital' and 'nation' do not erase the richness and contradictions of initiatives into virtual space" (p. 2). I carry this argument further to note the need for a reading of identity as both historicity (objectivity) and subjectivity in cyberspace.

THE IMAGINING OF INDIVIDUAL, COMMUNITY, AND NATION

While postmodern feminist scholars such as Haraway (1985) and Ito (1997) have argued for the fragmentation and hybridity of machines and bodies in the late twentieth century, postcolonial scholars (e.g., Appadurai 1990, 1993;

Bhabba 1993; Chattergee 1986) have noted the collapse of concepts such as state and nation, and with the advent of the Electronic Age, the collapse of space and time in the global moment. With the demise of the modern concepts of bodies and identities (Ito 1997), borders and territories, and the emergence of telematics and globalization, imagined communities of citizens create the modern nation-state (Appadurai 1993; Martin-Barbero 1993). From these changes the tension and contradictions in ideas such nationalism and patriotism become more apparent.

Still, as Appadurai (1993) has keenly observed, "No idiom has emerged to capture the collective interest of many groups and in translocal solidarities, crossborder mobilizations, and postnational identities. Such interests are many and vocal, but they are still entrapped in the linguistic imagery of the territorial state" (p. 418). While none of these theorists have noted the end of the political, the end of a modern colonial period is obvious and thus necessitates a new understanding of social orders and movements. As Appadurai (1990) notes, "The image, the imagined, the imaginary—these are all terms which direct us to something critical and new in global cultural processes: *the imagination as a social practice*" (p. 5).

THE MODERN DILEMMAS OF SOCIAL MOVEMENT

In the confusion among temporalities, spaces, identities, and nation-states, the connection to political action and social movement seems tenuous at best. The construction of individual as citizen is arguably one of the primary organizing factors of social life, yet the panopticon of citizenship has become increasingly elusive. The connection between the individual and the social has not disappeared; in fact, as Gergen (1990) notes, it has grown stronger.

Still, as Melucci (1993) concludes, with the glut of communications technologies and quantities of information, all aimed toward the individual who must receive, analyze, and nearly always respond to this information flow, the traditional reference points that mediate individual identity and society (church, family, etc.), have weakened. We no longer can respond with certainty to the increasingly prevalent question, "Who/what are you?" that we are of this or that race, ethnicity, or nation. Melucci does not imply that this phenomenon signals the end of cultural identification and thus the end of social and political action. He notes that "the focus of social movement in the age of information has shifted from groups and collectivities (what he calls external planets) to the internal planet of the individual." He argues that "the emerging of a transnational dimension to issues and social agents, more than apolitical question, is a sign of the fact that human action is now capable of culturally creating its own space" (1993, p. 289).

Following this, Melucci (1993) notes that four dilemmas characterize contemporary social movements. I will discuss each dilemma briefly and then look at their relationship to the thread discussed in this chapter and to related arguments regarding democracy and cyberspace. The first dilemma can be characterized as that of autonomy and control "between the potential of individual capacities and choices versus the tendency to create capillary systems of behavioral manipulation, which today impact both the brain and the genetic structure itself" (p. 290). This tension relates as well to Bhabha's (1993) discussion of historicity and subjectivity and Sundaram's (1993) discussion of "radical contextualization." Here, the potential of individual capacities and creative choices is balanced by the increasing power to create and control the "virtual" subject.

This leads to Melucci's (1993) second and third dilemmas, which I see as somewhat similar: those of responsibility and omnipotence and irreversible information and reversible choices. With these dilemmas the tension lies "between the tendency to expand the capacity of human systems to intervene in their own development versus the need to take account of and respond (response-ability) to the limits of nature" (p. 290). Melucci's ideas are based on the power of scientific knowledge and the power of choices that must be acknowledged.[4] Although he is discussing science as power, the same tensions can be related to the choices made in representing cultures and nations.

Melucci's (1993) final dilemma, that between inclusion and exclusion, is the tension of defining and defying difference in contemporary society. Melucci notes that due to advances in technology that collapse time and travel there is no longer an "outside world": "territories, cultures, languages exist only as the internal elements of a planetary system" (p. 290). Thus, differences are internalized as inclusive, and processes that cover over and level identities are internalized as equally fragmented according to the cultural codes of the dominant elite or exclusive processes that resist the homogenization or silencing of cultural forms.

The usefulness of this framework for explicating the dynamics of contemporary social movements can be seen in how well it addresses both the macrosocial structures that frame cultural contexts and the micropractices that negotiate and recreate meanings within the larger framework. Looking back at the thread of discourse, we see that the initial call to action presented the highway action as a measure designed to suppress information (thus preventing free choice) about the destruction of an important natural habitat (issue of control). The dilemmas of responsibility (as a Panamanian citizen or expatriot) and reversing the choices made by the president thus placed a national issue in a global forum (a listserv with subscribers from all over the world).

The thread that followed the call for letters did not address the same tensions (choice, responsibility, and control) around corporate greed and threats to the environment—or the action itself, for that matter—but instead attempted to place boundaries on just who could or should be able to criticize the movement to stop the construction of the highway. The responsibility at this point seemed to lie more with representing oneself as authentic and one's interests as aligned with those supporting the action. Disagreement was allowable, but only if one first met the criteria for engaging in debate about the future of the country. Charlie and Gregorio obviously disobeyed these rules by critiquing first and providing justification (via identity) for their critique after they had been chastised by the group.

This is the implication of the inclusion–exclusion dilemma, which here functions on a multitude of levels. First, as mentioned, the criteria for providing support or critique served a function of boundary maintenance. Inclusion in the listserv group was the primary dilemma for Gregorio, given the exclusion he faced elsewhere. On a different level for Gregorio, inclusion and exclusion among the African-American and Hispanic groups in Seattle seemed to be based on skin color—and Panamanians, according to this criteria, were too dark to "fit in" to either category. Last, inclusion or exclusion functioned on the level of strategic essentialism. It was important for Gregorio to identify certain qualities as essentially Panamanian (e.g., language, skin color) in order to call for peace among the members of the group.

THE TECHNOLOGY OF JUSTICE OR THE JUSTICE OF TECHNOLOGY?

Within the theorizing of democracy and cyberspace these dilemmas can also be easily spotted. Discourse that portrays technology as the means to democracy carries with it the equally weighty implication that technology and democracy provide "citizens" with a forum for justice (social, political, and, in some cases, economic). Thus, all citizens have equal access to change policies and with this access have the freedom to represent any number of differing identities. Beyond the fact that only 3 percent of the world's population have access to the Internet (see Sassen [1996] for a breakdown of these numbers), the inclusion argument thus positions opposition to technology as equality as antidemocratic. Other dilemmas, such as autonomy and control, responsibility and omnipotence, are the tensions fundamental to the creation and maintenance of democracy in late modern society.

Traditional Marxist arguments about the lack of access to technology, also align themselves with these binaries, through starting with the exclusion (as opposed to the inclusion) argument and then working to address the other tensions. The focus of the Marxist arguments thus center around (1) the failure of democracy to include the people, and (2) the relationship between control over electronic space and the flow of transnational capital.[5] Thus, the responsibility of the disenfranchised people is to unite against the global omnipotent corporate interests and fight against the commodification and consumption of individual and national identities.

Working from these dilemmas to the idea of social movement in cyberspace, it seems that these tensions are present in the discourse. But do they adequately account for the complex negotiations necessary to track the movement mentioned earlier, from historicity to subjectivity? Do they provide a perspective on the disjunctive forms of representation that signify a people?

A form of living that is more complex than community; more symbolic than society; more connotative than country; less patriotic than petri; more rhetorical than the reason of state; more mythological than ideology; less homogenous than hegemony; less centred than the citizen; more collective than the subject; more psychic than civility; more hybrid in the articulations of cultural differences and identifications—gender, race, or class—than can be represented in the hierarchical or binary structuring of social antagonism. (Bhabha 1993, 292)

I believe that these tensions are a useful beginning for locating a dynamic that needs a more complex reading, incorporating all the factors cited but employing none as a justification or validation for analysis.

THE REPRODUCTIVE SIGNIFICATION OF NATIONAL LIFE

Bhabha (1993) describes the space of the people as the historical "objects" of a nationalist pedagogy, giving the "discourse an authority that is based on the pre-given or constituted historical origin or event," as well as the "subjects of a process of signification that . . . demonstrates the prodigious living principle of the people as that continuous process by which the national life is redeemed and signified as a repeating and reproductive process" (p. 297).

The stories of identity and social movement recreated here have been erased, contested, and reconstructed in new spaces, most recently in the debates on the same listserv over the future of the canal and of Panama. The purchase of the major ports in Colon and San Cristobal by the Hutchison-Whampoa Company, linked to the People's Republic of China, have raised new concerns among policy makers in both Panama and the United States over the threat of communist interests controlling the country. A bill introduced in Congress by Representative Hunter, "prohibits the US assistance to the RP if a defense site or military installation built or formerly operated by the US has been conveyed by the government of the RP to any foreign government-owned entity" (HR 2950, 105th Cong., 1st sess., 8 November 1997, sec. 2, part 5). In effect, this bill is an attempt on the part of the United States to force Panama's hand in the face of a potential communist threat and to ensure the U.S. presence in the canal zone in the years to come. This has, once again, renewed debates on the listserv between Panamanians living in Panama and elsewhere in the world over the role of Panamanian citizens (with or without the "help" of the United States) in creating a democratic future. This issue is complicated and deserves a deeper analysis than that proffered here; nonetheless, the dilemmas raise tensions similar to those already discussed.

SOMEWHERE BETWEEN TARZAN AND THE CYBORGS

Returning to the opening citation from Homi Bhabha (1993) and the question of what constitutes the bodies politic/political bodies, it is important to note that the current moment can neither be characterized as the end of the physical—of boundaries and bodies (what Melucci [1993] would call the natural) or the totality of the machine—the emergence of new forms and forums for democracy, or the totalitarian takeover of the multinationals (Sassen 1996). As Ito (1997) concludes in her discussion of diasporic identity politics and the displacement of on-line communities, "Certainly bits of code mobilized by silicon chips and transported through fiber optics and telephone lines do not have the same materiality as flesh and blood, hunger and organic pain" (p. 102). And yet, she queries, can there really be any "clean separation" between these things? From another vantage point, discussing the academic debates between and among First and Third World scholars, Loomba (1991) makes a similar observation, noting that in this "neocolonial" age "it seems stubborn and naïve to insist that the politics of colonialism and postcolonialism cannot be entirely dissociated from those of its various examinations today" (p. 305). Regardless of one's philisophical orientations, it seems the materiality of actions taken in the name of sameness or difference, in the name of one's country or of one's listserv group, have important consequences for social movement.

In the spirit of imagined spaces, I argue that it is here that we need to make the connections between diasporic identity politics, embodied experiences, technology development, and international corporate politics. In these spaces the social encompasses the technological; language creates and gives meaning to technology in the cultural spaces of the virtual imagination.

NOTES

1. Scholars writing about virtual nations and diasporic spaces created on these listservs rarely acknowledge the recreation of dominance and hierarchy in the discourse. Mitra (1996), for example, notes "There is no Internet audience who is not also empowered to become an agent to mould the space as s/he wishes. . . . In this case the notion of using a text becomes particularly powerful because the audience can indeed take any text on the public sphere of the Internet and 'respond' to it or 'rewrite' it in a new way where the new text immediately becomes a part of the discursive space accessible to everyone" (pp. 49–50).

2. An interesting exception here would be Zonians, white people born and raised in Panama whose families have worked on and for the canal. Many Zonians have never learned Spanish, although they continue to live and work in the country.

3. A majority of the group's members identify as academics, lawyers, students, journalists, and professionals in computer-related fields.

4. I should note here that relative to national identity Melucci's (1993) dilemma corresponds somewhat to Bhabha's (1993) notion of the liminality of cultural subjec-

tivity; that is, the awareness of a Freudian double (self) in the time and space of a cultural unconscious. Bhabha asks whether "the emergence of a national perspective—of an elite or subaltern culture can ever articulate its representative authority" (p. 295). The response ability of representation—of the sign that points to something else—is always countered by the essentialism it invokes (the tendency to naturalize language as both channel and object—thought and the thing itself).

5. Sundaram (1993) groups cyberpublics into three categories: those of the nationalist state, of the transnational elite and of the space between the market and the state occupied by the various bulletin boards and social-movement networks.

REFERENCES

Appadurai, A. 1990. Disjuncture and Difference in the Global Cultural Economy. *Theory, Culture and Society* 7: 295–310.

———. 1993. Patriotism and Its Futures. *Public Culture* 5: 411–429.

Beniger, J. 1987. Personalization of the Mass Media and the Growth of Pseudo-Community. *Communication Research* 14: 352–371.

Bhabha, H. 1993. DissemiNation: Time, Narrative, and the Margins of the Modern Nation. In *Nation and Narration*, edited by H. Bhabha. London: Routledge.

Chattergie, P. 1986. *Nationalist Thought and the Colonial World: A Derivative Discourse.* Tokyo and London: Zed Books for United Nations University.

Clifford, J. 1988. *Predicament of Culture.* Cambridge: Harvard University Press.

———. 1992. Travelling Cultures. In *Cultural Studies*, edited by L. Grossberg, C. Nelson, and P. Treichler. New York: Routledge.

Conquergood, D. 1991. Rethinking Ethnography: Toward a Critical Cultural Politics. *Communication Monographs* 58: 179–194.

Corey, F. C. 1998. Crossing an Irish border. In *Readings in Intercultural contexts*, edited by J. N. Martin, T. K. Nakayama, and L. Flores. Mountain View, Calif.: Mayfield.

Crawford, L. 1996. Personal Ethnography. *Communication Monographs* 63: 158–170.

Gergen, K. 1991. *The Saturated Self: Dilemmas of Identity in Contemporary Life.* New York: HarperCollins.

Haraway, D. 1985. A Cyborg Manifesto: Science, Technology and Socialist-Feminism in the Twentieth Century. In *Simians, Cyborgs, and Women*, edited by L. Nicholson. New York: Routledge.

Herring, S. C. 1994. Gender and Democracy in Computer-Mediated Communication. *Electronic Journal of Communication* 3 (2). <http://cios.llc.rpi.edu/getfile/ HERRING_V3N293>.

Ito, M. 1997. Virtually Embodied: The Reality of Fantasy in a Multi-User Dungeon. In *Internet Culture*, edited by D. Porter. New York: Routledge.

Kaplan, C. 1996. *Questions of Travel.* Durham: Duke University.

Lebesco, K. 1998. Revolting Bodies? The On-Line Negotiation of Fat Subjectivity. Ph.D. diss., University of Massachusetts, Amherst.

Loomba, A. 1991. Overworlding the Third World. *Oxford Literary Review* 13: 164–191.

Martin-Barbero, J. 1993. Latin America: Cultures in the Communication Media. *Journal of Communication* 43 (2): 18–29.

Melucci, A. 1993. The Global Planet and the Internal Planet: New Frontiers for Collective Action and Individual Transformation. In *Cultural Politics and Social*

Movements, edited by M. Darnovsky, B. Epstein, and R. Flacks. Philadelphia: Temple University Press.

Mitra, A. 1996. Nations and the Internet: The Case of a National Newsgroup, "soc.cult.indian." *Convergence* 2 (1): 40–75.

Peck, M. E. 1987. *The Different Drum: Community Making and Peace.* New York: Simon and Schuster.

Sassen, S. 1996.The Topic of e-Space: Global Cities and Global Value-Chains. Paper delivered at the DEAF symposium "Digital Territories," 19 September, Rotterdam.

Sundaram, R. 1993. *Beyond the Nationalist Panopticon: The Experience of Cyberpublics in India.* Delhi, India: Centre for the Study of Developing Societies.

Index

About the Editor
and Contributors

Benjamin J. Bates is an Associate Professor in the Department of Broadcasting, College of Communications, University of Tennessee, Knoxville. His research efforts focus on the development of media systems, telecommunications economics and policy, and the economics and social impacts of information, information systems, and information policy. He has published more than thirty articles and book chapters.

Jeffrey Layne Blevins is a doctoral candidate at Ohio University. He holds a master of science degree from Southern Illinois University at Edwardsville, where he taught mass-media systems. His research interests include political economy and critical studies of mass media.

Leda Cooks is an Assistant Professor in the Department of Communication at the University of Massachusetts, Amherst. Her research and teaching interests are directed toward exploring the articulations of power, culture, and identities in global and local scenes.

Bosah Ebo is Professor in the Department of Communication at Rider University where he teaches international communication, communication ethics, and media and popular culture. He is the author of *Cyberghetto or Cybertopia: Race, Class, and Gender on the Internet* (Praeger 1998).

Margot Emery is a doctoral student in communications at the University of Tennessee and research associate of the university's Central and East European Center and Center for International Networking Initiatives. Her research interests are in social and political dynamics of information technologies and the role of information in open, closed, and transitional societies. <http://web.utk.edu/~memery>.

David J. Gunkel is Assistant Professor of communication technology at Northern Illinois University. His critical investigations of computer-mediated communication and cyberculture can be found in *Critical Studies in Mass Communication, The Journal of Mass Media Ethics*, and *Configurations*.

Ellen S. Kole is currently working on her Ph.D. She is researching the optimum way to organize computer network transfer to developing countries in order to meet the needs of nongovernmental organizations. She received sponsorship from the Carolus Magnus Fund to support her research in East Africa. The organization financially supports the top ten beginning researchers in their field. Her publications include "Supporting Small Enterprise with New Technology" in *Appropriate Technology* (1998) and "Myths and Realities in Internet Discourse: Using Computer Networks for Data Collection and the Beijing World Conference on Women" in *The Gazette: The International Journal for Communication Studies* (1998).

Marwan M. Kraidy is an Assistant Professor and Director of Graduate Studies in the School of Communication at the University of North Dakota. He teaches international communication, emerging media technologies, and popular culture and media theory. His publications include "Broadcasting Regulation and Civil Society in Post-War Lebanon" in the *Journal of Broadcasting and Electronic Media*. His current research interests include developing a theory of glocalization, and technologies and the public sphere in non-Western countries.

Laura B. Lengel is an Assistant Professor in the Department of Communication at the American International University in London, where she teaches writing with new technologies, digital video art, intercultural communication, field research methods, and international film. As a Fulbright Scholar and an American Institute of Maghreb Studies Fellow she examined the impact of the Internet on North Africa. She has published in *Convergence: The Journal of Research into New Media Technologies* and the *Journal of Communication Inquiry*, and has a forthcoming book titled *Culture and Technology in the New Europe*.

Jonathan Mendilow is a Professor in the Department of Political Science at Rider University. He is the author of two books, *From the French Revolution to the Rise of Fascism* (1984) and *The Romantic Tradition in British Political*

Thought (1986). His articles have appeared in numerous journals, including the *American Journal of Political Science, Political Studies*, and *Comparative Politics and Political Theory*.

Patrick D. Murphy is an Assistant Professor at Southern Illinois University, Edwardsville, where he teaches media criticism, transnational media, and video production. For the past nine years he has studied mass media and cultural change in Latin American, earning a Fulbright–Garcia Robles fellowship in 1993–1994 to research television in popular culture in Mexico. His articles have appeared in *Cultural Studies, Howard Journal of Communication,* and the *Journal of International Communication.*

Rodger A. Payne is Associate Professor of Political Science at the University of Louisville and Director of the $150,000 Grawemeyer Award for Ideas Improving World Order. He has published numerous articles and book chapters on security policy and global environmental politics and is working on a book about the democratization of multilateral development institutions.

Frank Louis Rusciano is Professor and Chair of Political Science at Rider University. He is a three-time Alexander von Humboldt Fellow and a former guest professor at the University of Mainz, Germany. He is the author of two books, *Isolation and Paradox: Defining "the Public" in Modern Political Analysis* (Greenwood, 1989) and *World Opinion and the Emerging International Order* (Praeger, 1998). His articles have appeared in numerous journals, including the *International Journal of Public Opinion Research, Comparative Politics, Western Political Quarterly,* and the *Harvard International Journal of Press/Politics.*

Glen Segell is a senior research fellow at the Institute of Security Policy in London. He is the author of fifteen books covering a wide range of topics, including economics, politics, the Internet, and war and international relations. He is on the editorial board of the *Electronic Journal of Conflict Analysis,* and is a member of the Council for Arms Control, the British International Studies Association, and the Society of Authors.

Deborah Tong is a graduate student in communications at McGill University, Canada. She is currently working as a senior editor for the Prague-based magazine *Think!* and is the multimedia editor for the online journal CTHEORY (<http://www.ctheory.com>) and CTHEORY MULTIMEDIA (<http://ctheory.concordia.ca>).

Vasja Vehovar is an Assistant Professor in the Faculty of Social Sciences at the University of Ljubljana, Slovenia. He has been the principal investigator for a national research project on the Internet in Slovenia. He was a Fulbright scholar at the Institute for Social Research at the University of Michigan in 1998. The ministry of science and technology of the Republic of Slovenia supported the research for his chapter.

Robert G. White is Professor and former Chair of the Department of Government and politics at Humboldt State University. He specialized in African politics and international development, and is a member of the U.S. African Studies Association and the Royal African Society of the United Kingdom. He is the author of "Using H-Africa in a Virtual Course" in *Great Ideas for Teaching About Africa*, edited by M. L. Bastian and J. L. Parpart (1999).

Chung-Chuan Yang teaches in the Department of Marketing and Distribution Management at National First Kaohsiung University of Science and Technology, Taiwan. His teaching areas include internet marketing, telecommunications policy, and international advertising. His research focuses on the social impacts of new communications technology, and electronic commerce system design and assessment. His works have appeared in the *Journal of Mass Media Studies, Human Communication, On the Internet, Global Internet Magazine, Journal of Communication & Culture, Journal of Television & Radio Studies, Journal of Marketing Communication,* and *Journal of Advertising Studies.*